JAPAN'S 19 TECHNOPOLIS

Hokkaido Island

HAKODATE
(Hokkaido)

AOMORI
(Aomori)

Sea of Japan

AKITA
(Akita)

NAGAOKA
(Niigata)

TOYAMA
(Toyama)

WESTERN HARIMA (Hyogo)

KIBI HIGHLAND (Okayama)

HIROSHIMA CHUO (Hiroshima)

UBE (Yamaguchi)

**Honshu
Island**

UTSUNOMIYA
(Tochigi)

Tokyo

Nagoya

Seto Inland Sea

Osaka

KURUME-TOSU
(Fukuoka/Saga)

HAMAMATSU
(Shizuoka)

GOBO
(Wakayama)

SASEBO
(Nagasaki)

WESTERN KAGAWA
(Kagawa)

KUMAMOTO
(Kumamoto)

NORTHERN OITA
(Oita)

Shikoku Island

KOKUBU-HAYATO
(Kagoshima)

MIYAZAKI
(Miyazaki)

Kyushu Island

Pacific Ocean

○ Technopolis Zone

▪ Mother City

(Prefecture)

Source: MITI, Industrial Relocation Guidance Division

The Technopolis Strategy: Japan, High Technology, and the Control of the Twenty-first Century

The Technopolis Strategy

Japan, High Technology, and the Control of the Twenty-first Century

Sheridan Tatsuno

A Brady Book
Published by Prentice Hall Press
New York, New York 10023

Copyright © 1986 by Sheridan Tatsuno
All rights reserved
including the right of reproduction
in whole or in part in any form

A Brady Book
Published by Prentice Hall Press
A Division of Simon & Schuster, Inc.
Gulf + Western Building
One Gulf + Western Plaza
New York, New York 10023

PRENTICE HALL PRESS is a trademark of Simon & Schuster, Inc.

Designed by Michael O'Brien
Manufactured in the United States of America

2 3 4 5 6 7 8 9 10

Library of Congress Cataloging-in-Publication Data

Tatsuno, Sheridan, 1949—
   The technopolis strategy.

   "A Brady book."
   Bibliography: p.
   Includes index.
   1. High technology industries—Japan—Technological
innovations. 2. Research institutes—Japan—Location.
3. Science and industry—Government policy—Japan.
I. Title.
HC465.H53T38   1986   338.4'762'000952   86-9300
ISBN 0-89303-885-7

To my wife Muneko
and my parents,
for your inspiration
and encouragement.

C O N T E N T S

ACKNOWLEDGMENTS

Each book has its roots in the minds of many people. For their friendship and insights, I am deeply indebted to the members of Dataquest for encouraging me to burn the midnight oil in true Silicon Valley style in order to write this book. In particular, I would like to thank my colleagues in the Japanese Semiconductor Industry Service (JSIS) who have become like a family to me: Gene Norrett, Vice-President and Director; Osamu Ohtake, Associate Director; Patricia Cox and Nagayoshi Nakano, research analysts; and Maureen Davies, Chieko Yamane, and Maria Gonzalez, our secretaries and effervescent cheerleaders.

I am also grateful to Dataquest's management for its continuing encouragement and sincere efforts to involve employees in the company decision-making process: Manny Fernandez, Fred Zieber, Ralph Finley, Jewel Peyton, Frank Sammann, Greg Goodere, Howard Bogert, Stan Bruederle, Bob McGeary, Tom Bredt, Wil Felling, Victor Krueger, Cliff Lindsey, Don Roberts, and Jane Lawes. Without Dataquest's superb libraries and in-house data bases, I would not have been able to track down the myriad of facts about Japan's electronics industry.

A guiding light in Silicon Valley is Stanford University, which has provided much intellectual leadership in these years of turbulent U.S.-Japan relations. I pay special tribute to Professor Daniel Okimoto, Stacy Tanaka, and our departed friend Henry Hayase for organizing excellent roundtable discussions at the U.S.-Japan Forum.

This book is truly a Japanese-American venture and my appreciation goes to my friends across the Pacific. I would like to thank the officials of the Ministry of International Trade and Industry (MITI) for their assistance and openness in frankly discussing Japanese industrial policies and U.S.-Japan trade: Nobuhiro Miyake, Jotaro Abe, Yoshiharu Kunogi, Naomichi Suzuki, Hideki Ogawa,

Shuji Kato, Eichi Hasegawa, Takayuki Matsuo, Makoto Kobayashi, Masao Fujita, Seiji Hirota, Kenichi Ito, Susumu Honobe, and Fumihiko Kato. Above all, I shall always be indebted to Dr. Sadakazu Iijima of the Japan Industrial Location Center, who was a major source of information on the Technopolis program, and Dr. Kenichi Imai of Hitotsubashi University, who shared his thoughts about Silicon Valley and Technopolis.

For the chapter on the Tsukuba Science City, my gratitude goes to several people: Tetsuzo Kawamoto of the Tsukuba Research Consortium, Hitoshi Murakami of the Tsukuba Information Lab, Dr. Shunichi Watanabe of the Ministry of Construction, and Kimihisa Murakami of the Department of Agriculture, Forestry, and Fisheries. For the Technopolis chapters, I wish to thank the government officials of the following prefectures, who welcomed me and guided me through their emerging technopolises: Aomori, Akita, Iwate, Yamagata, Miyagi, Niigata, Toyama, Shizuoka, Okayama, Hiroshima, Yamaguchi, Kumamoto, Oita, Kagoshima, and Miyazaki.

And finally, I would like to remember my mentor, Professor Chitoshi Yanaga of Yale University, who so carefully reviewed my first draft, and my editors, Ron Powers, Chris Williams, Terry Anderson, and Robin Eckhardt, for guiding this book through a major corporate reorganization. Without you, and many others, this book would have never been published.

PROLOGUE:
BEYOND PROTECTIONISM

In 1954, Akira Kurosawa, Japan's internationally acclaimed film director, made *The Seven Samurai*, a legendary film that has taken on symbolic importance for Americans clamoring for protectionism against the rising flood of foreign imports. Set in feudal Japan, the movie focuses on an impoverished village under attack by marauding bandits. In an effort to defend themselves, the villagers listen to an ancient elder who counsels them to hire *ronin*, masterless samurai without work. They are at a loss as to how to select the best swordsmen, so the village leader devises a test. He hides a bodyguard armed with a club at the entrance to the interviewing room. To his satisfaction, the ruse works. The first samurai swaggers into the room and is knocked out cold by the guard. Needless to say, he fails the test. A second samurai, more skillful and alert, fights off the attacker, but he too is rejected. Finally, a third samurai is summoned. A bit inebriated, he almost falls for the trap, but he stops before entering the door. "Drop your club," he warns the hidden assailant, "if you want to live." His years of training and experience warn him that danger lies in not being vigilant. He is chosen because he never draws his sword.

In a similar manner, America has been put to the test by Japanese industries during the last thirty years. Like the first samurai, we have been knocked out in industry after industry—steel, cameras, televisions, and VTRs—without ever knowing what hit us. We cried foul, blaming cheap labor, copying, industrial spying, and unfair "dumping" for our economic woes; but that did not help us regain our industrial competitiveness, because we failed to anticipate the moves of our growing economic rival across the Pacific. Now, like the second samurai, we have a clearer understanding of Japan's export drives, vertically-integrated companies, and hidden protectionist barriers. We are demanding more open markets and fighting back with tariffs, quotas, and domestic content laws. But these are only temporary, stopgap measures. For vote-seeking congressmen up for reelection, the sword of protectionism may play well in Peoria, but it is an elusive and cruel deception. Protectionism has never saved industries that have failed to anticipate market trends, retrain their workers, and modernize their plants. It may save some jobs and congressional seats for a few years, but it will not make our industries competitive again. It will only delay the painful process unless we make a decisive turnaround in our management policies and national and regional industrial strategies. As we learned in the 1930s, protectionism only breeds protectionism. Left unchecked, our unilateral actions threaten to touch off a backlash of protectionism that could cripple world trade.

Thus we are in a dilemma. America is an economic superpower, but unlike the third samurai, we have not learned vigilance. In our search for national security we spend billions of dollars on the latest military technology, but we fail to keep abreast of the massive economic and technological changes reshaping the globe. We have a highly sophisticated military intelligence-gathering network, but we have not strengthened our commercial listening posts to monitor Japan and other technological powers. We pride ourselves on our superior technology without bothering to find out what our competitors are doing. We talk about becoming more internationally competitive, but we have not encouraged our young people to study foreign languages, cultures, and business practices. For example, although most Japanese high-school graduates can read enough English to understand technical documents, only a handful of our top college graduates can read or speak passable Japanese—or French, German, Russian, Arabic, Chinese, or any other language. In Silicon Valley, Japanese-speaking engineers are a rare breed, even though Japan is our major competitor. But in Tokyo, English-speaking Japanese engineers are everywhere. At major international conferences and trade shows, we are a tongue-tied nation in an increasingly multilingual world.

As a result, we often fail to understand our trading partners and become easily frustrated with their business practices. We wait for foreign products and technologies to land on our doorstep before we act, but by then it is too late. We are beaten at our own game before we begin. Now we are demanding a more level playing field, but even if Japan concedes to our every demand, our projected bilateral trade deficit in 1986 would only be reduced by several billion dollars at most. We would still lose industries because we fail to realize that, in a fast-moving world, victory goes to the fleet-footed and the well-informed, for information and vigilance are power. This is our Achilles' heel; we are like the first samurai, swaggering through the door.

For years we could console ourselves with the thought that we were at least more imaginative and creative than our trading partners. Japan may be a fierce competitor, but we still view it as a second-rate copycat. We like to believe that without western science and technology—be it the "Yankee ingenuity" of Deming's quality control techniques or Silicon Valley's chip revolution—Japan would have remained in the dark ages. Despite the fact that foreigners are being granted a growing number of patents here, we still believe that most inventions and discoveries are being made by Americans, as measured by the Nobel prizes we have won.

I fear that we Americans are in for a rude shock. We may have been the leading innovators in the past, but this situation is rapidly changing. Today, Japan is undergoing a major transformation that promises to question some of our most cherished beliefs about the uses of science and technology. In field after field—ceramics, semiconductors, fashion design, biotechnology, solar energy, video and stereo equipment, optical communications, new metals and alloys, supercomputers, lasers, pharmaceuticals, factory automation, and robotics—Japan is catching up with and passing us, not only in product development but also in basic research. Japanese researchers are beginning to explore areas where few westerners have trod, such as optical computers, biochips, underwater robots, and automated aquaculture. They are introducing new approaches to science that have not been seen in the West. The fifth generation computer is only the tip of the iceberg. Japanese companies are already studying the feasibility of a sixth generation computer—the biocomputer—that will have the sophisticated memory and processing speeds of the human brain. Indeed, we are seeing a fundamental shift from "Japan Inc." as we knew it in the 1950s and 1960s to the "Japan

Tech" of the 1990s—a transition from imitation to innovation, from copying to creativity.

Ten years ago, when I worked and studied in Japan, people were depressed over the oil shock, rapid inflation, and environmental pollution. Minamata, where hundreds were severely retarded by mercury poisoning, was the symbol of everything that was wrong with "Japan Inc." Today, when I visit Japan on research, the mood is totally changed. I hear less about "catching up" or "sinking into the ocean" and more about exploring new frontiers and producing creative people. In magazines, newspapers, television programs, and everyday conversations, there is a sense of searching and urgency in the air. Creativity seems to be on everyone's mind—from schoolteachers and parents to taxi drivers and company presidents. Indeed, creativity has become an industrial slogan for the 1980s, just as quality was the watchword some years ago. "We cannot afford to remain imitators," say my friends and relatives. "We must become more creative, like the West." Some Japanese researchers are more pointed: "Frankly, we've hit the bottom of the barrel. There's not much in the West that we don't already know about. In fact, in many areas, we're ahead."

Many of my Japanese counterparts, especially those who have studied and lived overseas, want a more creative, well-balanced education for their children. They are frustrated with the regimentation and conformity of Japanese schools. They want a change, but there are many obstacles. Probably the major roadblock is the educational system. In personal discussions, many Japanese businessmen and officials at the Ministry of International Trade and Industry (MITI)—Japan's industrial watchdog—confide that they have given up battling with the Ministry of Education (MOE), which maintains a tight grip on the nation's educational system. "MOE is so hopelessly old-fashioned," they sigh. "We just ignore it or go around it." This sentiment is shared by growing numbers of Japanese demanding educational reform.

Given this situation, how will Japan make the shift from copying to creativity? How will it educate more creative people? What are its plans for encouraging innovative research?

In 1980, MITI attempted to answer these questions by announcing the Technopolis Concept, an audacious plan to build a network of nineteen high-tech cities throughout Japan. Based on

Silicon Valley's spinoff development pattern and the Tsukuba Science City outside of Tokyo, the new technopolises will be the engines for Japan's economic growth in the twenty-first century. They will be the focal point for advanced research in "sunrise" industries, such as biotechnology, fine ceramics, electronics, new materials, robotics, mechatronics (electronic machinery), computers, and software. Companies relocating to these technopolises will be eligible to receive tax incentives and Japan Development Bank loans, and special retraining programs will be available for people returning from larger cities. But these technopolises will not just be sterile, unfeeling science cities peopled by computer nerds. They will blend science, technology, and traditional Japanese culture into new communities that emphasize the development of creative, well-rounded people. Unlike Japan's crowded cities, they are located in unspoiled rural areas. They will offer ample housing, shopping malls, schools, recreational areas, life-long learning centers, and a relaxed lifestyle more typically found in the West. Telecommunications networks and online data bases will link researchers to the latest developments around the world. In ten years, the basic infrastructure of these new cities will be complete. During the twenty-first century, MITI expects the technopolises to become the greenhouses for creative new researchers and technologies. "For us," says one of the Technopolis planners, "this is the first good news in ten years. It's like the light at the end of the tunnel. So many people have high expectations that we are working hard to make it a success."

To Americans, MITI's plan to build a nationwide network of technopolises may sound overambitious or naive. After all, how can a government agency with limited funds like MITI possibly hope to recreate the free-wheeling, innovative environment of Silicon Valley? Won't more government intervention merely stifle creativity and bring about a welfare society for the rich? Even if technopolises are built, will companies relocate to these isolated industrial parks and pursue original research? Or will the technopolises become albatrosses around the necks of MITI and local governments, like the scheme to "remodel the Japanese archipelago" that failed so miserably under former Premier Kakuei Tanaka?

These are valid questions, but they overlook the fact that many countries and several American states have successfully built research cities to enhance their industrial competitiveness. The Research Triangle Park in North Carolina, Louvain University Science City in Belgium, Sophia Antipolis in southern France, and the Novosibirsk Science City in the Soviet Union are examples of government-planned cities that have created a critical mass of researchers and scientists. New Silicon Valleys are popping up throughout the world. The United Kingdom has developed a "Silicon Glen" in Scotland, Milton Keynes and Cambridge in England, and a high-tech center in Ireland. France is building high-tech zones in Grenoble and outside of Paris. West Germany has set up "technoparks" in Berlin, Stuttgart, and Munich. South Korea is building the Daeduk Science City near Taejon, a hundred miles south of Seoul, while Taiwan is hard at work building its Hsinchu Science City southwest of Taipei. Even mainland China has gotten into the game with Shenzhen, a new research city and university across the border from Hong Kong.

What makes the Technopolis Concept unique, however, is Japan's experience with building the Tsukuba Science City and Atsugi Research City, its competitor south of Tokyo. In industry after industry, Japan's method of promoting joint research—in short, "teamwork"—has proved a tough combination to beat. The Technopolis Concept expands on this idea by promoting private capital investment and joint research in high-tech industries. It shifts the focus of national policy from promoting specific industries to fostering creativity and the process of innovation.

Columnist Leigh Weimers of the *San Jose Mercury* puts it succinctly: "What the Japanese are trying to do is build nineteen Silicon Valleys. They're just saying, 'Here's what we're going to do—see if you can keep up.' We've been worrying about losing individual secrets, as in the Hitachi-IBM case. Maybe we should have been worrying about the whole valley."

The idea of "cloning" foreign cities is not new in Japan. A thousand years ago, during the Nara and Heian periods, Japan adopted numerous ideas and theories from China, then the most advanced civilization in the world. The ancient capitals of Nara and Kyoto were patterned after the T'ang capital of Ch'ang-an. During the Meiji Period Japan built the city of Sapporo in northern Hokkaido with the help of American planners. In the early 1960s the Japanese government studied foreign cities to build its Tsukuba Science City. Now MITI is cloning Silicon Valley and "Japanizing" it.

The Technopolis Concept is only the latest phase in this legacy of city-building by adapting foreign ideas. Many Americans believe it cannot be done. But most people said the same thing about Silicon Valley thirty years ago. There was no way that one could transform a sleepy farm town in the "Valley of the Heart's Delight" into a center of American high technology. It was a quixotic dream for wild-eyed dreamers like Fred Terman and Dr. William Shockley.

Now Japan has caught "Silicon Valley fever"; but in Japan it is called "Technopolis fever." Sixteen prefectures have been given the green light by MITI and are rapidly building their new high-tech cities. Japanese companies are opening new plants and research centers in these technopolises. By 1990, the technopolises will complete their basic infrastructure of universities, industrial parks, airports, and roads. In twenty years, some of the nineteen cities will succeed in achieving their goals. Some will even make dramatic breakthroughs in science and technology. But the real challenge facing Japan is not whether the technopolises can be built, but whether the Japanese can become creative. Can they discover a style of creativity that is truly their own? Can they trigger a flood of creativity in their communities, schools, and industries? Can they discover new ways to unleash the tremendous frustrations and dreams that lie percolating below the surface? Or will they always look to the West for new ideas and inspiration? In the long run these are the questions that will ultimately determine the success or failure of the technopolises. Japan alone must answer these questions if it is to become a nation of creativity and vision—a nation with the capacity for big dreams.

And for Americans the challenge is clear. We are witnessing a transformation of our Pacific partner in ways that will fundamentally change the nature of our relationship. How will we respond to this new challenge? Will we wield our sword of protectionism? Or will we find new ways to make our industries more innovative and internationally competitive? Will we be able to improve our schools and create new jobs for people being displaced? Will we find ways to channel the energy and dreams of our people? This country has a wealth of people and resources on which to draw. Our problem has not been a lack of opportunity and choice, but of vigilance and resolve. Which way are we going? How will we get there? These are questions we must address now if we are to remain an economic superpower in the twenty-first century.

Recently, I was visited at Dataquest by a 53-year-old engineer who wanted to discuss what his company could do to meet the Japanese challenge. His semiconductor company, like many others in Silicon Valley, has lost market share to Japanese competitors and he was worried about the future of his company and the valley. "I'm scared," he said. "We lost our steel industry, our ship-building industy, our TV industry—almost every major industry—to the Japanese. Now we may be losing our semiconductor industry. If I lose my job, how will I be able to raise my family and send my kids to college? What will they do when they grow up if we keep losing our industries? How can we maintain our competitiveness? How can we keep our heads up?"

I share this engineer's worries, not only because of my concern for the future of American industries, but because of my close personal ties to Silicon Valley—my birthplace and home. From childhood, I watched the valley grow from the "Valley of the Heart's Delight" to the heart of American high technology. I shared the joys of its many successes—from the Apollo Project to Apple Computer—and witnessed the agony of its recessions and layoffs. I rooted for its gutsy entrepreneurs and lamented as major companies gave pink slips to my colleagues and friends. Japan may be one of our closest allies, but I don't want Silicon Valley to become another Detroit. The last time the United States and Japan fought, my family and 112,000 other Americans of Japanese ancestry were thrown into detention camps in the desert for four years. That is why I have written this book—to give Americans a better understanding of our Japanese partners and to avoid another fruitless backlash of "Japan-bashing" and anti-Japanese sentiment. The United States and Japan are powerful countries, and we have much to lose in a heated trade war. We must act now and move beyond protectionism.

Sheridan Tatsuno
Fremont, California

PART I : TECHNOLOGY

Entering the Race

Since World War II, Japan has worked hard at catching up with the West in advanced technologies. In the lean postwar years, copying from the West—not reinventing the wheel—was seen as the surest and quickest road to recovery. But the Japanese added a twist: they made improvements to the foreign technology. Under the guidance of the Ministry of International Trade and Industry (MITI), Japanese companies invested heavily in new plants and equipment, and developed new manufacturing techniques to produce low-cost products. Quality became a national obsession.

Today, Japan finds itself in a dilemma. Westerners are reluctant to share their technology for fear of the "boomerang effect," and other Asian nations are undercutting Japan with low-cost products. Japanese researchers have caught up with and even surpassed the West in many fields. For the first time, Japan must innovate to maintain its competitiveness. Creativity has become its new industrial slogan.

MITI's industrial policies reflect this changing environment. In its *Visions for the 1980s*, MITI urged Japanese industry to shift from copying to creativity. Centralized policies will give way to corporate initiatives and regional high-tech strategies, such as the Technopolis program. "Japan Inc." as we know it now will cease to exist; it will be transformed into the "Japan Tech" of the twenty-first century.

1

CATCHING UP WITH THE WEST

> Business is not an individual
> game; it is teamwork. Nothing
> can be accomplished without har-
> monious collaboration.
>
> *Akio Morita*
> *President of Sony Corporation*

FROM ASHES TO TRANSISTORS

Akio Morita trudged up the rickety stairway of the burned-out
Shirokiya department store in Tokyo's Ginza district and stared
out the window of his third-floor office. In all directions the city
was in ashes. To the north the financial district of Marunouchi and
the shops in Nihonbashi had been burned to a crisp; to the east,
beyond the twisted railroad tracks, were the charred ruins of the
Takarazuka Theater. Aside from a few gutted concrete buildings
still standing in the gray rubble, General Curtis LeMay's massive
carpet bombings and the ensuing firestorms had totally leveled
the city in March 1945. The war was over, but the enormous task
of rebuilding the nation lay ahead. In its haste to catch up, Japan
had blindly copied from the West and been soundly beaten at the
foreigners' game. Now it had to learn how to survive using its
own wits.

In the streets below, armies of ragged people begged for work
in order to feed their starving families. Morita and his partner,
Masaru Ibuka, could only afford to hire a few people to run the
small electronics company they had established in October 1945,
a month after Japan's surrender. Calling themselves the Tokyo
Telecommunications Engineering Corporation (better known as
Sony), Morita and his threadbare team set out to make and repair

radios, short-wave converters, and phonographs for Tokyo's music-hungry population. Combing the city, they gathered all the scraps and electrical parts they could find to start their new business, and settled into their Spartan quarters.

With pluck and persistence, the Sony team worked long hours inventing and testing new products, stumbling temporarily with an ill-fated electric rice cooker. In wartorn Japan, electronic goods were scarce, so they were forced to devise products of their own. Gradually, the bustling little company secured orders for its vacuum tube voltmeters, tape recorders, and mixer-consoles from the Japan Broadcasting Company (NHK), the Japan National Railway, and other government agencies. Despite numerous setbacks, the Sony team persevered, growing into a company of seventy employees. Its future looked bright. Then, in 1950, Sony fired the public's imagination with the first portable tape recorder, a novel little machine that quickly made its way into businesses, homes, and schools, giving voice to a whole new generation of people. Japan's postwar electronics industry was finally on its way.

Meanwhile, excitement was brewing across town. At the Electrical Basic Research Laboratory of the Ministry of Commerce and Industry (MCI), researchers Michio Hatoyama and Makoto Kikuchi were avidly following the development of the transistor that had been announced by Bell Labs in December 1947. Hatoyama, now an advisor to Sony, had been involved in nuclear and microwave research during the war. He encouraged the younger Kikuchi (now the head of Sony's central R&D lab) to join him at MCI. Teaming up with Professor Hiroshi Watanabe (Tohoku University), Hiroshi Kiyomiya (Fujitsu), and Goto Yoshida (NEC Seiki), the small group began studying technical papers on the transistor at the American Occupation Headquarters Library in Tokyo. They were especially intrigued by an article that appeared in the July 12, 1948 issue of *Time* magazine describing Bell Labs' transistor. Although none of them had ever seen a transistor or had the foggiest idea how it worked, their curiosity was piqued. They wanted to develop a device of their own—one that would enable them to catch up with America, which had beaten them once on the battlefield, and now in the laboratory.

By late 1948, Japanese researchers were intensely studying the transistor. Professor Watanabe of Tohoku University formed a study group of researchers who eventually became the leaders of Japan's infant electronics industry: Masaji Kobayashi (NEC), Hiroe Osafune (NEC), Tomono Masami (Hitachi), Akio Kobayashi (Toshiba/Tohoku University/MITI), Jiro Yamasaki (Tokyo University), and Namio Honda (Tohoku University). Although Professor Watanabe believed that the transistor would replace the vacuum tube, others were skeptical, except for young Kikuchi who took the ideas being tossed around and conducted experiments of his own. To his dismay, germanium, which was being used by Bell Labs, was an extremely scarce material in postwar Japan. Hatoyama suggested he try another material that had been used in microwave devices during the war: silicon. Kikuchi took his advice and, in early 1950, achieved startling results; the transistor worked! Although the device needed to be refined, Hatoyama wasted no time. He presented their findings at Japan's first transistor symposium later that year.

The turmoil in their laboratory, which was, in Kikuchi's words, no more than a "horse stall," mirrored the momentous changes being wrought by General MacArthur as part of his overall program to break up the heavy industrial combines (*zaibatsu*), rewrite the Japanese Constitution, and restructure government ministries. In 1949 General MacArthur abolished the Communications Ministry and split it into the Ministry of Telecommunications and the Ministry of Posts. At the end of the Occupation in 1952, these ministries were merged into the present Ministry of Posts and Telecommunications (MPT). Japanese officials also merged the prewar Trade Agency and the Ministry of Commerce and Industry into a new ministry called the Ministry of International Trade and Industry (MITI) in an effort to reduce Japan's reliance on American aid and to fight postwar inflation. MITI's main role was to direct the rebuilding of Japan's devastated economy. In 1949, MITI's authority was bolstered by the passage of two laws—the Foreign Investment Law and the Foreign Exchange and Foreign Trade Control Law—which gave it the power to approve imports, joint ventures, foreign exchange transactions, and foreign investments. By uniting all powers under one "super-agency," MITI exercised almost total control over Japan's indus-

trial recovery and international trade relations. Ironically, it was
this concentration of power—a vestige of the American Occupation—that came to be known in the West as "Japan Inc."

The reorganization divided the responsibilities for electronic
research between the two new ministries. Communications
research was assigned to the Electrical Communication Laboratory (ECL) of Nippon Telegraph and Telephone, a public corporation created by MPT in 1952 to rebuild the nation's telephone
system. Electronics research was handled by MITI at its newly
created Electrotechnical Laboratory (ETL), which was formed by
researchers from the old MCI lab and directed by MITI's Agency
for Industrial Science and Technology. NTT and MITI pursued
different approaches. NTT developed transistors for its new communications systems, while MITI focused on computers and consumer goods because of its responsibility for expanding foreign
trade. Although this division of labor seemed logical at the time, it
led to duplicate research and turf battles over funding and
authority.

Japan's first transistor symposium in 1950 sparked an explosion
of activity among Japanese researchers. Among these were
Yoshida Goto of NTT and two researchers, Shingo Iwase (now
with Tokyo Sanyo) and Toshifumi Asakawa (head of Ricoh's technology division). Asakawa and Iwase set out to develop their own
transistor. They noted, as Kikuchi had earlier, that germanium was
unavailable in Japan. But following their instincts, they searched
the sidewalk stalls of Akihabara, a black market that specialized in
electrical components, where they found a used American-made
germanium amplifier. They took the valuable germanium out and
fashioned a crude transistor. The low quality of the germanium
posed problems, but the device eventually worked. In February
1951 they presented their findings at a physics symposium in
Osaka. With this paper, the race between MITI and NTT to produce the first practical transistor was on!

During the next three years, both groups devoted all their energies to developing the transistor. The Hatoyama-Kikuchi team
(MITI) focused on silicon, while the Iwase-Asakawa team (NTT)
tried to build a germanium transistor—a prudent choice, since
little was then known about the conductive properties of silicon.
The NTT team made rapid progress and developed an alloy junction transistor that was displayed at the Fifth Electronics Exhibi-

tion in June 1953. MITI officials were dismayed at the prospect of being shown up by this "new kid on the block" and redoubled their efforts, leading to the strong rivalry between the MITI and NTT research labs that still exists today.

In the early 1950s, Japan's fledgling electronics industry received an unexpected boost. The Korean War and the consequent lifting of restrictions imposed by the Occupation Forces created a military procurement market and triggered a demand for consumer goods. Private radio broadcasting was resumed in 1951, followed by television broadcasting in 1953. To protect Japan's infant electronics industry, MITI imposed restrictions on foreign investments and American transistor imports in 1952. Japanese companies signed agreements with foreign firms to obtain the latest transistor technology—an approach encouraged by MITI. Toshiba and Hitachi signed technology agreements with RCA and Western Electric, and Matsushita with Philips and Western Electric. Ignoring MITI's advice, Sony signed up with Western Electric. By 1955, Fujitsu, Hitachi, Matsushita, Nippon Electric (NEC), and Toshiba were all producing transistors under license.

THE TRANSISTOR BOOM

In August 1955, Sony displayed a gleaming little product that shook the consumer world. Thin and compact, the TR-55 portable transistor radio was half the size of a carton of cigarettes. Its sound quality left something to be desired (a fatal flaw in the eyes of the critics), but young people didn't seem to mind. To them, portability and convenience, hallmarks of the 50s generation, were more important. Their carefree lifestyle and swooning over Elvis Presley made an impact on the corporate bottom line. In the first year Sony sold half a million transistor radios, grossing $2.5 million. With its pocket-sized model, Sony's sales soared even higher and its staff grew from 400 to 1,200. Other Japanese companies copied Sony, choosing names such as "Sonny" and "Somy" for their products. Soon the transistor radio overwhelmed Japan with the force of rock and roll.

In the United States, the boom did not have the same impact on American manufacturers such as General Electric, Motorola, RCA, and Zenith, who dominated the consumer market with their large table radios and consoles. They viewed transistor radios as tinny electronic curiosities from Japan that would be only a passing fad. Because of their heavy investment in tube radio plants, they were reluctant to pursue the new transistor technology. After all, why invest in a short-lived gimmick?

The Japanese, however, saw the transistor radio as a wedge into world markets and a means for earning scarce foreign currency. Companies made a conscious decision to transistorize their consumer products, a decision that was critical in bolstering Japan's fledgling electronics industry. Between 1957 and 1962, Japanese production of electronic equipment increased almost five-fold. Transistor radios accounted for 20% of all electronic equipment manufactured. About 80% of all transistor radios were exported, with half going to the United States.

Transistor technology not only fueled the growing consumer market, but also stimulated computer research. In 1951 Tokyo University and Toshiba developed a vacuum tube computer, though it was far behind the Mark I vacuum tube computer that had been developed in the United States in 1944. The urgency of this research was highlighted in 1954 with the arrival of American computer imports. In 1955, at the request of electronics companies such as Fujitsu, Hitachi, Matsushita, NEC, and Toshiba, MITI formed a Computer Research Committee to chart the direction of Japan's computer industry. The committee recommended limiting foreign computer imports, promoting transistor and computer research, and importing foreign technology through licenses and technical assistance.

Two computer projects were organized: one at MITI's Electrotechnical Laboratory and a joint project involving Tokyo University, NTT's Electrical Communication Laboratory, and Kokusai Denshin Denwa (KDD), NTT's international affiliate. MITI developed the ETL-MARK series of computers, which laid the groundwork for Japan's commercial transistor computers. In 1958 NTT introduced the MUSASHINO-1 parametron computer, which was quickly commercialized; because of its slow operating speed and high power consumption, it was soon replaced by transistor computers. This time MITI, which had developed transistor computers, was vindicated in the technology race with NTT.

To catch up with the United States, the Japanese government actively promoted the nation's computer industry. In 1956 the Machinery Temporary Measures Act provided for direct grants and low-interest loans for R&D investments and foreign technology acquisitions. In 1957 this law was expanded into the Electronics Industry Provisional Development Act, which authorized direct subsidies and special tax depreciation for R&D and capital investments, government loans for newly introduced products, selective exemption from antitrust laws, and raw material cartels. To implement these laws, MITI created the Electronics Policy Division and the Electronics Industry Deliberation Council (EIDC). EIDC was supported by the Japan Electronics Industry Development Association (JEIDA), a group of chairmen from twenty-five top electronics companies.

This restructuring of the industry under MITI guidance led to the introduction of small business computers, such as Nippon Electric Company's NEAC-1200 and Hitachi's HIPAC-1, which used parametron technology. In 1958 transistor versions of these computers were introduced in Paris at the first International Information Processing Conference (AUTOMAS). Despite their commercial viability, computers remained a secondary concern for MITI, not a national economic priority.

This situation changed in 1959 when IBM announced its Model 1401, a low-priced, powerful office machine that signaled the shift to the second generation of computers. IBM and Sperry-Rand planned to build manufacturing plants in Japan, and they held basic patents that Japanese manufacturers desperately wanted. By 1960 foreign imports captured 70% of the Japanese computer market, causing alarm among industry leaders. MITI responded with a series of counterattacks. First it raised tariffs from 15% to 25% and imposed "Buy Japan" procurement policies and tougher foreign exchange controls. In 1961 it organized the FONTAC Computer Project (1961–1964) and assigned Oki Electric and NEC to develop the hardware and Fujitsu to write the software. To compete with IBM's sophisticated leasing system, MITI encouraged Japanese companies to form the Japan Electronics Computer Corporation (JECC), a computer leasing company that bought computers from the computer manufacturers and rented them to users. This program was crucial, since 80% of the installed computers in Japan in 1961 were rented. Financed by

private companies and Japan Development Bank loans, JECC enabled Japanese manufacturers to compete against IBM and other
foreign firms which rented their computers at 1/40 to 1/60 of the
purchase price. By 1970 JECC had bought $250 million worth of
computers, a figure that leaped to $7.3 billion by 1981, not
including rental revenues of $5.6 billion.

MITI guidance and JECC purchases provided a badly needed
boost to the industry, but Japanese computer makers saw they
were still far behind American companies, especially IBM, which
dominated the market. Journalists called the situation "IBM and
the Seven Dwarfs." Under the Foreign Investment Law of 1949,
MITI had the power to deny IBM's request to build a manufacturing plant in Japan, but IBM had a powerful bargaining weapon—
the ability to block Japanese computer production. After lengthy
negotiations, MITI granted IBM manufacturing rights and foreign
exchange guarantees in return for IBM's licensing its patents to all
interested Japanese computer makers. In 1960 IBM signed cross-
licensing agreements with thirteen Japanese manufacturers; these
were renegotiated in 1971 with fifteen companies.

Japanese computer makers licensed technology from other
American companies: Hitachi from RCA (1961), Mitsubishi from
TRW (1962), NEC from Honeywell (1962), Oki Electric from
Sperry Rand (1963), and Toshiba from GE (1964). In almost
every case, Japanese manufacturers copied the American prod-
ucts, then gradually added their own features.

Although these agreements enabled Japanese companies to
compete against American companies, this advantage soon dis-
appeared. Between 1955 and 1967, Japanese wages in the electrical machinery sector jumped 128%, compared to 51% in the
United States. Moreover, American firms moved their production lines to Hong Kong, Taiwan, Korea, Singapore, and other
Southeast Asian countries, further undercutting Japan's labor
cost advantage. To maintain their competitiveness, Japanese
companies increased their R&D spending and plant investments.
Funding for electronics research labs boomed in 1961, and
major firms raided each other for top researchers. IBM's Watson
Labs attracted Sony's Reona Esaki, who later won the Nobel
Prize in physics. Michio Hatoyama of MITI went to Sony and
NTT's Shingo Iwase was hired by Sanyo. Pressed by "the Ameri-
can challenge" that was also overwhelming Europe, Japanese

industry buckled down to the tough task of becoming more cost-efficient. Despite its rapid progress in consumer electronics, Japan was still behind the West, which had far better research facilities, more funding, and creative scientists. The race to catch up now turned into a sprint with the advent of integrated circuits (ICs).

THE SHIFT TO INTEGRATED CIRCUITS

During the 1950s, while Europe and Japan produced germanium-based transistors for consumer products, the United States focused its research on silicon. The American direction was heavily influenced by the Department of Defense and NASA, which sought rugged, miniaturized devices for their different missions. In 1959 the Air Force contracted Texas Instruments to develop integrated circuits (ICs) for the Minuteman II missile, while NASA awarded contracts for the Apollo spacecraft computer to Fairchild, whose planar process (which involves etching IC designs on chemically-treated silicon wafers) was critical for large-scale IC production. In the early 1960s, twelve key military and space contracts were issued as U.S. production of ICs jumped from $4 million to $80 million. By 1963, worldwide industry sales passed the $1 billion mark. During this period, Fairchild spun off new companies, such as National Semiconductor, Signetics, and Siliconix, which pursued new IC technologies.

By contrast, the Japanese semiconductor industry developed completely around the consumer market. Without the demand created by military and space programs, silicon technology was extremely expensive to develop, and IC production remained small-scale—only $58,000 in 1963 and $1.6 million in 1966. Japanese manufacturers were stuck with transistor technology until MITI forced NEC to sublicense the planar technology that it had purchased from Fairchild. With the new technology, Japanese manufacturers quickly jumped into IC production: Mitsubishi Electric and NEC (1965), Toshiba (1966), Fujitsu and Oki (1967), and Sharp (1969). Japanese IC makers received a strong boost in demand from the emergence of the calculator market. In 1964, Sharp and Sony announced transistor-based calculators, which were followed by Casio's memory calculator in 1965. Competition between Sharp and Casio rapidly escalated into the famous "calculator war."

THE AMERICAN CHALLENGE

While electronics makers battled for a share of the lucrative consumer market, Japanese industry was again jolted out of its complacency by several events. In 1964 IBM introduced the System 360, a third generation computer that was a quantum leap over Japanese computer technology, and highly visible because it was used at the Olympic Games in Tokyo and at many Japanese banks. At the same time, Texas Instruments demanded that MITI approve its petition for a wholly-owned subsidiary in Japan in exchange for being required to license its new IC technology to Japanese companies. Then, in 1965, TI applied for a patent for its IC technology (the Kilby patent), which was called the "TI Shock" because the technology was crucial for producing ICs. In 1964, Machines Bull, France's largest computer manufacturer, was purchased by GE in what the French called *Le Défi Américain* (The American Challenge). These events convinced industry leaders that the United States was out to swallow up Japan's infant computer industry.

From 1964, MITI began vigorously promoting the Japanese computer industry. To blunt the American offensive, the ministry requested the Electronic Industry Deliberation Council (EIDC) to recommend a computer strategy that would enable Japan to achieve technological excellence and increase its local market share. MITI established a computer data and policy analysis center, and encouraged the top six manufacturers to form the Japan Information Processing Center (JIPC), a private research institute. The two groups were instrumental in organizing the $28 million Super High-Performance Electronic Computer Development Project (1966–1971) under the guidance of MITI's Electrical Technical Laboratory. In this project, the "Big Six" computer makers were assigned to develop computer mainframes, disk drives, display terminals, and other peripherals. Nippon Telegraph and Telephone organized the Dendenkosha Information Processing System (DIPS) project in 1968 to connect timesharing computers to electronic exchange and transmission systems. MITI also created the Information Technology Promotion Agency, which lent money to start-up software houses. Forty private software companies were founded in 1971 alone.

The computer industry received top priority, but MITI protected the semiconductor industry as well because of its critical link to computer development. MITI's strategy was to limit foreign imports and acquire foreign technology through patent agreements. The "TI Shock" was the first test of MITI's resolve. Japanese manufacturers, already paying a 4.5% patent royalty to Fairchild for its planar technology, argued that excess royalty payments to TI would make domestic ICs uncompetitive. They asked that the patent be denied. MITI took the manufacturers' request into advisement and waited until 1967 before replying to TI's request with the following conditions: (1) the Kilby patent would be made public with reasonable royalty rates; (2) TI would establish a joint venture with a Japanese company and limit its participation to 50%; and (3) TI would not challenge domestic companies by increasing its production.

Texas Instruments rejected these conditions and refused to license its IC patents, but this did not prevent Japanese manufacturers from jumping into the market. By 1967, Japanese companies began exporting electronic calculators and other goods, while TI's patent request was enmeshed in government procedures. Worried that TI might file suit, MITI asked domestic companies to withhold exports. In 1968 the deadlock was broken when TI capitulated to MITI's conditions. But by then, the damage was done. Japanese manufacturers had captured most of the emerging IC market. TI was forced to compromise to avoid being shut out of the Japanese market altogether. The finally settlement included a 50/50 joint venture with Sony, licensing the Kilby patent to Hitachi, Mitsubishi, NEC, Sony, and Toshiba, and limiting production to 10% of the Japanese market. It was the TI incident that firmly fixed MITI's image in the West as "Japan Inc."

With the TI issue resolved, the Japanese IC industry grew rapidly. Total IC production among the top twelve manufacturers leaped four-fold, increasing from $30 million in 1968 to $114 million in 1970. Demand for ICs was generated by the booming desktop calculator market, which absorbed more than 60% of the domestic Japanese IC production in 1969.

Despite the industry's expansion, several events threatened to undermine Japan's position in ICs and computers. In the mid-1960s, thirty-six new U.S. semiconductor companies, such as Avantek, Intel, and Mostek, were founded, and older companies like Fairchild, National Semiconductor, and Texas Instruments pursued aggressive pricing strategies. Then, in 1970, import controls on ICs and computers were lifted as a result of international trade talks, causing IC prices to drop to one-fourth of their 1969 price by the summer of 1970. Japanese producers petitioned the government for protection against U.S. "dumping," but this effort failed. Then, to top it all off, IBM introduced its Model 370 series in late 1970, which slashed computing costs by 60%.

In response, MITI pursued several policies to expand local computer production and reduce foreign domination. In 1971 MITI pushed through the Japanese Diet the Law for Provisional Measures to Promote Electronic and Machinery Industries (*Kidenho*). This focused R&D investments in three areas: computers and ICs, magnetic disks and facsimile equipment, and advanced production techniques. These projects received direct MITI funding and low-interest Japan Development Bank loans, while MITI provided guidance in procurement, industrial standards, and technology upgrading. Under the *Kidenho*, which permitted corporate mergers, MITI encouraged Japanese manufacturers to pair off into three groups: Oki/Mitsubishi Electric (COSMOS Computer Series), Toshiba/NEC (ACOS Computer Series), and Fujitsu/Hitachi (M Computer Series). MITI hoped to take advantage of the cross-licensing agreements these companies had signed with American computer makers. For example, Honeywell, NEC's licensor, had merged with General Electric, Toshiba's licensor. The Mitsubishi-Oki venture linked Mitsubishi to Univac, Oki's joint venture partner. Despite MITI's financial support during the early 1970s, there was a falling-out among several these groups. In 1975, Oki split off from Mitsubishi, which joined Hitachi and Fujitsu to conduct semiconductor research. The Fujitsu-Hitachi alliance fell apart when Fujitsu introduced the M-180-2 model and Hitachi its M-162 and M-200 models.

Nippon Telegraph and Telephone (NTT) had better luck with its 35 billion yen Pattern Information Processing System (PIPS) computer project (1971–1980), which focused on developing a fourth generation computer that could recognize complex Japanese characters, three-dimensional objects, and human speech. In this project, Hitachi, Fujitsu, and NEC developed the components for their office automation (OA) products, laying the foundation for the next step in technology—the fifth generation computer. Japan still had a long way to go, but it was quickly catching up.

DESIGNING NEW CHIPS

In 1975 Japanese industry was confronted with yet another challenge from the West. American mainframe computer manufacturers introduced inexpensive plug-compatible machines that offered large-scale integrated (LSI) circuits and IBM-compatible software. IBM flexed its technical muscle with its Future System computer, which incorporated very large-scale integrated (VLSI) circuits designed with leading-edge electron beam equipment. For Japanese manufacturers, these new products came at an inopportune time. In 1974 the government had begun liberalizing imports of semiconductors, computers, software, and peripheral equipment. Controls were also being eased on foreign investments in computer manufacturing plants in Japan. There was fear in Tokyo that American companies, especially IBM, would continue to dominate Japanese industry.

These events sent shock waves throughout Japan. To meet this new challenge, Nippon Telegraph and Telephone (NTT) and MITI organized separate research projects to develop VLSI circuits. In April 1975, NTT formed a consortium with Fujitsu, Hitachi, and NEC to develop advanced communication systems. The first phase focused on photolithography and submicron (less than one millionth of a meter) device technologies. The second phase covered special VLSI circuits for NTT's communications systems. The three participating companies invested R&D funds in their own labs, where research was conducted under the guidance of engineers from NTT's Electrical Communication Research Laboratory. NTT did not provide direct funding, but subsidized them through its massive procurement program.

The second and most well-known project was MITI's VLSI Project. Early in 1975 MITI officials and members of the Japan Electronic Industry Development Association (JEIDA) discussed the need to meet the IBM challenge. At the time, computer makers, NTT, and MITI were working independently on the 64K dynamic RAM (64 thousand bits of directly accessible memory). Professor Shoji Tanaka of Tokyo University suggested that they join forces, but the companies hesitated because of the difficulties they had encountered earlier in jointly developing the ACOS, COSMOS, and M Series computers. Moreover, MITI officials were reluctant to tackle the highly complex VLSI technology because of the public's distaste for giving subsidies to large corporations. But the specter of IBM's growing domination worried industry leaders. Everyone realized that no single company could tackle "Big Blue" alone. Thus, after a series of talks led by Dr. Yasuo Tarui of MITI's Electrotechnical Laboratory, the JEIDA members decided to cooperate.

On July 15, 1975, the five leading computer companies (Fujitsu, Hitachi, Mitsubishi Electric, NEC, and Toshiba) formed the VLSI Research Association, with Masato Nebashi, a former MITI official, as its executive director, and Dr. Tarui, as research director. The Association began its operations in March 1976, but without NTT's participation. MITI had suggested a joint project, but NTT declined because it already had the most advanced VLSI lab and was unwilling to sacrifice its telecommunications research for the more general goals of computer development. Moreover, the historic rivalry between these two agencies posed major organizational obstacles.

Initially, there were disagreements over research goals. The companies wanted to focus on the 64K dynamic RAM, which could be quickly commercialized, while MITI favored more long-term, basic research in the 256K and one-megabit (one million bits) DRAMs. Both parties compromised. The VLSI Association chose six areas covering basic and applied research—microfabrication technology (electron beam and X-ray), low-defect, large-diameter silicon wafer processing, computer-aided design (CAD), VLSI process techniques and equipment, VLSI testing equipment, and VLSI logic and memory devices (64K DRAM).

The VLSI Project consisted of six research labs, organized into three groups (see Appendix A). Basic research was conducted at four joint laboratories, where engineers from the participating companies worked with researchers from MITI's Electrotechnical Laboratory. Researchers were handpicked by Dr. Tarui and numbered 300 by March 1977, of whom 100 were assigned to the joint labs. The VLSI Project was unique; it was the first time that researchers from rival companies worked side by side. But company rivalries created serious barriers to the free flow of information. The mutual distrust was so great that some engineers installed locks on their doors. Although the Association held monthly seminars to exchange information, this arrangement was too formal. Finally Nebashi resorted to taking small groups of scientists out for drinks in the evening to break the ice. After a while, the barriers began to dissolve.

The late-night fraternizing may have improved communication, but it did not lessen the intense rivalry among the participating companies. Indeed, the VLSI Project triggered an "investment race" that led to a serious industry overcapacity in 1985—right in the middle of the industry's worst downturn. Between 1978 and 1984, capital spending by the top 10 Japanese semiconductor firms leaped from $298 million to $2.9 billion (see Appendix B). Japanese manufacturers also invested 13 to 16% of their sales on research, compared with only 8 to 10% for U.S. firms. On the average, Japanese companies invested 60% more per sales dollar than American companies. This heavy R&D and capital spending contributed to their growing market share during the 1980s.

MITI supplemented corporate investments with interest-free conditional loans (hōjōkin), repayable with profits derived from the project. MITI provided about 40% of the $300 million lent to the members of the VLSI Project. But more important than low-cost loans were NTT's massive procurement programs. In 1978 NTT procurement accounted for about 10%, or $230 million, of local semiconductor consumption.

The Japanese government also provided legislative support and industrial financing. In 1978 the Diet passed the Temporary Law for the Promotion of Specific Machinery and Information Industries (Kijōhō), which gave priority to three categories of leading-edge technology—prototype R&D (ICs, computers, laser equipment), commercial production (bubble memories, mass storage systems, liquid crystal displays, and high-performance remote processors), and manufacturing improvements (computers, magnetic recording media, and electronic switching systems).

The VLSI Project was responsible for helping Japan catch up with the West in three important semiconductor areas: patents, research papers, and market share. By 1980 about a thousand patent applications had been submitted. The number of Japanese research papers presented at the prestigious International Solid State Circuits Conference (ISSCC)—the "Superbowl" for IC makers—jumped from 9 papers in 1976 to 49 in 1985, when Japanese companies surpassed the United States. Most of these papers focused on leading-edge technology, such as megabit memories, superfast gallium arsenide, and image sensors.

Participants in the VLSI Project grabbed major shares of the 64K DRAM market. By the first quarter of 1979, Fujitsu began limited production of 64K DRAMs, and Hitachi and Mitsubishi Electric circulated samples. They were soon joined by NEC, Oki, and Toshiba. By the second quarter of 1981, the "Big Six" began commercial production. Despite a worldwide recession, shipments of 64K DRAMs grew rapidly in 1982. Prices for the 64K DRAMs dropped from $25 to $30 per chip in early 1981 to $4.25 in late 1982. By late 1981, Dataquest, a high-tech market research company in Silicon Valley, estimated that Japanese manufacturers had captured 70% of the worldwide market. This figure dropped to 64% in 1982 as American firms entered the market.

The phenomenal success of the VLSI Project has elicited cries of unfair industrial "targeting" from the West, but this appears to be a case of being a bad loser; MITI merely had a good idea and beat us to the draw. Since then, American companies have put aside their differences and organized their own joint R&D projects: the Semiconductor Research Cooperative (SRC) in North Carolina's Research Triangle Park and the Microelectronics & Computer Technology Corporation (MCC) in Austin, Texas. The Europeans have set up the ESPRIT program (European Strategic Program for Research and Development in Information Technologies) and the Mega Project to develop megabit chips. If one looks at the past, an interesting pattern emerges: the alternating challenge from the United States and Japan has always spurred the other side to greater efforts and achievements. On both sides, the impacted industry has cried foul, asked for government assistance, and organized cooperative action. In many ways, the U.S.-Japan rivalry has been a positive force—without Japan, the United States would not have pushed to develop new technologies so quickly, and vice versa. It has been a symbiotic, though contentious, relationship.

In retrospect, Japanese chip makers succeeded for a variety of reasons. The VLSI Project funding was instrumental in reducing basic research costs and risks to participating companies, who were also eligible for low-cost loans, special depreciation allowances and tax benefits, and greater access to private bank loans. Applied research was focused along narrow product lines that could be rapidly commercialized by companies involved in a wide range of electronic products.

But lack of American preparedness was also a contributing factor. During the 1974–1975 recession, American chip makers laid off workers and reduced plant and equipment investments, while Japanese firms kept their staffs and increased R&D spending significantly. Japanese and U.S. semiconductor investments diverged after 1978. Moreover, key U.S. firms deemphasized the 64K DRAM markets or jumped in too late. Due to the complexity of their "elegant" chip designs, several U.S. manufacturers had quality and yield problems, forcing IBM and Hewlett-Packard to buy from Japan when quality chips were unavailable from American makers in large quantities. By contrast, Japanese firms used simpler designs, larger chips, and inexpensive packaging.

Thus, the VLSI Project succeeded due to a fortuitous turn of events. American firms underinvested in production lines in the late 1970s, leaving a gaping hole in the market which the Japanese rapidly filled—just as they had done with transistor radios in the 1950s. Although Americans point to predatory pricing and dumping, these one-sided views are not substantiated by the facts. Preparation and good luck, plus Americans "caught napping," were the reasons for Japan's success in the 64K DRAM market.

But the VLSI Project is only the beginning. Because of its commercial success, MITI began forging new high-tech policies in the late 1970s. MITI's key priority is to encourage Japanese industries to shift from copying the West to developing their own in-house creativity. MITI has organized new joint R&D projects, such as the Supercomputer Project and Fifth Generation Computer Project, to effectuate this change. When queried about their goals, MITI officials vaguely refer to "making contributions to international science and technology." But their real intent is no secret in Tokyo: MITI bureaucrats are trying to regain their former power by helping Japanese industries take the lead. The shift from copying to creativity is only a vehicle for this overall industrial strategy. (Ironically, American protectionists are helping to resurrect the old MITI by investing it with greater authority over high-tech industries and foreign trade.)

Thus, Japan has come a long way in rebuilding itself since the war. By improving on foreign technology, not reinventing the wheel, Japanese electronics companies were quickly able to catch up with the West. But in copying foreign technology, Japanese have been "creative copiers"—creative in improving product designs and manufacturing techniques. Now they are trying to become creative scientists.

2
FROM JAPAN INC. TO JAPAN TECH

Japanese industrial policy is intended to encourage creativity—and a technology-intensive industrial structure that is pollution-free, resource-conservative and consumer-responsive.

Sadanori Yamanaka
Minister of International Trade
and Industry
April 1983

In 1982 Dr. Sheldon Weinig of Materials Research Corporation of New York stood before the Japan Press Club in Tokyo to announce his plans to build a semiconductor materials plant in Japan. After months of trying to obtain approval from Japanese government ministries, he was fed up with the bureaucratic red tape and decided to take his case straight to the public. He wanted to express his frustration over the inordinate delays and endless paperwork that virtually guaranteed the exclusion of foreign manufacturers from the Japanese market. "If I were a Japanese company in the United States," he said, "I wouldn't have to obtain permission from the federal government to open a new plant. Local governments would be tripping over each other to welcome me with open arms. But here it's different. You can't do anything without central government approval."

If Dr. Weinig had held his press conference five years earlier, that might have been true. But Japan was changing under the onslaught of the 1979 oil shock, slowing economic growth, and foreign pressure for more open markets. With jobs disappearing in traditional heavy industries, Japanese were scrambling for new

21

sources of jobs and revenues. And come running they did. After the press conference Dr. Weinig was bombarded with phone calls from six Japanese governors who invited him to open a plant in their economically-depressed prefectures. During the next few months he was wined and dined, taken on tours of industrial parks and universities, and treated like royalty in the finest hotels. Without realizing it, he had touched off a battle of the prefectures. Then, in late 1982, Dr. Weinig held a second press conference that would deeply influence the direction of Japanese industrial policies. With Governor Morihiko Hiramatsu, he announced that MRC would open its plant in Oita Prefecture on the southern island of Kyushu, only five miles from Texas Instruments' integrated circuit plant. Moreover, as a result of Governor Hiramatsu's lobbying at MITI, the Japan Development Bank (JDB) agreed to extend a $1.5 million loan to MRC and its Japanese partner, Midoriya Electric—the first JDB loan ever granted to a majority-owned foreign company.

This announcement was big international news, but what made it really significant was one fact that the press failed to report. Fifteen years earlier, as a top-ranking MITI official, Hiramatsu had strongly opposed Texas Instruments' entry into the Japanese market. Responding to local industry calls for protection from the "TI Shock," MITI had demanded that TI enter a 50% joint venture with Sony, license its famous Kilby patent to Japanese companies, and limit its IC production to 10% of the Japanese market—an invisible ceiling that still exists for many American semiconductor makers. This was the price of admission to the Japanese market. TI balked at these unreasonable demands, but after Japanese IC makers began grabbing market share it finally capitulated. This catapulted Hiramatsu into the role of watchdog for keeping out foreign high-tech companies.

Today Governor Hiramatsu is singing a different tune. Since his election as governor in 1979, he has made a complete about-face in his trade philosophy. Instead of stonewalling foreign investments, he is actively promoting them in Oita Prefecture— a trend that is spreading throughout Japan. His strategy is simple; using a vast network of personal contacts built up during his twenty-five-year career at MITI, he cuts through government red tape, negotiates financing and tax breaks, and invites high-tech executives to Oita where they are given the red-carpet treatment. He is a Japanese version of Chicago's former Mayor Daley, using MITI's "administrative guidance" for his own purposes. Indeed, Governor Hiramatsu was so eager to attract MRC that he took the unprecedented step of flying all the way to New York to meet with Dr. Weinig. In the past, such unabashed promotionalism was unheard of. But Governor Hiramatsu's change of heart symbolizes the gradual change in Japanese industrial policies that has been germinating since the mid-1970s. Once an unrepentant protectionist fighting to keep out "the black ships," he is now an internationalist trying to open Japan to the West. For many Japanese, his forthright, unorthodox style of political leadership is appealing, and in many quarters he has become known as "Mr. Japan Tech."

MITI'S CHANGING ROLE

During the last few years, Japanese industrial policies have come under increasing fire in the West because of Japan's phenomenal commercial successes abroad. Critics have leveled a variety of charges against Japan, ranging from "dumping" and "industrial spying" to "targeting" and "unfair trade practices." At the center of this ongoing dispute is MITI, which, because of its controversial role in setting industrial policies, is probably the most scrutinized, and most widely misunderstood, ministry in the Japanese government. Over the last twenty years, Japanese industrial policies have changed dramatically; but western perceptions of MITI remain stuck in the mid-1960s, when MITI was at its zenith as the protector of "Japan Inc." Most westerners still view MITI as an omnipotent ministry that maintains rigid control over the Japanese economy and dictates the fate of Japanese industries. Yet nothing could be further from the truth. Since 1980, MITI has been stripped of substantial legal powers, and the growing strength of Japanese industry has diminished its influence. Ask any manager of a major Japanese corporation and they inevitably chuckle at western exaggerations of MITI's power. To them, MITI is struggling to recapture its lost stature with new policy initiatives. Nevertheless, the myth of Japan Inc. still persists in the West. Why is this? How has MITI changed over the years? And what impact will its new industrial policies have on the United States?

Formed in 1949 as the result of the reorganization of the pre-war Ministry of Commerce and Industry (MCI) and the Board of Trade, MITI has gone through five phases during its tumultuous thirty-seven-year history: postwar reconstruction, the high-growth era, environmental pollution and two oil shocks, the shift to high technology, and the regional era. During each period MITI modified its industrial policies to respond to the changing environment. To better understand Japan's latest policy initiatives, let's look at how MITI has evolved over the years.

In the early 1950s, MITI was the economic high command responsible for directing the reconstruction of Japan's devastated economy. During the Occupation, it was granted enormous legal powers by General Douglas MacArthur, whose main objectives were to reform Japanese ministries and reduce Japan's economic dependence on the United States. In December 1949, the Japanese Diet passed the Foreign Exchange and Foreign Trade Control Law, which gave MITI control over international trade, foreign exchange and investments, joint ventures, and technology transfers. General MacArthur thought the law was only temporary; but as Professor Chalmers Johnson of the University of California, author of *MITI and the Japanese Miracle*, points out: "Far from being gradually relaxed, the law persisted for the next thirty years and was still on the books during 1980. It was the single most important instrument of industrial guidance and control that MITI ever possessed." He cites Leon Hollerman: "The Supreme Commander of the Allied Powers (SCAP) naively presided not only over the transfer of its own authority but also over the institutionalization of the most restrictive foreign trade and foreign exchange control system ever devised by a major free nation."

Under the 1949 law, MITI gained absolute control over all international trading activities in Japan. To protect struggling infant industries, it imposed high tariffs, import quotas, strict inspection procedures, and investment controls. These protectionist measures alone would have reduced competition and slowed technological development, so MITI stoked the heated rivalry that already existed among Japanese companies by providing advice and selectively offering financial assistance. Key strategic industries were targeted, including steel, shipbuilding, machinery, and petrochemicals. In 1951 the Japan Development Bank (JDB) was created to provide funding for specific government programs; it soon became MITI's most important tool for industrial policy. In 1952 the Enterprises Rationalization Promotion Law authorized MITI to offer subsidies and accelerated depreciation to companies investing in new equipment and machinery, and provided for the construction of new industrial parks. The Ministry of Finance (MOF) assisted by combining all postal savings accounts into one investment pool, the Investment and Loan Plan (FILP), which became a major source of cheap industrial financing. To promote exports, small businesses were encouraged to form export cartels in 1953, a policy reinforced by the Export-Import Transactions Law in 1955, which strengthened general trading companies and required compulsory cartels for small exporters. The fledgling electronics industry also received a boost with the passage of a special promotion law that offered cheap, long-term loans and direct government subsidies. Thus, by 1957, MITI's key industrial policy tools were in place. It had gained control over foreign exchange and capital, cartels, banking groups, industrial siting, direct subsidies and loans, and industry restructuring councils. Because of its broad powers over major sectors of the economy, MITI came to be known as "mighty MITI."

During the high-growth period of the 1960s, MITI refined its industrial policies, helping Japanese industries to achieve rapid expansion under Prime Minister Hayato Ikeda's income-doubling plan. MITI was not the main reason for Japan's commercial success; it only provided the policy framework and financial support for private industry, which invested heavily in new technologies, training, and new plant and equipment. Working closely with big business, MITI developed a system of nurturing new industries—known as *ikusei*—that involved several steps: investigating industry trends and formulating basic policies, granting foreign currency allocations and Japan Development Bank loans, issuing licenses for the import of foreign technologies, granting accelerated depreciation allowances for strategic industries, providing cheap industrial sites, offering tax incentives, and creating cartels to regulate competition and coordinate investment. These policies were coordinated through MITI's Industrial Structure Council, a joint government-industry advisory group that made policy recommendations to MITI. Although this close business-government relationship—known as "Japan Inc." in the West—is often cited as the reason for Japan's success, it was more of a feedback mechanism devised to ensure that MITI's policies stayed in tune with big business interests.

Despite its heralded consensus-making and planning, MITI's policies were discredited during the 1970s when Japan's high-growth economy was derailed by environmental pollution, two oil shocks, and inflation. Severe pollution struck the heavy industrial zones along the Pacific belt where MITI had encouraged concentrated development of petrochemical refineries and steel mills. Within several years, new diseases entered the national lexicon—*itai-itai* (ouch-ouch) disease, Yokkaichi sulfur dioxide poisoning, and, most frightening of all, Minamata mercury poisoning, which left its victims mentally and physically retarded. Mass citizen protests erupted over noise pollution along the bullet train lines, and over the lack of proper planning and citizen input at Osaka and Narita international airports. Prime Minister Kakuei Tanaka's plan to remodel the Japanese archipelago with large-scale public works projects triggered land speculation and kickback scandals, eventually leading to his resignation. Public disgust with the high social costs of rapid industrialization sparked demands for stricter environmental and consumer regulations. In response, MITI supported demands for the creation of an Environmental Agency in the Prime Minister's office to regulate industrial and noise pollution, and for more investments in better housing, sewers, and other public works. Of course, MITI was not the sole culprit; environmental pollution and consumerism were worldwide phenomena. But these events dramatized the weakness in MITI's closed-door policymaking approach.

The oil shock of 1973 gave MITI's heavy industry policies a final blow, sending the Japanese economy into an inflationary tailspin. Even more than the United States, Japan had based its entire economy on the availability of cheap oil. In the early 1970s, about 85% of that oil came from the Middle East. With that lifeline threatened, the Japanese cabinet ordered a crash conservation program and enacted two laws that gave MITI broad powers to restrict industrial production: the Emergency Measures Stabilization Law and the Petroleum Supply and Demand Normalization

Law. These laws temporarily bolstered MITI's waning control over the economy and legitimized its use of "administrative guidance" (measures not backed by legal statutes) to guide industrial activities.

But these powers only salved a deep wound. During the mid-1970s MITI a serious crisis of confidence, in the course of which its industrial policies came under harsh criticism from a public fed up with the agency's emphasis on heavy industrial development at the expense of the country's well-being. Professor Chalmers Johnson notes:

> One issue after another plagued the ministry in this era—industrial pollution, revolts against its administrative guidance, charges of corrupt collusion with big business, inflation, public dismay at some of the consequences of its industrial location policy (especially the virtual depopulation of some Japan Sea coast prefectures . . . and the overcrowding of the Tokyo-to-Kobe industrial zone), and serious damage to relations with Japan's main economic partner, the United States, because of trade imbalances, and undervalued yen, and Japanese procrastination in implementing capital liberalization.

In short, MITI's industrial policies were no longer viewed as an answer to vexing economic and industrial problems, but as a source of Japan's troubles.

MITI underwent a period of intense soul-searching to find its way out of this policy mess. One source of new ideas was Naohiro Amaya, a young bureaucrat who had written two provcative treatises calling for a shift to "knowledge-intensive industries." In 1969, in *Basic Direction of the New International Trade and Industry Policy*, Amaya argued for strengthening the service sector, consumer markets, and medical and educational technology. He believed that MITI's proper role was to promote internationalization of the economy, antipollution measures, and consumer protection.

MITI officials initially dismissed his ideas as naive and idealistic, but the Industrial Structure Council expanded on them in its new industrial policy for the 1970s, which called for phasing out smokestack industries and developing high-technology industries. These policies were reaffirmed by MITI's Industrial Policy Bureau, which issued *Visions for the 1970s*. This report stressed the need for Japan to reduce its dependence on imported oil and raw materials, and to promote computer, semiconductor, and other

advanced technologies. Industry was encouraged to relocate from
the overcrowded Tokyo-Kobe megapolis to the outlying regions.
Liberalization of capital flows and imports, begun in the
mid-1960s, was viewed as a means to transform the nation's
industrial structure. These two policy documents provided the
intellectual foundation for MITI's *Visions for the 1980s*, which
emphasized high technology as the key to economic growth.

MITI's move into high technology was given a swift kick by
political events and the second oil shock. In late 1979 the Japanese Diet revised the Foreign Exchange and Foreign Trade Control Law of 1949, depriving MITI of many of its statutory powers.
Under the revised law, Japanese companies no longer need MITI
approval to make foreign exchange transactions or enter into
joint ventures and licensing agreements; they only have to give
prior notification. With the gradual liberalization of financial markets and import controls, this revision has triggered a rapid
increase in capital outflows, joint ventures, and licensing agreements with the West since 1980 (see Appendix C). To achieve its
policy goals, MITI is now forced to rely on "administrative guidance"—directions, warnings, persuasion, encouragement, and
requests. As many observers note, MITI is a lion without teeth.

Despite this setback, MITI has not given up, but is trying to
stage a comeback. In late 1979, MITI issued its famous *Visions for
the 1980s*, which emphasized the need for Japan to shift to creative new technologies and energy security. According to MITI
Minister Keiichi Konaga: "Up to now, Japan's technological development has relied heavily on using foreign technology. Such a
pattern will not be allowed to continue. We will have to make
original developments on our own. We will push technological
advances with creative and problem-solving type people. This will
involve a greater risk, a longer development period, and far more
financial resources than in the past." One powerful reason for this
shift to creative technologies is the drying-up of technology flows
from the West. In the past Americans were lax about selling technology to Japan, but now we are concerned about the "boomerang effect"—selling our technology, only to be bombarded by
Japanese exports which employ it. Moreover, the Reagan Administration is limiting technology transfers to Japan, which some fear
is a "leaky bucket" to the Soviet Union. In some fields, such as
gallium arsenide and optical fibers, Japan has caught up with the

West and is even being sought as a possible supplier of technology to the U.S. Department of Defense. As a result, Japan is developing its own creative technologies to use as bargaining chips in exchange for western technologies—and as a potential source of new revenues as worldwide protectionism threatens to reduce Japan's exports of goods and services.

Since 1980, MITI has targeted fourteen high-technology industries for accelerated development: aircraft, space, optoelectronics, biotechnology, computers, robotics, medical electronics, semiconductors, word processors, new alloys, fine ceramics, medicine, software, and electronic machinery (mechatronics). To achieve technological superiority in these fields, MITI has organized ten-year national R&D projects in supercomputers, fifth generation computing, robotics, software, new materials, fine ceramics, optoelectronics, biotechnology, biocomputers, and semiconductors. According to Professor Daniel Okimoto of Stanford University, MITI plays a constantly-changing role in developing new technologies. Using its traditional *ikusei* method, MITI nurtures and protects these infant industries until they are strong enough to achieve take-off status, then lets the market take over. As shown in Figure 2-1, robotics, computers, and semiconductors were considered infant industries in the 1970s, but achieved take-off in the early 1980s. Now MITI is concentrating on software, biotechnology, and other new infant industries. An obvious weakness in this strategy is that protectionist barriers are required to shield these industries from international competition, a situation that has caused trade friction with the West. Although MITI is encouraging market openings to reduce trade friction, strong industry pressures (in the form of nontariff barriers, such as the old-boy network within the vertically-integrated companies) will slow the entry of foreign competition, forcing MITI to use less protectionist policies, such as increased R&D funding and information sharing, to help infant industries.

For declining or sunset industries, MITI has traditionally organized depression cartels to reduce overcapacity and eliminate weaker companies. During the high-growth era, failing companies could easily identify new opportunities in related fields, but with slower growth, MITI must now help heavy industries make the shift to high technologies. For example, steelmakers are encouraged to move into new materials and alloys. Petrochemical

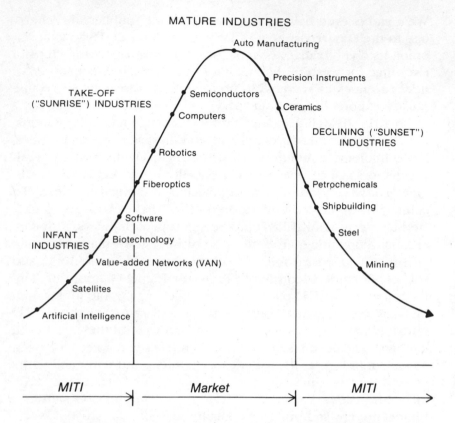

Figure 2-1. MITI's role in the industrial life cycle.

companies are moving into biotechnology, flexible manufacturing systems, and new chemicals. Shipbuilding companies are developing underwater robots, software, and mechatronics. MITI's new R&D projects are specifically tailored to help sunset industries make this difficult transition.

Although highly visible, MITI's R&D projects are only the tip of the iceberg. MITI's real goal is to transform Japan into a high-tech archipelago by the year 2000. As we shall see in the next chapter, Japanese ministries have devised a six-pronged industrial strategy to put Japan ahead of the United States in the twenty-first century. Its core strategy is the Technopolis Concept, which is aimed at decentralizing industrial development and creating a nationwide network of Japanese-style Silicon Valleys. Developed in cooperation with industrial, academic, and political leaders, these techno-polises will serve as the incubators for Japan's next-generation technologies. Taken together, these "take-lead" strategies repre-sent Japan's grand design for the twenty-first century.

Although 1990 is still four years away, MITI is already at work on its *Visions for the 1990s*. What will this new industrial policy look like? MITI Minister Konaga says nothing concrete has been decided, but he emphasizes five factors that will influence its for-mulation: the technology revolution, the shift to an information society linked by telecommunications, an aging population and the shift to service industries, increasing diversity in Japanese val-ues, and the growing internationalization of Japanese society. In recent years MITI has frequently referred to the emergence of a "regional era," in which industry and people will move from the Tokyo-Osaka megapolis to the regions. Given its emphasis on the Technopolis program, there is a strong likelihood that the 1990 *Visions* will focus on the regionalization of high technology, which MITI calls "Silicon Archipelago," or, more broadly, "High-Tech Archipelago."

Thus "Japan Inc." as we knew it in the past is rapidly fading away, a victim of the massive changes transforming the global economy. On the horizon is "Japan Tech," which promises to bring revolutionary new technologies to our doorsteps in the twenty-first century.

3

JAPAN'S TAKE-LEAD STRATEGIES

> The next revolutionary advance in
> technology should come by the
> beginning of the next century,
> most probably from Japan.
>
> *Dr. Michiyuki Uenohara*
> *Executive Vice President and*
> *Director of Research,*
> *NEC Corporation*

COUNTDOWN 2000

In mid-1985, at the height of Tsukuba Expo 85, the influential
Japan Industrial Journal ran a full-page advertisement by a major
corporation that reflected Japan's current thinking about high
technology. "The countdown has begun," it read. "Only fifteen
years to the twenty-first century. Are you ready? We are!" Below
the headline was a summary of the company's major achievements in advanced technologies, ranging from semiconductors
and computers to telecommunications and robotics, and its
splashy vision for life in the year 2000.

At first glance, there was nothing special about this advertisement amid the cacophony of others touting similar achievements
in science and technology. During the last few years, Japanese
newspapers have become a battleground for high-tech companies, which offer everything from compact disks to large-screen
televisions and satellite antennas. But what was different about
this ad was its cocky, challenging tone. Only five years ago, Japanese companies were much more circumspect in their advertis-
ing, stressing the quality, reliability, and low prices of their
products. Companies rarely boasted about their creativity or

innovativeness, which admittedly was their Achilles' heel, and even fewer made references to the twenty-first century, which was viewed as a utopian phrase thrown about by MITI bureaucrats.

But today these attitudes are rapidly changing. The Japanese are visibly confident and proud of their high-quality products and phenomenal comeback from the war, and researchers are less reluctant to brag about their achievements. "I don't think that we are far behind," says Kazuhiro Fuchi, director of MITI's fifth generation computer project. "Certainly on the big, online systems, our skills are as good as any." Today many Japanese even believe that Japan has moved ahead in some high-technology fields. "The time when you could buy the technology you needed is past," says Dr. Michiyuki Uenohara, research director at NEC Corporation. "We no longer select new technology from abroad. We must create new technologies by ourselves." His feelings are shared by Dr. Mitsuo Kawashima, former project research manager for MITI's New Electron Devices Project: "Frankly, we've hit the bottom of the barrel. There's not much we don't know about in western semiconductor technology because we subscribe to all of your electronics magazines and technical journals. But few western researchers bother to read Japanese technical journals, if they can at all. In fact, most westerners I meet don't even know what the leading Japanese journals are in their own field!" In the fast-moving world of high technology, the Japanese clearly have an advantage over us because of their ability to closely monitor our technologies. Like experienced poker players, they already know our entire hand before the first draw, while we can only guess at theirs.

And the stakes of the high technology game are rapidly going up. Until the 1970s, Japan's main goal was to catch up with western technology. Small in size and poor in natural resources, it was like a second-rank marathoner trying to keep up with the world's best. Now it has caught up and is itself being chased by the "new Japans"—South Korea, Taiwan, Singapore, Hong Kong, Malaysia— and, more recently, by India, mainland China, and Sri Lanka—who are gunning to replace Japan as major suppliers of high-quality, low-cost products. Even in advanced technologies, such as semiconductors and computers, South Korean conglomerates such as Hyundai, Dae Woo, Samsung, and Gold Star are buying the latest

American technology and making massive investments to overtake Japan by 1990. Japan can no longer afford to rest on its laurels.

JAPAN'S SIX-PRONGED PLAN

As Japan's sunset industries decline and the "new Japans" challenge it in international markets, the choice for Japanese industry is clear: to move up the technology stream ahead of its competitors. The Japanese euphemistically call this "contributing to the benefit of mankind," but the real goal is to pass the United States, which is focusing much of its energies on the Strategic Defense Initiative, or "Star Wars," and other military projects. Here the Japanese see an opening, and are quickly moving to take advantage of it. In this frontrunner position, Japan must move with lightning speed to capitalize on its leading-edge technologies, since the advent of supercomputers, expert systems, and satellite communications will reduce its lead to no more than a few days or even hours. Soon information will be available to whomever is willing to pay for it.

Moreover, in the future the Japanese government will no longer be able to force industry to march to its tune; that heavy-handed approach is too time-consuming and has not worked with fast-moving, high-technology companies. Instead, government ministries, such as MITI, the Science and Technology Agency, and the Ministry of Posts and Telecommunications, must anticipate, cultivate, and promote emerging technologies and markets in which Japan has a competitive advantage. Anticipation, not reaction, will be the name of the game, and government's new role will be that of catalyst, strategist, cultivator, and advisor—a cross between a "think tank" and a consulting firm.

How does Japan plan to take the lead technologically? By pursuing a six-pronged industrial plan that builds on its past experience and industrial strengths. This plan, which represents the Japanese government's grand design for leading the country into the twenty-first century, consists of the following strategies:

Strategy #1: Parallel-Track R&D Projects
Strategy #2: Strategic International Alliances

Strategy #3: The Technopolis Concept
Strategy #4: Telecommunications Networking
Strategy #5: Venture Capital and Venture Businesses
Strategy #6: Selective Import Promotion

Unlike past practice, these take-lead strategies are not based on large budget increases, nor on the Japanese government's previous method of directing and restructuring industry. Rather, they are designed to take maximum advantage of the major changes occuring within Japanese society and the trend toward private investment. But for an inside look at Japan's take-lead strategies, let's examine them one by one.

Strategy #1: Parallel-Track R&D Projects

At the heart of Japan's take-lead strategies are its joint research and development (R&D) projects, which are designed to give Japanese industry a competitive edge internationally. MITI's fifth generation computer project is probably the best known, because it has attracted the lion's share of media coverage, but it is only the tip of the iceberg. Tucked away in government laboratories and corporate R&D centers around Tokyo are over thirty national projects, which are currently developing a wide variety of leading-edge technologies, including supercomputers, new semiconductors, jet engines, biotechnology, optoelectronics, new alloys, biochips, fine ceramics, communications satellites, robots, and solar energy, as shown in Figure 3-1. Because of their long planning horizon and focus on basic research, these projects are viewed by industry leaders as the main engines for Japan's economic growth in the twenty-first century. They are principally sponsored by MITI, Nippon Telegraph and Telephone (NTT), and the Science and Technology Agency (STA), but other ministries have recently jumped into the R&D race, including the Ministry of Posts and Telecommunications, the Ministry of Education, and the Ministry of Construction.

In 1983 Japan spent $29 billion on R&D, or about 2.6% of its GNP, of which the Japanese government directly funded about 25%. The government also provides indirect subsidies for private investments in the form of R&D tax credits, accelerated depreciation for new R&D facilities, and low-interest loans from

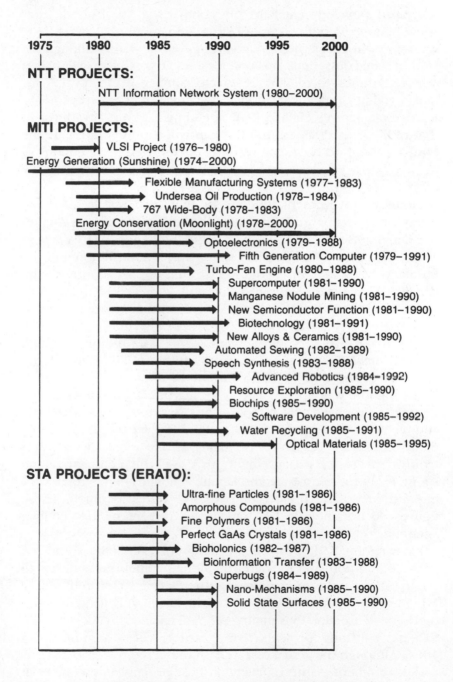

Figure 3-1. Japan's parallel-track R&D projects.

the Japan Development Bank. By comparison, the United States spent about $83 billion on R&D in 1983, about 2.7% of its GNP, with government spending accounting for over half. Although the United States outspends Japan on total R&D, we divert over half of our R&D funds to military research, compared to only 2% for Japan, giving Japan a tremendous advantage in commercial fields. As a result, Japan's civilian R&D spending is about two-thirds of that of the United States. And this gap will soon disappear. Prime Minister Yasuhiro Nakasone recently encouraged private industry to help boost Japan's total R&D spending to 2.9% of its GNP by 1995.

Japanese government funding for high-tech research is relatively small compared with that of the United States (see Appendix E). In 1984 the Science and Technology Agency (STA) spent about $1.1 billion, while MITI spent only $250 million and the Ministry of Education about $210 million. By contrast, the recently privatized Nippon Telegraph and Telephone (NTT) spent around $580 million, plus $2.8 billion in procurement. The Japanese Self-Defense Forces spent $12 billion, of which research and procurement accounted for $3.2 billion, bringing Japan's total R&D budget to about $7 billion. U.S. defense-sponsored research totaled $26.5 billion in fiscal 1984, of which $12.1 billion was spent on electronics R&D. In addition, the Pentagon procured $87 billion in missiles, jets, ships, satellites, and vehicles that contained $26.8 billion worth of advanced electronics. (see Appendix D). Thus, if one looks just at electronics R&D and procurement in 1984, the Pentagon alone spent $38.9 billion, versus the Japanese government's total R&D expenditure of $7 billion, or over five times as much. These figures do not include R&D and procurement by U.S. civilian agencies.

Japan's joint R&D projects are long-term, generally six to ten years in duration, and they are run along parallel tracks to create competition and synergy among the various research teams. MITI's current projects, begun in 1981, are now halfway to completion and are already spinning off patents and technical papers. STA has nine new projects, five of which will be completed in 1986. Although the actual research is conducted in corporate labs and government institutes, many of these projects open offices in downtown Tokyo to maintain close contact with the participating companies. Once a month researchers from MITI, NTT, and member companies meet to present papers and discuss technical issues, often inviting researchers from related national projects. For example, researchers from the Supercomputer Project regularly consult with members of the New Semiconductor Elements Project, which is located in the same building, not far from the U.S. Embassy.

Contrary to popular opinion, Japanese R&D policy is not formulated only by MITI or a monolithic "Japan Inc.," but is the result of many government agencies fiercely competing for funding and jurisdiction over promising research areas. Top-level policy-making is carried out by the Council for Science and Technology, chaired by the Prime Minister, which lays out the major outlines of Japan's scientific research and coordinates the plans of the various ministries. Working closely with the Council is the Science and Technology Agency (STA), which is responsible for managing the Tsukuba Science City outside of Tokyo and preparing an annual white paper on Japanese scientific trends. STA funds three public corporations whose staff are not civil servants: the Japan Atomic Energy Research Institute, the National Space Development Agency, and the Power Reactor and Nuclear Fuel Corporation. In 1985 almost $1 billion was spent on civilian nuclear power and space development, about 46% of Japanese government R&D spending.

STA also provides partial funding for a public corporation called the Japan Research and Development Corporation (JRDC), which transfers technology from national laboratories and universities to private industry through contracts and licensing agreements. In 1981 JRDC established an innovative research system called the Exploratory Research for Advanced Technology Organization (ERATO), which will spend about $70 million during the 1980s to develop revolutionary new technologies, many of which have not even found their way into the public lexicon yet (see Appendix F). ERATO's major goal is to overcome strong industry skepticism about the quality of basic research being done in Japan. It has created projects not rigidly organized into hierarchies, as in Japanese universities or industry, and has brought in foreign and corporate researchers. Moreover, its project directors are given broad authority, and, to gain credibility with the West, ERATO makes its research results available to foreign businesses.

The second largest research body in Japan, next to NTT's Electrical Communication Laboratories, is MITI's Agency of Industrial Science and Technology (AIST), which runs sixteen national laboratories staffed by 3,500 researchers. Nine of these labs, staffed with 2,600 researchers, are located in the Tsukuba Science City northeast of Tokyo. MITI projects fall into three major categories: subsidized projects, large-scale projects, and national projects. In subsidized projects, such as the VLSI Project, MITI funds up to 50% of the research costs through the use of *hojokin*, or conditional loans that are repayable only if the recipient companies accrue profits from the technologies. Large-scale projects, first begun in 1966 under the National Research and Development Program (NRDP), focus on emerging technologies that are too expensive and risky for companies to undertake alone. MITI funding for these projects is limited, averaging about $10 million per year. Currently, MITI has large-scale projects in scientific supercomputers, optoelectronics, advanced robotics, automated sewing, and twenty-two other fields (see Appendix G). Finally, MITI sponsors national projects that focus on long-term research requiring large amounts of funding, such as the fifth generation computer ($250 million) and the SIGMA software project ($100 million). These ambitious projects are MITI's "media darlings," designed to stimulate creative research and appeal to the public's imagination, very much like NASA's Apollo Project.

During the 1980s, MITI's budget constraints have required participating companies to shoulder a greater burden of the project costs. For example, MITI funded 40% of the VLSI Project (1976–1980), but is funding only 25% of the New Semiconductor Elements Project (1982–1990). Moreover, as Dr. Mitsuo Kawashima, former R&D manager for the New Semiconductor Elements Project, observes: "Most of the joint research is being done in corporate laboratories, not MITI labs, to reduce government expenses." As government funds become tighter, MITI projects are becoming increasingly "privatized," with MITI acting as project organizer and coordinator, not financier. Instead of direct financing, MITI is emphasizing indirect measures, such as special depreciation allowances, R&D tax credits, and access to research facilities and government-owned patents.

MITI projects are usually limited to the top companies in a given field, exempting them from the Antimonopoly Law. This oligopolistic approach limits excessive competition and makes the projects more manageable, but MITI has frequently been criticized for excluding small, innovative companies with leading-edge technologies. To address this problem, MITI has proposed a Venture Business Promotion Law that would grant start-up companies R&D subsidies, tax breaks, and a buildup of investment loss reserves. In addition, MITI has opened its laboratories in the Tsukuba Science City to promote joint research with smaller companies, allowing them to use MITI's equipment or to bring in their own. This is a major policy shift, since private researchers were prohibited from entering MITI labs in the past.

Proposals for national R&D projects are usually floated past trade associations and MITI councils for up to three years, a consensus-building process known as *nemawashi* (literally, wrapping the roots for transplanting). If approved, AIST then organizes a research association to manage the project. Most MITI projects run in three phases, using the successful VLSI Project as a model. During the first phase, MITI plays a major role, organizing the project and assigning basic research tasks. During the second phase, MITI laboratories and private researchers establish broad product specifications to give each company an equal starting position. Companies work closely with each other on specific tasks, but are not required to disclose proprietary information. Once the basic technology is developed, MITI files the patents and licenses them to the participating companies, which then fiercely compete to beat each other to the marketplace, a process that takes anywhere from twelve to twenty-four months.

The pressure for Japan to keep at the head of the technology stream requires that it produce a steady flow of patents, new products, and new technologies. By establishing parallel-track projects, MITI and other ministries have ensured themselves of innovations down the road. For example, the four-year VLSI Project generated 1,000 patents, or an average of 250 patent applications per year. In March 1984, the Next-Generation Industries Project, established in October 1981, announced that 435 patent applications had been submitted, or an average of 175 patents per year. Assuming MITI and STA's thirty R&D projects (with an average duration of eight years) each generate up to 250 patents a year, they will produce about 60,000 patents by 1990! Recently, the Japanese Patent Office has prepared for this patent deluge by automating its operations. Indeed, it can be argued that the Japanese government plans to systematically use statistical indicators, such as patent applications and technical papers, to monitor its creative research policies, just as Japanese companies have used statistical quality control methods in mass production. Already, this approach is working. In 1982 Japanese applied for 218,261 patents, compared with 149,500 in the Soviet Union, 106,413 in the United States, 46,579 in West Germany, and 39,214 in Britain. Thus, the potential for a Japanese patent deluge, followed by a product deluge, is very real.

Americans are often skeptical about whether these joint R&D projects will produce creative research. In their view, truly creative research is not planned, or programmed, but occurs when an individual researcher is allowed total freedom to explore and experiment. This approach may work for start-up companies, but it is an unreliable way to maintain the international competitiveness of major corporations. Most scientific breakthroughs occur after sustained periods of rapid, incremental improvements to existing technology. Sudden, out-of-the-blue breakthroughs are extremely rare. America's romanticized notion of the rugged individual, the lone scientist/inventor like Albert Einstein, or Apple Computer's Steve Wozniak, is giving way to the more pragmatic reality of large, corporate R&D teams conducting joint research. As American researchers have long known, unbridled individualism alone does not guarantee creative research. Adequate funding, supportive management, excellent laboratories and equipment, "shoptalk," seminars and conferences, teamwork, and a sense of purpose are the crucial ingredients for success. These are areas in which the MITI and NTT research teams excel. As the old adage goes: "Two heads are better than one."

Strategy #2: Strategic International Alliances

"If you can't beat 'em, join 'em." For years, this phrase captured the feeling of Japanese companies in their race to catch up with the West in science and technology. Coming from a position of weakness after the war, they had little choice but to pay substantial royalties to foreign companies for the latest technologies. During the 1950s and 1960s, MITI encouraged these technology imports as a way to rebuild Japan's devastated industries and accelerate the pace of technological development, thus giving rise to Japan's copycat image. But given Japan's desperate economic situation, this "don't-reinvent-the-wheel" strategy made eminent sense, and it was accomplished in two ways: MITI used its control over foreign exchange transactions to channel corporate spending into the licensing of foreign technologies, while foreign companies such as IBM and Texas Instruments were forced to license their key patents as an admission fee to the Japanese market.

For over thirty years this one-way flow of technology worked brilliantly, enabling Japan to quickly catch up with the West. But now the technological free ride has come to an end. Many western companies are reluctant to license their technologies to Japanese companies for fear of the boomerang effect; and under the Reagan Administration, the Pentagon has cracked down on the flow of advanced technologies to Japan. According to Kazuo Miyazawa, director of MITI's Supercomputer Project, this technology boycott is beginning to be felt. "It is getting harder to follow leading-edge American technology because the Pentagon often requests American scientists to withdraw sensitive papers from international conferences and has closed many American conferences to foreigners altogether. We are concerned about this stifling of scientific exchanges."

To get around this obstacle, the Japanese government and major corporations are changing their strategies. Instead of depending on one-way flows from the West, they are pursuing joint research and mutual technology exchanges to ensure a continuing flow of technology. Advanced technologies, once viewed as freely exchangeable intellectual property, are increasingly being used as bargaining chips in the high-stakes game of industrial technology. At the government level, MITI, the Science and Technology Agency (STA), and Nippon Telegraph and Telephone (NTT) are pushing strategic alliances in three areas: high-technology working groups, MITI and NTT research projects, and technical information exchanges.

At the Versailles Summit in June 1982, Japan participated with Canada, France, West Germany, Italy, the United Kingdom, and the U.S. in setting up a Working Group on Technology, Growth, and Employment. The Working Group proposed twenty-two international collaborative projects in high-technology research, four of which Japan agreed to organize: safety research on light water nuclear reactors, photovoltaic solar energy, photosynthesis, and advanced robotics. Japan is using these projects to keep in touch with the latest developments in the West. Since the Williamsburg Summit in May 1983, these projects have begun taking shape.

Participation in MITI and NTT research projects has been a stickier matter. In February 1982, following Hitachi's offer of 64K dynamic RAM technology to Hewlett-Packard, then-MITI Minister Shintaro Abe issued a statement encouraging technical cooperation between Japan and the United States. The first major test came when the Japanese government invited foreign companies to participate in MITI's Fifth Generation Computer Project in late 1982. MITI only welcomed Japanese companies that had been founded by foreign firms which had R&D capabilities in Japan. The U.S. government contested MITI's screening criteria, requesting that MITI open the project to foreign firms without local R&D capabilities. But MITI refused, contending that such an arrangement would be unfair to smaller Japanese firms that had been excluded. Instead, MITI asked Britain to participate because of its "Alvey" fifth generation computer project. This decision elicited strong criticism from Japanese computer makers, who noted MITI's failure to get the Americans involved. "Why Britain?" they asked, pointing out that Britain's · computer technology was behind America's. They argued that the project should be less academic and open to small, innovative software houses. No mention was made of IBM Japan, which had offered to join but was turned down by MITI after the Hitachi sting operation. Instead, MITI offered minor concessions, such as buying Digital Equipment computers for the fifth generation project; but this gesture amounted to technology importing, not genuine international cooperation. In August 1985, MITI made another concession to deflect growing trade friction. After five years of negotiations, it agreed to license to IBM some patents from its supercomputer, fifth generation computer, and other projects. But IBM was still not invited to join the fifth generation project, nor were MITI patents available to other foreign companies.

Nippon Telegraph and Telephone (NTT) has been slightly more open to foreign participation as a result of trade negotiations. In June 1983, NTT promised to exchange information and engineers with the National Bureau of Standards (NBS), and sent procurement missions to the United States and Europe to placate growing criticism of its "buy Japan" policies. Recently, NTT has entered into joint research with foreign companies such as Eaton, a U.S. semiconductor equipment maker, and Energy Conversion Devices, an innovative firm that developed the amorphous silicon used in solar-powered calculators. Although NTT President Hisashi Shinto agreed to increase NTT procurement of foreign products, he still acknowledges that it probably will not grow rapidly. Thus, MITI and NTT give much lip service to international alliances, but concrete action is slow in coming.

In the early 1980s, John Naisbitt, author of *Megatrends*, predicted that we would see a boom in corporate tie-ups between the United States and Japan. Since 1980, his predictions have come true due to Japan's revision of the 1949 Foreign Exchange and Trade Control Law, which loosened MITI's control over joint ventures and capital flows. Previously, MITI had the authority to approve all joint ventures and technology licensing agreements, which were closely scrutinized for their consistency with national policies. Now Japanese companies are only required to give MITI prior notification before signing agreements, a change that has led to an explosion of joint ventures, cross-licensing agreements, and joint development activities in all fields. The most notable has been in the car industry, with the GM/Toyota and Chrysler/Mitsubishi alliances. But in semiconductors, Japanese-U.S. agreements have leaped from only four in 1980 to thirty-two in 1984 (see Appendix H). Japanese companies have become alternate sources for U.S. microprocessor companies, such as Intel, Motorola, and Zilog, while U.S. companies are trading their chip designs for Japanese wafer processing technology. Other companies, such as RCA and Sharp, have set up joint ventures to produce chips for markets on both sides of the Pacific. With the recent spate of tie-ups between South Korean and American companies, Japanese companies are now under pressure to quickly link up with South Korean firms in order to avoid being iced out of the South Korean market by a growing U.S.-South Korea alliance.

Thus, international business relations are becoming extremely complex in the Pacific Basin, forcing Japan to promote strategic alliances to protect its technological base and market opportunities. With the emergence of the Southeast Asian nations, Japanese companies are beginning to enter into a variety of new alliances with old rivals. But the real dark horse in this technology race is an age-old rivalry—Japan and mainland China—which has now turned into one of the closest technological alliances. This is the strategic alliance that will surely give the United States a run for its money.

Strategy #3: The Technopolis Concept

The third prong in Japan's take-lead plan—and the major theme of this book—is the Technopolis Concept, MITI's ambitious plan to create nineteen ultra-modern Silicon Valleys throughout the Japanese archipelago by the year 2000. Coined in 1980, the word *technopolis* symbolizes the merging of two key ideas driving Japan's industrial strategies in the 1980s and 1990s. The first idea (technology) calls for modernizing Japan's sunset industries with an injection of creative, grassroots technologies. The second idea (*polis*) comes from the ancient Greek city-states, which emphasized a balance between private industry and the public sharing of ideas and responsibilities. Building on these ideas, MITI has developed a national industrial strategy that aims at strengthening Japan's regional economies through the planned development of new high-tech centers. Like Boston's Route 128 and North Carolina's Research Triangle, the Technopolis Concept is based on the idea of forging a working partnership among businesses (*san*), universities (*gaku*), and local governments (*kan*).

However, MITI has taken this idea one step further. Instead of relying solely on the initiative of governors, mayors, and corporate leaders, MITI is orchestrating a nationwide dialogue over the future direction of Japan's industrial policies. Coordinated through the Technopolis process, MITI has encouraged heated competition among the prefectures for new programs and policies, realizing that the best ideas usually come from the people directly affected. This massive pooling of ideas—a Japanese version of the Greek forum—is MITI's key industrial strategy for the twenty-first century. Through this public dialogue, MITI hopes to develop new industrial policies that will guide Japan for the next twenty years. MITI's ultimate goal—often called its "Super Vision for the Twenty-first Century"—is to transform Japan into a high-tech archipelago of new research cities (see Figures 3-2 and 3-3). These technopolises will be scattered throughout Japan to disperse industrial growth from the overcrowded Tokyo-Osaka megapolis to the emerging regions of Japan Tech. These cities will offer a variety of research, educational, and cultural facilities to attract and spawn new companies in Japan's next-generation industries—electronics, biotechnology, new materials, ceramics, software, and robotics.

The Technopolis program is not a totally new idea. In the 1960s, the Japanese government passed the New Industrial City Law (1962) and the Industrial Improvement Special Regional Development Law (1964) to build industrial centers for heavy manufacturing and petrochemical industries in coastal areas. The chief promoter of these programs was the central government, which poured huge sums of money into ports, highways, and other heavy infrastructure. Later, in the early 1970s, former Prime Minister Kakuei Tanaka proposed remodeling the Japanese archipelago with a network of bullet trains, highways, telecommunications networks, and new information cities. Both schemes failed because of their prohibitive costs, severe industrial pollution, and two oil crises that crippled Japan's high-growth economy.

In its *Visions for the 1980s,* MITI first announced the Technopolis Concept, which offered a new approach to regional development. Unlike the New Industrial City scheme, the Technopolis program emphasizes the creation of a "soft" infrastructure of trained people, new technologies, information services, venture capital, and telecommunications networks. People and services, not massive public works projects, are the focus of this new program. Moreover, local governments play the central role in actually planning and constructing the technopolises, while MITI's role is limited to setting basic criteria for the program and providing technical assistance, advice, tax incentives, and Japan Development Bank loans.

In 1983 MITI established development guidelines, the basic rules that will guide construction of the technopolises. Generally,

Figure 3-2. ''Japan Inc.'' (1950s-1970s): Megalopolis.

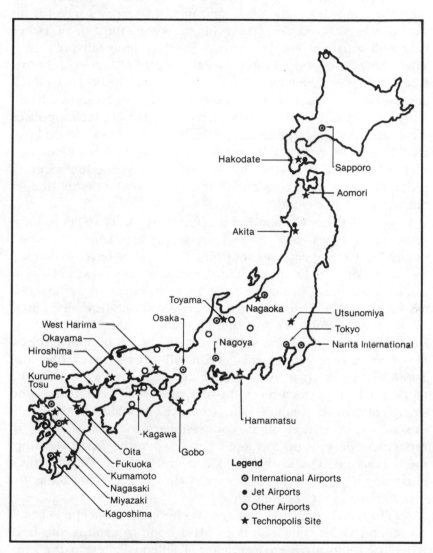

Figure 3-3. "Japan Tech" (1980s-1990s): Technopolis.

the nineteen technopolises must meet several criteria. They must
be located within thirty minutes' drive of their "mother cities"
(regional cities over 200,000), and within one day's travel from
Tokyo, Nagoya, or Osaka. The technopolis zone must be no larger
than 500 square miles, or about the same size as Silicon Valley.
These new cities should offer a balanced mix of high-tech industrial complexes (*san*), universities and research institutes (*gaku*),
and pleasant residential areas and cultural and recreational facilities (*juku*). Unlike Japan's major cities, the twenty technopolises
are being built in scenic areas and designed in harmony with local
traditions and the natural environment. Finally, they must be completed by 1990, although the Ministry of Construction recently
recommended an extension to the year 2000 due to budget
cutbacks.

How will the technopolises be financed? MITI expects local
prefectures, cities, and towns to raise the estimated $1 billion
needed to finance each technopolis. The regions have responded
by setting up "Technopolis Funds" raised by local taxes and corporate donations. The central government offers some financial
assistance in the form of a special depreciation allowance (30%
on machinery and 15% on buildings during the first year) for
investments in plant and equipment in the technopolis zones.
However, this investment tax credit will only be available until
1989. For research activities, existing subsidy programs can be
tapped when prefectural industrial research laboratories and
small companies conduct joint research. In addition, the Small
Business Corporation offers concessionary loans at 2.7% with
repayment periods up to fifteen years, while the Japan Development Bank (JDB) and the Hokkaido and Tohoku Development
Financing Corporation offer special, low-interest financing for
investments in technopolis areas.

MITI officials concede that the Technopolis Concept is based
on Silicon Valley; but how does MITI hope to capture the free-
wheeling, innovative environment of Silicon Valley in the conservative, follow-the-leader atmosphere of Japan? Will people
move to the technopolises? Where will Japan's entrepreneurs
come from?

This is where our western values color our perceptions of Japanese industrial policy. MITI is not trying to recreate Silicon Valley,
warts and all, but to adapt the best features of America's high-tech

regions to a uniquely Japanese model of high-tech development. The key to understanding the Technopolis Concept lies in MITI's idea of *ikusei*, or nurturing of people and industry. Based on the Japanese kanji characters *iku*, meaning to *nourish* or *educate*, and *sei*, meaning *to bring into existence*, the term refers to MITI's method of systematically nurturing infant industries through careful guidance and financial backing. In the past *ikusei* referred to the transfer of technology and manufacturing techniques; in the 1980s it is aimed at stimulating the process of innovation—the process of cultivating people and high-tech cities. In its new role, MITI is acting as catalyst, father-confessor, and consultant, offering ideas and assistance to local governments that are going through the throes of building their technopolises. The key difference between the Technopolis Concept and Silicon Valley is one of culture and style; while Silicon Valley developed spontaneously and at times chaotically, the technopolises are being systematically planned and cultivated by local governments. As Technopolis planners often told me during my visits: "You say we can't plan for innovation. We say that one cannot run a business without a business plan."

This approach reflects the historical and cultural differences between California and Japan. Located on the westernmost edge of the continent, Silicon Valley embodies the frontier of American industrial thinking. It is fast-moving, spontaneous, individualistic, transient, and nonconformist—noted for its rebellious start-up companies and frequent industry shakeouts. People and companies are evaluated not only by who they are but by how they perform, and success is not measured in years but in quarters. This hotbed of entrepreneurial activity is quintessentially Californian. It is a twentieth-century Gold Rush. However, to the Japanese, who are more accustomed to permanence and stability, Silicon Valley is the "Wild West" incarnate, with its overnight millionaires, high-priced lawyers, spouse-hopping, pill-popping plant workers, hidden sweatshops, and INS factory raids.

MITI officials claim they are emulating Silicon Valley, but the Technopolis Concept is a totally different approach. Silicon Valley was never planned; it just happened. Any government planning occurred after the fact, a *laissez-faire* approach that we are paying dearly for today. By contrast, the Technopolis Concept is more similar to North Carolina's Research Triangle, which was created through a partnership of government, business, and academia. But Japan's technopolises are more deeply influenced by traditions and customs that go back hundreds of years. Indeed, the Technopolis Concept can be viewed as a modern version of castle building because of the central government's major role. Like the Tokugawa shoguns who oversaw the construction of castle towns in the sixteenth century, MITI originated the Technopolis Concept and selected the prefectures that would build the technopolises. And just as Japan's feudal castles spawned new castle towns, the universities and research institutes in these technopolises are expected to generate a contingent of talented workers and new start-up businesses.

Strategy #4: Telecommunications Networking

If MITI's strategy for the twenty-first century is the Technopolis Concept, Nippon Telegraph and Telephone (NTT)—Japan's recently privatized phone company—has an equally grand vision for revolutionizing Japanese society with its advanced telecommunications systems. Known as the Information Network System (INS), the program is designed to link Japan's major cities to the technopolises and other regional cities with a nationwide fiber optics network, backed by direct broadcasting and communications satellites. This system will eventually replace the existing telephone lines laid since the war. The goal of the INS program, which was first introduced in 1981 by NTT's Executive Vice-President Yasusada Kitahara, is to fully digitalize and upgrade Japan's telephone services by 1995 with the latest information processing techniques, including supercomputers, expert systems, video signal processing, and fifth generation computers. To achieve this ambitious goal, NTT has launched a full-scale R&D and construction program that uses the leverage of its strong financial base and research capabilities. Over the next twenty years NTT plans to invest $125 to $150 billion to install the INS network in Japan's crowded cities and mountainous regions. The project will be difficult to build, but the potential payoffs are great; besides increasing NTT's revenues, INS is expected to create a $200 to $300 billion market for new telecommunications equipment and services, a major boost to Japan's slow-growing economy. INS has already spawned a rush of companies, both domestic and foreign, competing to provide add-on services in the emerging value-added network (VAN) market. Because of the massive investments involved and the prospects for creating new industries and jobs, INS is widely hailed as the "bullet train of telecommunications"—Japan's new *Shinkansen* program for the 1980s and 1990s.

In light of Japan's huge budget deficits, why has NTT chosen to totally rebuild Japan's telecommunications system now? And why didn't it choose a less expensive approach? The answers are partly financial and partly political. Since World War II, the Japanese telecommunications system has lagged behind that of the United States and Europe. In 1952 the Japanese government created NTT as a public corporation to rebuild the country's devastated phone system, placing it under the auspices of the Ministry of Posts and Telecommunications. During the next twenty-five years, NTT and its international affiliate, Kokusai Denshin Denwa (KDD), repaired telephone connections and installed new switching equipment and phones. Surrounding itself with 200 suppliers known as the "NTT family," NTT succeeded in installing phones in virtually every home and business in Japan by 1978. With its rapid growth in telephone revenues, NTT was able to expand its work force and reinvest heavily in new equipment and research facilities.

However, by the early 1980s it became apparent that NTT's prosperous days were over. Excessively bureaucratic, technologically outdated, and bloated with 330,000 lifetime employees who could not be fired, NTT's costs began rising faster than its revenues, raising widespread concern that it would go into the red by the mid-1980s. Poor management had caused major cash flow problems, forcing NTT into debt to pay dividends. Like the financially-beleaguered Japan National Railway (JNR), NTT threatened to become another financial burden on the national treasury, and major corporations, supported by MITI, began clamoring for NTT to be made a private company. Its immediate prospects were dismal. Telephone services, which accounted for almost 90% of its revenues, leveled off as telephone subscriptions reached the saturation point. Unless NTT found new sources of revenue quickly, it would become financially insolvent.

Moreover, there were strong political pressures for NTT to develop a new system. In 1981 foreign telecommunication suppliers began criticizing NTT's "buy Japan" procurement practices that prevented them from entering the tightly-regulated Japanese telecommunications market. This issue quickly welled up into a political firestorm, threatening to worsen Japan's growing trade friction with the West. In the middle of this turmoil, Hisashi Shinto was brought in from a major shipbuilding company to make NTT more efficient. Nicknamed "Mr. Reorganization," Shinto had few political obligations to the NTT family, and promised to increase NTT procurement of foreign goods. But NTT officials hesitated. Cutting back the domestic share of NTT's $3 billion in annual procurement would be political suicide, since most NTT officials join these companies upon retirement, a practice known as *amakudari* (literally, "descent from heaven"). NTT needed a way to increase foreign procurement without jeopardizing the NTT family, and INS seemed like a viable option. Although it would be expensive, INS would force every Japanese household and business to buy new digital phones, providing NTT with immense opportunities to sell new services.

Another motivating force was MITI's Fifth Generation Computer Project, which suddenly gave NTT an incentive to improve both its technology and its public image. Long viewed as a stodgy, conservative organization, NTT has nevertheless been a major rival of MITI in computer research. Since the early 1950s NTT's Electrical Communication Laboratory has vigorously competed to surpass MITI's Electrotechnical Laboratory. When MITI announced its Fifth Generation Computer Project in November 1981, NTT quietly formed its own Base Intelligence Research Group at its Yokosuka ECL to pursue the same research. NTT has much stronger research capabilities in electronics: while MITI had a budget of $100 million and 700 researchers at ETL in 1984 (of a total research budget of $260 million and 2,600 MITI researchers), NTT spent $525 million on electronics research and had 2,000 people at its four ECL sites: Atsugi (semiconductors), Ibaragi (fiber optics), Musashino (digital switching), and Yokosuka (computers). Moreover, NTT's research programs are closely tied to its procurement program, which in effect subsidizes leading-edge research, giving NTT an enormous edge over MITI. To capitalize on this research base, NTT decided that developing the INS program would utilize the most advanced technologies coming out of its research laboratories. Because of its challenge and scope, INS would give NTT a renewed sense of purpose and focus.

Simply stated, the INS program is designed to give Japan the most advanced telecommunications system in the world. By developing an integrated network of fiber optic cables and satellites, NTT hopes to boost its revenues and hold off rivals in the hotly competitive Japanese telecommunications market, which was deregulated in April 1985. INS will combine the latest in computer and optical communication technologies to make the transition from verbal communication (words) to audiovisual communication (images), paralleling work on the fifth generation computer. When INS is completed, the Japanese home-of-the-future will be offered a variety of new services, including mini-facsimile machines, videotext and videophones, telemetering and telecontrol for monitoring water and gas utilities, medical information systems, home shopping and banking, computer-aided instruction (CAI) for home study, and home security systems. Offices will be equipped with digital sketch phones, teleconferencing, video response systems (VRS), and optical storage systems. Rather than supplanting face-to-face contact, these systems will enable the Japanese to exchange information more quickly and efficiently.

NTT has already begun laying the foundation for the INS network. In 1979, twenty-three wards in Tokyo were offered a fixed-image teletext system called CAPTAIN (Character Pattern Telephone Access Information Network System), which provides news and weather forecasts, stock reports, travel information, games, mail-order requests, banking services, and teaching materials from 220 companies. In the early 1980s NTT commercialized circuit switching and packet switching (a system that transmits information units in packets to reduce costs), followed by D-60 digital switching for long distance calls and D-70 switching for local calls.

Actual work on INS commenced in 1983 when NTT began testing an eleven-mile system in Kawasaki, south of Tokyo, and laying the 1,250-mile Japan Transverse fiber optics trunk line from Sapporo on the northern island of Hokkaido to Fukuoka City on the southern island of Kyushu, which was completed in late 1984. A 1.6-gigabit (billion bits of information) per second cable will be laid between Tokyo and Osaka by 1988. By the end of the 1980s all major Japanese cities will be linked by trunk lines, and KDD will lay submarine cables across the Pacific Ocean, as well as to Japan's smaller islands. By 1995, NTT envisions that the entire Japanese archipelago will be linked to the INS system.

Under the VAN Deregulation Law which took effect in April 1985, private companies will be allowed to compete against NTT by laying their own cables or leasing time on NTT's line to provide value-added services. Competition in this area is fierce, and NTT is already faced with a growing list of rivals: Daini Denden (the "Second NTT"), AT&T and the Mitsui Group, GTE Telenet and Intec, the Japan National Railway, the Federation of Economic Organizations (Keidanren), and others. These groups are planning to "cream" the lucrative Tokyo-Nagoya-Osaka-Kobe corridor, where 36% of the population and 46% of industry is located, by installing their own systems. For example, the "Second NTT," spearheaded by Kyocera, Mitsubishi Corporation, and Sony, plans to build a separate fiber optics cable by 1987.

In 1984 NTT inaugurated an INS model system that offers services to 10,000 subscribers in the Mitaka-Musashino area in western Tokyo. The experiment involves testing new home terminals that employ digital phones and facsimile, interactive videotext, telewriting and data terminals, video phones, and video response systems. Despite the state-of-the-art technology, NTT is working to identify and resolve problems that have cropped up with the system. For example, many participating companies had to order their employees to sign up for the experiment, since only a few households volunteered. Most of the volunteers were businesses. Another problem is the video response system, which has an insufficient number of lines to handle the customer load. On the other hand, homeowners like the digital video telephone, which has a readout that keeps a running cost of phone calls, and businesses find that video conferences keep attendees alert. These findings will be summarized and analyzed to make improvements in the nationwide INS system.

Currently, Japanese agencies are developing new technologies that will be incorporated into the INS program. The Ministry of Posts and Telecommunications has plans to develop a telephone system with automatic language translation capability, using voice recognition, machine translation, and speech synthesis techniques. The project will begin in 1986, and will employ fifth generation computer technology. NTT has launched two other programs. One is a national data net for personal computers, which allows them to communicate through the national public phone system, using NTT's digital data exchange (DDX) packet switching network. The second is an expert system for medical diagnosis, which covers nineteen fields, including pediatrics, internal medicine, plastic surgery, and gynecology. The system will be installed in NTT's Kanto Teishin Hospital in 1988.

Japan is years behind the United States in satellite technology, so NTT and the Japan Broadcasting Corporation (NHK) are working with Japan's National Space Development Agency (NSDA), which has a $470 million budget to develop satellites. In 1983 NASDA launched the Sakura CS-2, Japan's first communications satellite, and plans to launch two more in the future: the CS-3 in 1988, which will handle up to 25,000 phone calls, and the CS-4 in 1993 for up 200,000 calls. For radio and television broadcasting, NASDA launched the BS-2a direct broad satellite (DBS) in 1984; but two of the three transponders used to transmit signals broke down, setting back the program. The failure also ignited a debate over the purchasing of foreign satellites, a bone of contention in the current trade talks, since the satellite was built by the Toshiba/GE team. Many Japanese corporations prefer to use advanced foreign parts, but critics charge that NASDA is using technology "over its head" for DBS satellites (60% foreign content), while its own communications satellites (less than 30% foreign) are woefully outdated. Others don't care what percentage is foreign-made as long as the satellites work. After the Sakura B-2a failed, observers joked that Japanese companies were selling their small-dish DBS receivers as Chinese woks in Akihabara, Tokyo's electronics street bazaar.

Thus, the INS program has its ups-and-downs, and much of the excitement surrounding it is pure media hype; but because of its potential for dramatically changing Japanese society, INS and the booming VAN market are worth watching closely. Like the cheap toys and radios from Japan that were once ridiculed for breaking down, INS is still in the throes of infancy. Experience and time will change all of that. INS has already begun to be felt in Japan's semiconductor industry. According to Jerry Crowley, President of Oki America: "Japanese companies are increasing their capital spending plans, because they believe INS procurement will create a long-term, virtually risk-free market that will develop independently of business cycles and technology trends in the United States."

Strategy 5: Venture Capital and Venture Businesses

Another strategy in Japan's take-lead plan—one taken directly from the United States—is the promotion of a thriving venture capital market and start-up companies, or "venture businesses." On the surface, Japan's goal is to accelerate the diffusion of new technologies and to create new industries and jobs in a slow-growth economy. But underlying these economic considerations is a more deeply-rooted motivation: to demolish Japan's copycat image by nurturing grassroots technologies and reawakening the country's entrepreneurial spirit, which has lain dormant for years.

Since the early 1950s, risk-taking and entrepreneurialism have been forgotten stepchildren in Japan's cautious, follow-the-leader business environment. Worried about security and prestige, Japanese young people compete fiercely for limited positions in major corporations, leading to the infamous "exam hell" approach to education. Small businesses were viewed as secondary players in Japan's economic recovery, a trend reinforced by MITI policies which gave short shrift to its small business agency. But historically, Japan has not always been so big-business oriented. In the early 17th century, a flourishing business class (*chōnin*) sprang up in the castle towns around the Tokugawa warlords and their retainers. These merchant families and peddlers supplied the castles with rice, sake, fish, and armor as well as arts and crafts. In the nineteenth century, Japan's opening to the West triggered a groundswell of small businesses and trading companies in Tokyo and Osaka. This entrepreneurialism was closely linked to the country's enthusiasm for western learning, popularized by the term *bummei kaika* (civilization and enlightenment).

In the postwar period, dynamic start-ups such as Sony, Hanae Mori, and Kyoto Ceramics (Kyocera) created totally new products and industries, often in defiance of Japan's stifling business environment. The Kyoto region, in particular, has been a fertile ground for venture businesses, while the trendy Shinjuku district in Tokyo is known for its entrepreneurial software firms. Recently, to understand the dynamics of homegrown entrepreneurialism, MITI has studied such venture businesses as soft-ware supplier Cosmos 80, Sord Computer (Japan's Apple Computer), and the booming fashion industry. As Japan's heavy industries decline, MITI looks to these businesses as sources of future economic growth. Venture capital is now such a high priority that MITI sponsors conferences, proposes tax breaks for investors, and even offers low-rent commercial space to entrepreneurs. Over thirty of Japan's forty-seven prefectures have also jumped into action, offering venture capital funding and sponsoring venture business associations.

But Japan faces an uphill struggle because it still lacks a well-developed, over-the-counter (OTC) stock market to finance venture businesses. In the early 1970s Japan experienced its first venture capital boom, which saw the formation of eight venture capital companies. As shown in Appendix I, these were owned primarily by major Japanese banks, securities companies, and trading companies. Unlike American venture capital firms, they were staffed exclusively by traditional financial analysts who had little experience with new technologies. Moreover, many of these funds were run by semiretired people who were shunted off to venture units, and did not offer management consulting or marketing services.

This first venture boom fizzled in the mid-1970s for a variety of reasons. In 1976 the Ministry of Finance clamped down on new company listings and trading after a series of wild investment schemes rocked the country in the aftermath of the 1973 oil shock. To protect investors, companies had to meet minimum capital, earnings, and dividend requirements to be listed on the Tokyo or Osaka stock exchanges. As a result, daily trading volumes were miniscule and the OTC market became known as a graveyard for financially troubled firms. Moreover, few of the early venture capital firms wanted to invest in high-risk, leading-edge technologies, but preferred to put their yen into more mature retailing, wholesaling, and consumer manufacturing companies that were preparing to go public.

In 1975 MITI tried to overcome these obstacles by setting up a Venture Enterprise Corporation (VEC) to lend up to $400,000 to small businesses for R&D purposes at 4% interest from a commercial bank, with VEC guaranteeing 80% of the loan for up to eight years. By 1984 VEC had guaranteed over 200 loans worth about

$27 million; but most entrepreneurs shied away to avoid the paperwork and MITI interference. Without regulatory powers, MITI had little influence in directing venture capital companies to high-technology startups.

Since 1982, Japan has experienced a second "benchaa boomu" because of the rapid growth of high-tech industries and consumer demand for custom products. Moreover, investment funds are shifting away from declining heavy industries. There are signs that this boom may be more successful. Over thirty new venture capital firms have opened shop, and there has been a rapid influx of foreign venture capital firms. According to MITI's Venture Capital Research Group, venture capital investments in high-tech ventures jumped from $10 million to $160 million in 1983 (though this is miniscule compared to the $1.8 billion in U.S. venture capital financing). Foreign venture capital firms invested about $40 to $80 million of this amount.

In November 1983 the Ministry of Finance approved the creation of three American-style OTC markets at the Tokyo, Osaka, and Nagoya exchanges. The change came after much lobbying by MITI and the Japan Securities Dealers Association. The new rules require a net worth of about $850,000 and pretax profits of over 4 cents a share for listing. About 12,000 companies would qualify under these liberalized rules. However, as Jon Choy of the Japan Economic Institute notes: "Competition to find good venture investments is extremely intense. Fund managers have combed the 60,000 Japanese small businesses and rejected all but 1,500 of them. An announcement of a promising invention prompts a flood of telephone calls and visits from interested investors. There are clearly more lenders than borrowers in the venture market, a point that might presage a shakeout if venture capitalists continue to increase."

Recent liberalization of Japan's capital market, which was intended to stimulate foreign investment in Japan, has rebounded in the other direction. Because of high U.S. interest rates, Japanese investors are putting their money into U.S. Treasury bills and other safe, high-yielding instruments. This massive capital outflow is draining Japan of investment funds and is forcing Japanese venture capitalists to seek investment opportunities overseas.

Despite the slim pickings, foreign venture capital firms such as Hambrecht & Quist, Pacific Technology Ventures, International

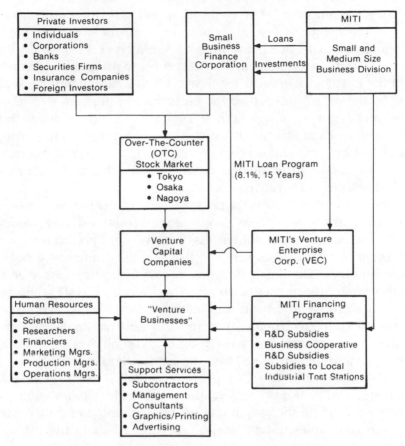

Source: Dataquest, Inc.

**Figure 3-4. MITI's venture capital and venture
business programs.**

Data Group, Baring Brothers, and Burr, Egan, Deleage & Co. have
opened branches in Japan, and promise to introduce new investment strategies and management consulting techniques. Some
companies are entering into joint ventures with Japanese financiers to establish an "insider" presence in Tokyo. Baring Brothers
and Hambrecht & Quist, for example, have teamed up with Orient Leasing Company.

During this second venture boom, MITI is downplaying its
interventionist role and emphasizing market incentives, as shown
in Figure 3-4. In February 1984 MITI and the Small Business

Agency announced a "venture business" subsidy program consisting of four financing systems: a new Small Business Finance Bank program that will issue loans up to $1.5 million at 8.1% for fifteen years to high-tech companies; a R&D subsidy program to finance half the development costs for new ceramics, biotechnology, and mechatronics; subsidies to eighteen small and medium-size business cooperatives engaged in new ceramic research projects; and subsidies to local industrial testing stations for purchasing mainframe computers. These programs are designed to help venture businesses underwrite the high costs of conducting basic research and developing innovative products.

MITI is proposing several laws to promote small businesses. The Small Businesses' New Technology Promotion Law would grant a build-up of investment loss reserves and preferential tax treatment for businesses selected by local governments as high-tech ventures. The Small Business Credit Insurance Law would allow venture businesses to obtain unsecured loans. MITI officials are considering four criteria for qualifying firms for tax incentives: (1) research in electronics, mechatronics, new materials, biotechnology, or computer software; (2) R&D spending over 3% of total sales; (3) founded or moved into the high-technology field within the last ten years; and (4) plan to be listed on OTC stock exchange. MITI is also urging the Fair Trade Commission to remove its ban on the assignment of venture capital executives to start-up companies for the purpose of strengthening the managment of these firms.

Despite these latest developments, there are many obstacles blocking the development of a thriving venture capital market and venture businesses in Japan. Probably the biggest roadblock is Japan's highly group-oriented society, which discourages individual actions. From childhood, Japanese are taught that "the nail that sticks out gets hammered down." If an aspiring entrepreneur wants to jump ship, his parents, family, friends, and colleagues will often work together to discourage him. Indeed, entrepreneurs in Japan are called *datsusara*, meaning "salarymen who have broken loose," suggesting rebels who cannot work well with other people, rather than groundbreaking pioneers. Japan's famous lifetime employment system reinforces this loyalty to the company by discouraging job-hopping and severely penalizing those who leave. Consequently, startup ventures have an extremely difficult time finding qualified scientists, researchers, and other technical staff. This is compounded by a general reluctance to hire "head-hunters" and by the absence of a strong network of lawyers, consultants, venture capitalists, and successful entrepreneurs.

However, this situation is gradually changing in high-tech fields, such as computers, software, and communications. More entry-level and mid-career professionals, especially those educated in the West and exposed to foreigners, are becoming dissatisfied by the rigidity and slow promotions within large corporations, and are beginning to start their own ventures. Within the last few years, for example, over 500 software design houses have sprung up around the country. Shinjuku, Tokyo's youth mecca, and downtown Hiroshima have become two hotspots.

But there are still numerous legal and organizational roadblocks. Japan's Federal Trade Commission, for example, prevents venture capital firms from placing their employees on venture business staffs and prohibits venture capitalists from over 49% ownership. These rules enforce an "arms length" relationship, just the opposite of the kind that has been the lifeblood of Silicon Valley start-ups. Moreover, most Japanese venture capital companies act like finance companies, pursuing a low-risk, low-return strategy because of their close ties with major banks (*keiretsu*). Thus, for most entrepreneurs, family and friends are the major source of funds. But this "family operation" style has its own problems. Once having established a company, entrepreneurs are often reluctant to sell out in the OTC market because of family pressures. Yet in order to succeed, these start-ups usually need a vigorous shot of funding and marketing expertise, which most entrepreneur-scientists are unable to provide. Thus, they are caught in a vicious bind—good ideas, but no money and nowhere to go. Understandably, the mortality rate of these new ventures is rather high.

Despite these obstacles, the overall prospects for Japanese venture businesses look encouraging. The influx of American venture capitalists, the creation of an OTC stock market, the growing entrepreneurialism of young Japanese, and the boom in high-tech industries should provide a strong impetus for the Japanese venture capital market. More importantly, Japan's fierce determination to "catch up with the West" in venture capital may be the decisive factor. Combined with the country's herd mentality, Japan's venture capital market may be unstoppable once it gets going.

Strategy #6: Selective Import Promotion

Japan's most controversial strategy is its selective import promotion policies, which have led to growing trade friction with the West. Since the mid-1970s, Japan has slowly opened its doors to foreign imports under the General Agreement on Tariffs and Trade (GATT) guidelines. Computers and software imports were liberalized after 1974; tariffs on automobiles declined in 1978. Since the 1979 Tokyo round of trade agreements, the Japanese government has accelerated its tariff reductions to blunt growing criticism of its protected markets and ballooning trade surplus. In December 1981, import testing procedures were streamlined. In 1982, tariffs were reduced on 313 products, followed in 1983 by further reductions on 363 products. By the end of 1983, Japanese officials claimed that Japan had on average the lowest tariffs of any industrial nation. While this was true at a superficial level, it was apparent upon closer inspection that the tariff cuts were primarily aimed at low value-added foods and products that were already scheduled for liberalization. Emerging high-tech industries and certain farm products remained protected behind a wall of import quotas, tariffs, and strict testing standards.

In October 1983, Japan shifted gears. Prime Minister Yasuhiro Nakasone announced that Japan would "move beyond market-opening measures into the realm of active import promotion." This strategy involves a variety of new policy tools: the promotion of foreign investment, foreign plant siting in Japan's new technopolis regions, low-interest import financing by the Export-Import Bank and the Japan Development Bank (JDB), short-term yen loans for importers, revised standards and certification systems, improved distribution systems for imported products, and more business information from the Japan External Trade Organization (JETRO), MITI's overseas promotion arm. While these are positive, market-opening gestures, their underlying motive is pure political judo. Japan is quickly trying to turn the growing foreign demands for market access to its advantage by pulling in new jobs and investments. "If you can't keep 'em out, use them to your advantage" seems to be the latest thinking in Tokyo.

MITI has aggressively pursued these policies as a way to divert attention away from the more politically explosive issue of market opening. In 1983 the Japan Development Bank (JDB) accepted loan applications from foreign companies and issued $70 million in low-interest loans to thirteen companies, including Materials Research Corporation, Burr Brown, Nippon Motorola, Intel, and Fairchild. These were widely publicized in the press to suggest Japan's openness to foreigners. In 1984 the JDB announced a new loan program for foreign capital investments in high-tech companies, plant siting in Japan's technopolis regions, and the importation of computers, peripherals, medical equipment, and machine tools. In addition, Japan's twenty technopolis areas announced a variety of local tax incentives, land write-downs, and other subsidies to companies opening manufacturing plants and R&D centers. Some regions have had positive results. Monsanto recently announced a polysilicon plant in Utsunomiya, north of Tokyo, while Fairchild Japan opened a new semiconductor plant in Nagasaki.

While these are steps in the right direction, Japan's new import promotion strategy is heavily one-sided. On the one hand, Japan promotes low value-added imports, such as raw materials and agricultural products (except for oranges and beef, which are protected by the powerful farm lobby), high-tech goods that it does not produce (such as jet aircraft), and the foreign capital, technology, and plant investments needed to create new jobs and produce high-tech goods. On the other hand, government policies have discouraged the importing of satellites, telecommunications equipment, and other technology-intensive goods that pose a threat to Japan's infant industries. The high value-added imports being promoted, such as electronic cash registers, computers, and semiconductors, are mature industries where Japanese companies offer stiff competition. In short, Japan wants the benefits of foreign investments and technology without foreign competition. Indeed, its latest trade policies might be more accurately called "selective import promotion."

This latest strategy has failed to dampen foreign criticism of Japan's ballooning trade surplus. In July 1985, the imminent threat of a U.S. protectionist backlash forced Prime Minister

Nakasone to announce yet another round of market-opening measures. Scheduled to be implemented over three years, the "Improved Market Access Action Program" calls for removing tariffs on 1,800 products, accepting foreign test data for specified imports, increasing government purchases of foreign goods, removing interest rate ceilings on large deposits, and allowing foreign lawyers to practice in Japan. On paper, these measures sound good, but there are many problems with them. The key obstacle is one of omission. The tariff cuts overlook key items (such as oranges and beef) in which foreign countries have a strong interest, while the revised certification and testing standards still omit strategic products. Moreover, until the last minute, Japanese officials insisted on retaining the authority to exclude foreigners from the drafting or revising of industrial standards. Ministry resistance was so strong that even the prestigious *Japan Economic Journal* observed: "Instances like this make it all the more necessary for not only foreign countries but also Japan's private sector to keep a watchful eye on the bureaucracy so that it will implement the three-year program as promised."

How will Japanese officials respond to the latest market-opening measures? Will they follow through on their promises? For an idea of how Japanese industrial policies have been implemented in the past, let's take a look at two high-technology fields: semiconductors and software.

In July 1982 the U.S.-Japan High-Technology Working Group was established to resolve trade friction between the two countries. A special subcommittee was convened in April 1983 after the Semiconductor Industry Association (SIA), an American lobbying group, issued a report entitled *The Effect of Government Targeting on World Semiconductor Competition.* The report criticized MITI for targeting the semiconductor industry for accelerated development and protecting the Japanese market from foreign imports. Although both contentions are difficult to prove prima facie, SIA's lobbying was instrumental in eliminating tariffs on semiconductor imports. In November 1983, both countries endorsed the recommendations of the High-Technology Working Group: eliminate the 4.2% tariff on semiconductors, exchange semiconductor trade data, expand mutual trade and investment, increase technology exchanges, prosecute unfair copying of semiconductor designs, toughen patent protection procedures, and improve access for foreign firms into MITI's Technopolis program. In April 1984, tariffs were eliminated by both sides.

While these measures led to more amicable relations, they did nothing to correct the growing U.S.-Japan trade imbalance in this highly strategic industry. In 1981 the United States enjoyed a semiconductor trade surplus with Japan, but Japan's hot-selling memory chips pushed the U.S. trade deficit from $86 million in 1982 to a whopping $1.2 billion in 1984. Moreover, the Japanese share of the U.S. semiconductor market jumped from 6.7% in 1981 to 17.4% in 1984. Ironically, the trade imbalance and Japanese market share did not decline until early 1985, when the collapse of the U.S. personal computer market sent the semiconductor industry into a recession, reducing demand for Japanese memory chips.

Initially, the 4.2% tariff cut was viewed as a victory by the United States, but the agreement only lowered export barriers for Japanese firms, and the new trade statistics program has only served to monitor Japan's fluctuating market share. The key to reducing the trade imbalance is not government trade agreements, but increased U.S. sales and production in Japan. Given the intensely competitive nature of the Japanese market, the "old boy" network of Japanese customer-supplier relations, and the niche-market approach of U.S. companies in Japan, this situation is not likely to change overnight. Even Motoo Shiina, a top-ranking Diet member and chairman of the Liberal Democratic Party's Policy Research Council, admits: "MITI has requested 130 major corporations to develop affirmative action buying programs, but even if they increase their purchases of U.S. goods of all types, it would only reduce the the U.S.-Japan trade imbalance by $5 to $7 billion out of forecasted total of $50 billion in 1985."

The software rights battle illustrates the political problem with Japan's selective import promotion strategy. In December 1983 the Information Industry Committee of MITI's Industrial Structure Council proposed software legislation that would effectively push U.S. software makers out of the Japanese market. MITI's proposal called for mandatory registration and licensing of new software. Software developers would be required to disclose their programs to a new agency, and third parties could lease and modify these programs. Developers would have limited control over copying, licensing, and distribution of their programs for a period of fifteen years under a revised patent law, but all programs deemed vital to the public welfare (such as medical software) would come under MITI's control.

MITI's hardnosed legislation came in response to a series of events that shook the software industry. In 1983 there was a rapid rise in lawsuits over software rights; of the forty-four cases pending in Japanese courts, twenty were filed that year. In two cases (K.K. Taito v. Makoto Denshikoygyo K.I. and K.K. Taito v. ING Enterprises), district courts ruled that software was subject to copyright protection in Japan. Moreover, a survey conducted in mid-1983 by the *Japan Industrial Journal* revealed that IBM virtually dominated the domestic software industry. Among the top ten software programs for large-scale computer systems, IBM Japan held six spots (first, and fifth through ninth). MITI was concerned that the copyright approach would slow the dissemination and use of software programs. Unless another approach was used, IBM would maintain its dominance.

This concern was compounded by the Hitachi-IBM espionage case. In November 1983, IBM dropped its lawsuit against Hitachi after the latter agreed to pay IBM from $13 to 26 million to cover legal costs resulting from the industry spy case and Hitachi's previous use of IBM software. Earlier, Hitachi had maintained that it did not recognize IBM software copyrights; but Hitachi backed off when IBM pointed out possible infringement of its copyright. In settling the case, Hitachi agreed to allow IBM to inspect new Hitachi products for five years. The settlement sent off alarm bells at MITI, which feared that the Fifth Generation Computer Project's software development program would be compromised, since Hitachi is a key member of the project. Tsukasa Fukuma, author of a new book called *Information Imperialism*, observes that as long as IBM had access to Hitachi software programs, MITI officials believed that Fifth Generation findings would leak to IBM, and the project would slow down because of reluctance from other participants. The new software law would stop that leak by defining software as industrial property and requiring all companies (such as IBM) to disclose their software programs. Thus, MITI would maintain absolute control over all software deemed vital to the national interest, such as the Fifth Generation software.

The resulting battle between MITI and the Ministry of Education's Cultural Agency over MITI's proposal abolishes the myth of a united "Japan Inc." In January 1984 the Cultural Agency came out with a counterproposal defining software programs as intellectual property that should be accorded the same copyright protection as books and movies. The Agency sharply criticized MITI's proposal, arguing that mandatory disclosure and shortening of protection from the standard fifty years to fifteen years would discourage software development. Many software programs developed in the 1960s, it noted, are still in use. The Cultural Agency was joined by the Ministry of Posts and Telecommunications in exchange for support of its NTT telecommunications reform proposals. (Longtime rivals, MITI has called for liberalization of the value-added network (VAN) market that NTT wants to protect.) Thus, in two related issues, NTT and MITI stood on opposite sides of the fence.

The issue came to a tortuous and heated close in March 1984, several months after U.S. negotiators demanded that MITI withdraw its proposal. In a low-key announcement, MITI officials notified the U.S. Embassy in Tokyo that it would not submit its software rights bill to the Diet before the March 27th deadline. With that announcement, the software controversy was over, at least temporarily, until MITI could regroup its forces and formulate a compromise bill.

Thus, the *Japan Economic Journal*'s warning about Japan's new market-opening measures has been borne out in the past. Unless foreign governments take the initiative to carefully monitor Japanese policymaking activities and industry standard councils—as the "Japan lobby" has so successfully done on Capitol Hill—Japan is not likely to open up its markets. And as long as Japan pursues a selective import promotion strategy, there is a chance that foreign companies may be iced out of the Japanese market or indirectly used to deny others access.

PUTTING IT ALL TOGETHER

In this chapter we have reviewed Japan's take-lead strategies for the 1980s and seen how the various government ministries plan to implement them. Although many westerners may construe these strategies as a Japanese "conspiracy" to dominate the world, neither MITI nor any other ministry has the power to merge them into a single master plan. Bickering among ministries is as prevalent in Japan as anywhere else, preventing them from working closely with each other. For example, the heated rivalry between MITI and the Ministry of Posts and Telecommunications over software and telecommunications is well known, and often works to the advantage of the United States. Nevertheless, taken together, Japan's take-lead strategies will have a far-reaching impact on the West by 1990. What are these synergistic effects? And what impact will they have?

Japan's take-lead strategies can essentially be divided into two approaches: "inside" strategies and "outside" strategies. The inside strategies aim at developing the country's "soft" infrastructure of technology, research centers, venture capital, and telecommunications. For example, MITI's joint R&D programs are designed to form a critical mass of creative researchers who can enable Japan to surpass the West in leading-edge technologies. By 1995, these projects are expected to generate over 60,000 patents, providing numerous opportunities for venture capitalists. Although this patent deluge will primarily benefit large companies, MITI's small- and medium-business program will increase the "trickle down" by linking small companies with the large R&D participants, encouraging small business research consortiums, and providing technical advice through regional technology centers. Since over 80% of the Japanese labor force is in this sector, MITI is encouraging banks and venture capital companies to fund new ventures in software, audiovisual retailing, and telecommunications. These venture businesses will eventually form the economic core of Japan's technopolises.

The Technopolis Concept is the culmination of these diverse efforts by MITI to move Japan up the technology stream. The technopolises will be the center of Japan's future industrial growth. They will host the R&D centers and manufacturing plants introduced by major Japanese corporations, foreign companies, venture businesses, and existing small- and medium-sized businesses. NTT's Information Network System will link these technopolises to Tokyo and other major cities, forming a nationwide information network of teletopias, also known as MITI's New

Media Community cities. By the year 2000, these technopolises and teletopias will become the new centers of innovative research. They will be the engines for Japan's economic growth in the twenty-first century.

Strategic alliances and selective import promotion, Japan's "outside" strategies, are the most visible to foreigners because of their tie to international trade. Designed to reduce trade friction and maintain the inflow of foreign capital, ideas, and technology, they are a form of "political judo" in the sense that Japan is using the strong market-opening pressures being exerted by foreign governments and companies as a means of acquiring the foreign investments that it needs for economic growth. In this context, joint ventures, licensing agreements, and foreign participation in Japanese R&D projects are merely ways of monitoring and importing foreign technology.

Japan's most controversial strategy is its selective import promotion policies, which are designed to keep out high value-added products that threaten infant industries, but to encourage investments, plant siting, and technology imports. MITI's Industrial Location Guidance Division, the Japan Regional Development Corporation, and the prefectural governments are the main vehicles for this selective import strategy. By opening the door quickly and selectively, MITI and the prefectures hope to outsell foreign governments and American states in the race to attract high-technology companies.

The major weakness in Japan's outside strategy is obvious: selective import promotion threatens to derail international cooperation. By keeping out high value-added goods such as software and satellites, Japan risks intensifying trade friction and discouraging foreign companies from opening plants or investing in Japan. As they see it, the Japanese government only wants their money and technology, but not their products or competition. To an extent, this perception is accurate. Imported foreign plants may increase "Japanese exports," making them party to a loss of American jobs and worsening trade relations. On the other hand, Japanese plant investments in the United States partially counterbalance U.S. investments in Japan. But unless Japan stops practicing a discriminatory import strategy, foreign companies may lose interest in MITI's technopolises altogether. If Japan truly believes in free trade, it will have to scrap its selective import promotion strategy for a geniune market opening that welcomes high value-added imports as well as foreign plants and investments. In the long run, this strategy will pay the biggest dividends in terms of good will and increased trade.

PART II : POLIS

Building New Cities

In 1980, MITI announced the Technopolis Concept, a bold plan to build a network of high-tech cities linked to Tokyo by bullet trains, airports, and communications systems. To westerners, this plan may appear unworkable, but to the Japanese it makes perfect sense. Technopolis is only the latest step in a long tradition of city-building *(machizukuri)* that dates back to the nation's founding. To fully understand this tradition, one must look to the distant past, to the ancient capitals of Nara and Kyoto and the feudal castle towns of Osaka, Kamakura, and Edo, which form the basis for Japan's modern cities.

More recently, Japanese cities have evolved in new directions, reflecting the advance of technology. Sapporo, Nagoya, the Atsugi Research City, and the Tsukuba Science City have drawn heavily on western urban design and offer new ideas for the emerging technopolises.

Thus, what emerges from the pages of history is not a static process of remolding Japanese cities in tired, traditional forms, but a dynamic process of incorporating new ideas from abroad to create world-class cities. It is within this context that the Technopolis Concept must be viewed— not as a short-term policy to address immediate economic ills, but as a long-term strategy designed to lead Japan into the twenty-first century.

For the Japanese, patience and endurance are virtues. True success is not measured in months or years, but in decades and centuries. The seeds being planted now by MITI will be harvested in the next century, a practice that has its roots in the ancient capitals of Japan.

4

FROM ANCIENT CAPITALS

The imperial city of fairest Nara
Glows now at the height of beauty,
Like brilliant flowers in bloom!

Ono no Oyu (Manyō-shū)

NARA THE SEVENFOLD

Empress Genmei gazed over the Nara plain, the site of her new capital. To the east, west, north, and south, as far as she could see, farmers stood knee-deep in flooded paddy fields planting rice. Their backs were bent in supplication. She prayed for a plentiful harvest, for the country had been ravaged by famine and epidemics. Not even the royal family had remained untouched. In the previous year, 707 A.D., her son, the Emperor Mommu, had been struck down by illness, leaving his infant son Obito to inherit the Asuka throne. To ensure the family's ascendency, Genmei declared herself empress and assumed the awesome task of ruling the country, a task that she would eventually abdicate to her daughter, the Empress Genshō. In accordance with the ancient Shinto belief that the imperial palace was polluted by death, Genmei chose to move the 120-year-old Asuka capital to the northern end of the Nara plain. Heijō-kyō (the official name for Nara), as she called her new capital, would be patterned after the Chinese capital of Ch'ang-an, but unlike previous Japanese capitals it would be built on a scale then unimaginable. It would be the jewel of the Yamato state.

Thus, in the year 708 Empress Genmei declared: "The area of Heijō conforms with the laws of geomancy, three mountains protect it, and the result of the divination was good. The capital must be built here."

Ancient Nara is a prime example of government planning on a large scale, symbolized by the numerous Buddhist temples that surrounded the palace walls. These temples consisted of seven buildings—the pagoda, oratory, lecture hall, library, belfry, refectory, and dormitory. The new capital was a compromise that reflected the political and religious pressures of the day. Although earlier emperors had attempted to relocate the capital from the Yamato Basin, they encountered strong opposition from clans in the Asuka region and the powerful Buddhist temples, such as Hōryūji and Yakushiji. Empress Genmei was well aware of her reliance on these groups, especially the Buddhist monks who offered deliverance from the raging epidemics.

Although grander than its predecessors, Nara was not the Japanese government's first attempt at building a capital based on the Chinese model. In 645, the Emperor Kōtoku constructed his imperial palace at the port city of Naniwa (present-day Osaka), the main departure point for diplomatic and trade missions to the T'ang court. The ancient capital of Naniwa was laid out in a checkerboard pattern like that of Ch'ang-an, with its administrative offices, ministries, and imperial palace located in the north-central portion of the city.

In 694, the Emperor Tenchi moved the capital to the Fujiwara site at the southern end of the Yamato Basin, as shown in Figure 4-1. Like the Naniwa capital, the new capital was laid out in a grid fashion. It was surrounded by twelve gates and divided into two halves by the main avenue, which ran from north to south. The powerful Asuka clans controlled the residential blocks and the marketplaces. However, because it was surrounded by mountains on three sides, the Fujiwara site was too small to handle the rapid growth of the government bureaucracy. Empress Genmei sought a more spacious location that would allow the city to grow and permit easier access to the provinces. The Nara site to the north fit the bill.

In choosing the final site, Empress Genmei employed Chinese geomancy, the elaborate system of "avoiding calamities" that involved drawing connections between the Five Elements. During the Nara and Heian periods, Japanese life was heavily influenced by these superstitions. Chronicles of the period frequently refer

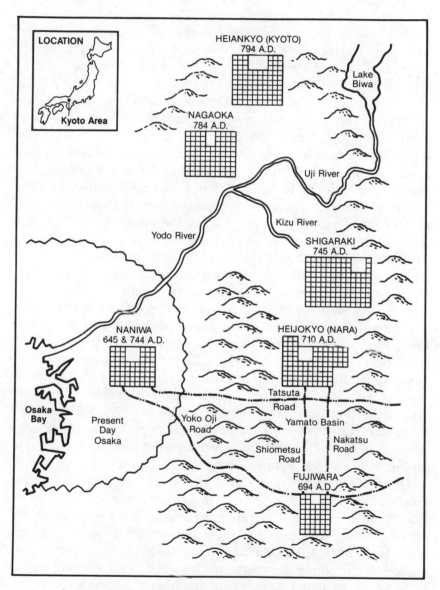

Figure 4-1. Japan's ancient capitals.

to "unlucky days" and "unlucky directions," depending on the astrological conditions of the day. The Nara site was chosen because the arrangement of the surrounding hills and streams, or what the Chinese called *Fenshui* (air and water) were considered auspicious. The site was close to several rivers, and a pond (a symbol of power) was located to the south.

Nara was laid out in the same checkerboard fashion as Ch'ang-an, but it was much larger than the Naniwa and Fujiwara capitals—approximately 2.5 miles by 3.1 miles. The city was divided by a main boulevard which ran from the Sujakumon gate in the north to the Rajōmon gate in the south, and consisted of eighty city districts subdivided into sixteen sections each. The emperor's palace (Daidairi) commanded the city from its position north of the Sujakumon gate. Within the palace walls were the imperial residence (Dairi), court hall (Chōdōin), and southern garden (Nan-en). Unlike the T'ang capital, Nara had no heavy walls surrounding the city. Two north-south roads linked Nara with the former capital of Fujiwara to the south.

The construction of Nara was unprecedented in scope. Initially, the imperial court conscripted labor from the provinces, but opposition was widespread because of the severe hardships and starvation endured by the workers. Runaways, looting, and political agitation threatened to halt construction of the new capital, so the imperial court relied on voluntary, paid labor and compulsory employment in which each village was responsible for sending a fixed number of laborers. However, this dependence on peasant labor attracted job-seekers and displaced farmers, contributing to an increase in street crime, gambling, and arson.

The most spectacular landmark in the city was the Tōdaiji, the Eastern Great Monastery, where the colossal statue of the Great Buddha was erected. Cast in bronze and gilded with gold, the statue stood fifty-three feet high and weighed over a million pounds. During the Nara period (710–794), Buddhist monks wielded enormous power over the imperial court. Playing on the Chinese belief that the emperor's failures were responsible for famines and epidemics, they implored the leaders to donate money for temple construction and to pray to the Great Buddha for relief. The imperial government responded by pouring large sums of money into the construction of the Tōdaiji and other temples. By the end of the Nara period, the Six Buddhist Sects (Jōjitsu, Sanron, Hossō, Kusha, Ritsu, and Kegon) exerted such great influence over the court that they elicited the outrage of the powerful Fujiwara family. It is estimated that of the 200,000 people living in Nara in 775, the cultural blossoming of the capital could be attributed to 20,000 people related to the courts and the monasteries. During this period, the *Fudoki*, a topographical survey of Japan, and the *Manyō-shū* (a collection of 4,000 poems), were prepared, and Buddhist philosophy flourished.

By 741, however, there were calls from the Fujiwara family to move the capital in order to escape the pervasive influence of the Buddhist monasteries. During the next forty years, the capital was moved to several different sites—to Naniwa in 744, Shigaraki in 745, and Nagaoka in 784—but for various reasons these new locations were abandoned. Finally, in 794, a new site was selected for the construction of yet another capital.

KYOTO: THE CAPITAL OF PEACE AND TRANQUILLITY

In 792, after a series of palace intrigues at Nagaoka, the Emperor Kammu decided to move the capital. Under the pretext of going on hunting trips, the young, athletic emperor explored the Yamase region to the north of Nara. After several trips, he discovered a plain at the juncture of the Kamo and Katsura rivers surrounded by mountains on three sides. He was pleased by the setting and on the 22nd day of the tenth month in 794, declared: "The rivers and mountains of the imperial site in Kuzuno are beautiful to behold; may our subjects from all over the country come to see them." To select a name for the new capital, he held a poetry reading at which every poet made reference to the word *Heian*, or peace. This, he decided, would be the name of his new capital—Heian-kyō, the Capital of Peace and Tranquillity—a place of peace among the feuding political factions. It was an auspicious choice, for Heian-kyō (present day Kyoto) would remain the capital for over a thousand years and become the center of Japan's cultural blossoming.

Kyoto was a magnificent city, a classic example of Japanese planning on a grand scale. Upon selecting the site, Emperor Kammu created a government agency, called *zōeishi*, with a staff of 150 officers to plan and construct the city. The agency laid out Kyoto according to the checkerboard pattern adopted from China. However, the city was slightly larger than Nara, measuring some 3.5 miles from north to south and 3.0 miles from east to west. Suzaku Ōji, the main north-south avenue, divided the city into the western and eastern halves, reflecting the division of the imperial government into the Ministry of the Left and the Ministry of the Right. Other streets ran parallel on either side, and nine streets ran from east to west. At the northern end of the city, surrounded by roofed mud walls with fourteen gates, were the imperial residence and the government ministries.

Before the city could be built, however, large-scale public works projects had to be undertaken. The most important task was to divert the Kamo and Takano rivers around the city to reduce the potential for flooding and political disunity. In addition, palace gates were built and the sloping ground leveled for the construction of the imperial palace and government ministries. Emperor Kammu ordered high-ranking officials to mobilize laborers from their provinces to build the city; these numbered 24,000 during the peak construction period. To reduce the influence of Buddhism in the new capital, Emperor Kammu issued an edict sharply limiting temple construction and donations of land to the local monasteries, two practices that had threatened the stability of the government and reduced tax revenues needed for the construction of the new capital.

Despite the ban, Kyoto inherited a number of Buddhist temples dating back to Prince Shōtoku (574–622), who had established Buddhism as the state religion. The Hata family, who had donated the land for the new capital, had supported Prince Shōtoku in promoting Buddhism in Japan, and had built several family temples overlooking the site of the capital. Kōryū-ji contained a statue of Amida, the Buddha of Mercy (a national treasure) and the Reihō-kan (Sacred Treasure Hall) housed the famous wooden statue of Miroku, the Buddha of the Future. Even Emperor Kammu was not beyond the reach of Buddhist influence. He had the Tō-ji (East Temple) and Sai-ji (West Temple) built on either side of Rashōmon, the city's main gate, to protect the city from misfortune. He also maintained close ties with the priest Saichō (767–822) who built his temple, Enryaku-ji, the center of Tendai Buddhism, to the northeast of the capital on Mt. Hiei. The location was important, because in Japan the northeast direction is feared as the "Devil's Gate," through which fires, epidemics, and other misfortunes are believed to spread. Emperor Kammu encouraged Saichō to build Enryaku-ji to protect the capital from malevolent forces.

In his effort to build a permanent capital, Emperor Kammu lavished great sums of money on the imperial palace and the eight government ministries. Covering one-fifth of the entire city, the imperial enclosure housed thirty large pavilions. At the massive wooden gate stood the Daigokuden, the main palace, and the Hōrakuin, the hall for state ceremonies. The contrast in architecture was striking. The imperial palace embodied the unadorned simplicity of Japanese architecture, with its unvarnished woods and thatched roofs; the government ministries imitated the splendor of T'ang architecture, designed with white plaster walls, vermilion pillars, and greenish-glazed tile roofs. This unusual juxtaposition reflected Emperor Kammu's effort to meld continental thinking with traditional Japanese values.

Kyoto, blessed with natural beauty and broad, tree-lined avenues, proved to be successful beyond Emperor Kammu's wildest dreams. Its founding attracted people from the surrounding provinces and marked the beginning of the Heian period (794–1185), an era known as Japan's "Golden Age" because of its cultural and religious blossoming. During the next four hundred years, Japanese society moved out of the shadow of Chinese culture and produced great works of art and literature that reflected a truly Japanese sensibility. Perhaps the greatest of these was *The Tale of Genji*, the world's first novel, which was written by Lady Murasaki Shikibu to describe court life in Kyoto. Using *kana*, or Japanese phonetics, Lady Murasaki and other women writers revolutionized Japanese culture by introducing a purely Japanese alphabet and style of written expression. The Heian court was marked by intense artistic activity in which taste and refinement were judged by the grace of one's poetry or a few strokes of the brush.

Buddhist thought also underwent profound changes as Japanese monks developed new philosophies. The priest Saichō studied in Nara, but rebelled against the formality and rigidity of the religious communities by seeking solitude atop Mt. Hiei. He believed in enlightenment through austerity and meditation, the basis for the Tendai school of thought and, later, Zen Buddhism. A second religious leader was Kūkai (774–835), who also studied in China, but formulated a new doctrine, Shingon, which postulated the existence of Buddha in all things. His belief that art was a means of revealing the divine led to a blossoming of Buddhist art in the capital. Under Emperor Saga, Kammu's successor, Kūkai established the Shingon sect within the imperial enclosure.

For court nobles, Chinese studies was still the passport to political office. In order to advance, young men had to take qualifying exams covering such classical works as the *Chou Li*, the *Analects*, and the *Classic of Filial Piety*. However, this interest in systematic learning took new forms in Japan. The Heian court established an educational system consisting of one central college (*daigaku*) and one provincial college (*kokugaku*) to prepare students for the exams, the forerunner of Japan's present educational system. Outstanding scholars were periodically gathered into special commissions to revise outmoded codes and study administrative problems. Independent scholars produced numerous encyclopedias, critical treatises, and legal commentaries, all of which provided the court with insight into adapting the Chinese system to Japanese society.

If Kyoto was a center of enlightenment and learning, it dazzled for only a brief period of time. The Heian Period reached its zenith during the reign of Fujiwara no Michinaga (966–1027), a powerful statesman who ruled with great vision. By the end of the eleventh century, however, the imperial court had degenerated to a "cloistered government" in which the emperor would abdicate the throne to a docile heir, usually a minor, and continue to rule from a palace or hidden retreat. This separation of power eventually split the country into competing factions, a weakness played upon by mountain priests who attacked the capital with armies of soldier-monks to intimidate the court. By the twelfth century, Kyoto had turned into a battlefield and poets wrote ominously of the coming of an age of violence, disorder, and war. Out of this turbulence emerged two military clans, the Taira and the Minamoto, who would lead the country into feudal warfare. The apocalypse had arrived, leaving Kyoto in its fiery wake.

THE ASCENDANCY OF KAMAKURA

The rivalry between the Taira and the Minamoto clans escalated precipitously during the twelfth century, each side gaining the upper hand for political control over the throne for a while, and then losing it to the other. Both families were descendants of the emperors and were closely matched in military strength. The Taira were strong in sea warfare and controlled the coastal areas of the Inland Sea, while the Minamoto excelled in land combat using mounted troops. The first test of strength came in the Hōgen Insurrection (1156), when the Minamoto attempted to occupy the imperial palace; they were soundly beaten by Taira leader Kiyomori, who mercilessly executed the Minamoto leaders. Although the Taira leader ruled for a short period, their victory incurred the wrath of the Minamoto who sought revenge. Yoritomo, the surviving leader of the Minamoto, moved his military headquarters to Kamakura, a small fishing village in the Kanto area to the east, where he rebuilt the Minamoto forces and exercised control over provincial warrior groups. Military action flared up again during the Gempei War (1180–1185). From his Kamakura headquarters, Yoritomo directed the Minamoto forces that finally annihilated the Taira in a dramatic sea battle at Dan no-Ura (at the northern end of the island of Kyushu). Victorious, Yoritomo became Shogun and established the capital at his military headquarters in Kamakura. Kyoto remained the cultural center and seat of the imperial palace, a symbolic role that would continue to the nineteenth century.

Kamakura embodied the chaos and ruthlessness of military rule in feudal Japan. Unlike Nara and Kyoto, which had been systematically planned in advance along Chinese lines, Kamakura was built in response to the immediate needs of a growing army of retainers and merchants. It was hemmed in by mountains on three sides and Yuigahama beach to the south, making the grid pattern difficult to create. But it was a natural fortress. Yoritomo used the mountains, river, and shoreline to his strategic advantage in defending the capital. He established a road maintenance bureau to cut a network of routes and defense posts into the surrounding mountains, and to build dikes along the river and coastline. The port of Waga was developed to handle military vessels and heavy commercial traffic, and large warehouses were built to store the cargoes of food, lumber, and materials shipped in from the provinces. Yoritomo constructed his imperial residence and the Hachiman Shrine, his family shrine, in a mountainous area in the northern part of the city, a move that encouraged the religious community to build a Zen Buddhist temple complex and the Ebara Tenjin-sha Shrine in the surrounding area. The main boulevard, lined by samurai residences, served as the city's axis, running from the Hachiman Shrine southward to the shoreline where merchant shops sprang up helter-skelter. During the Gempei War, Kamakura was the scene of great activity as Yoritomo staged the comeback of the Minamoto clan, forcing the military government to control the city's land use to reduce chaos and confusion.

The Kamakura Period (1192–1333) saw the rise of the warrior class. During this period, the centralized government of the Heian Period fell apart and was replaced by a feudal system of rural warlords (*buke*) who maintained standing armies of samurai warriors (*bushi*). These samurai evolved a system of ethics known as *bushido*, or way of the warrior, in which a samurai was obligated to show absolute and unwavering loyalty to his lord. In return, the lord would bestow favors and benefits, such as parcels of land and positions of power. Trained in the martial arts, the samurai were expected to eschew material comforts for the austerity and discipline of military life. Their code of honor embodied the basic tenets of Zen Buddhism: a sense of calm, trust in fate, submission to the inevitable, disdain for life, and a stoic composure in the face of calamity.

Yoritomo's move to Kamakura triggered the development of castle centers and a highway system. After defeating the Taira clan, he assigned military governors to twenty-six provinces to maintain control over local warrior groups. These governors built imperial villages that were protected by small castles erected on nearby hilltops. Limited to defensive purposes during battle, these castle centers were the forerunners of the later castle towns. To link these castle centers and the Kamakura Bakufu (a Chinese term meaning headquarters for the Commander of the Imperial Guard) to the imperial palace in Kyoto, three highway systems were constructed: the Tōkaidō, Tōsandō, and Hokurikudō. Small station towns were built along these roads to provide food and lodging for the Bakufu's troops and messengers. The Tōkaidō and

Hokurikudō lines are now the routes for Japan's famous bullet train, the *Shinkansen.* Thus, despite the chaos and incessant fighting of the Kamakura Period, the groundwork for Japan's future urban centers and transportation lines were laid by the Kamakura shoguns.

THE RISE OF CASTLE TOWNS

For all its military strength, the Kamakura Bakufu fell in 1333 to the Ashikaga family, a warrior clan from northeastern Japan who ruled the country for the next 240 years. However, riven by internal dissension, the Ashikaga shogunate split into the Northern and Southern Dynasties, which battled over the imperial throne. It was an age of unending warfare. Feudal warlords, forced to choose sides in the conflict, built large hilltop castles to house their growing armies. These castles were often located near existing temple towns, highway stations, or ports, and attracted merchants and craftsmen who formed entirely new towns. With the introduction of muskets and cannons, the castles were reinforced with thick earthen walls and stone gates, a process that was accelerated by the Ōnin War (1467–1477), which destroyed the power of the Ashikaga shoguns and set the stage for a century of civil wars under the Sengoku warlords. By the middle of the sixteenth century, Japan was dotted with dozens of small castle towns growing spontaneously at the base of hilltop castles.

The civil wars were finally brought to a violent end by the emergence of three successive military geniuses who beat the feuding warlords into submission: Nobunaga Oda, Hideyoshi Toyotomi, and Ieyasu Tokugawa. Under their leadership, Japan became unified into a single military government that lasted until the arrival of Commodore Perry in the nineteenth century.

Nobunaga Oda (1534-1582), the first of the unifiers, was a young man when he defeated several powerful warlords and marched into Kyoto in 1568 to claim the Ashikaga throne. After proclaiming his protector, Yoshiaki, as Shogun, he proceeded to subdue the warrior-monks of Mt. Hiei and the powerful warlords surrounding Kyoto. To protect the capital against invasion from the northeast and to conquer the remaining warlords in distant provinces, Nobunaga built his great castle of Azuchi on the shores of Lake Biwa. With its massive, seven-story fortress overlooking the Ōmi Plain, the castle town symbolized the concentration of power in one great military house. It acted as a barrier against attacks from the eastern provinces, where large standing armies of mounted soldiers and footsoldiers armed with muskets had been assembled. From Azuchi Castle, Nobunaga strengthened his grip over the country by establishing a network of smaller castle towns in conquered territories. These castle towns were used as bases to disarm enemies, collect taxes, and control the movement of people. In a departure from the past, free markets were permitted within the castle towns, giving rise to a flourishing business sector. However, this "free trade" policy was limited to the controlled castle towns, and was part of Nobunaga's overall effort to abolish guilds and set up a national system of weights, measures, and currency. However, before Nobunaga could consolidate his power, he was attacked by the troops of a disgruntled general and chose to commit suicide rather than be captured by a traitor.

With Nobunaga's death, Hideyoshi Toyotomi (1536–1598) took up the task of unifying the country. A brilliant general of peasant origin, Hideyoshi outmaneuvered potential rivals to the throne by entering into alliances with Nobunaga's 200 vassal lords and reconstructing Kyoto with the aid of local warlords and rich merchants. To legitimize his position, he built an imperial palace for the emperor and temples for the Buddhist monasteries. However, his ultimate goal of national unification was blocked by the presence of half a dozen warlords to the west. To bring them under his rule, Hideyoshi established his headquarters at a massive new castle on the Osaka plain and concentrated his growing army in the surrounding castle town. From this fortress, he launched numerous military campaigns against his rivals until he had achieved supremacy over the entire country. Once in power, he strengthened his grip by destroying castle towns in conquered provinces and redistributing fiefs to loyal vassals to prevent uprisings. These regional lords built their own castle towns, which replicated on a small scale life in the capital. Between 1580 and 1610—exactly 400 years before MITI's Technopolis program— over thirty castle towns were constructed in Edo, Osaka, Himeji, Hiroshima, Kanazawa, Okayama, Wakayama, Sendai, Kumamoto, Nagoya, and other provinces (see Figure 4-2), laying the founda-

Figure 4-2. Major Japanese castle towns (1580–1610).

tion for Japan's modern cities. Many of these castle towns are now "mother cities" for MITI's nineteen technopolises. Perhaps no other period in Japanese history had seen urban construction planned on such a massive scale.

This shift from scattered hilltop castles to castle towns symbolized the centralization of military and economic power under Hideyoshi. Osaka, which served as the model for other castle towns, followed the concentric pattern of construction used at Nobunaga's castle in Azuchi. The main castle area was divided into three areas: the central weapons storage area (*honmaru*), the lord's quarters (*ninomaru*), and the administrative offices and quarters for the senior samurai (*sannomaru*). It was protected from cannon fire by thick stone walls and deep moats built to a sufficient distance. Outside the walls of the castle was the castle town (*jōkamachi*), which was laid out in a grid pattern and provided living quarters for the lesser samurai, merchants, and laborers. Initially, castle towns were only small garrisons with few amenities, but they rapidly grew into major cities as whole communities followed their lords and established businesses under their special status as contract laborers. Over time these protected shopkeepers and artisans gave rise to a new merchant class (*chōnin*) who dominated the economy of the emerging castle towns. With its strategic location and wealthy merchant families, Osaka soon became a major center of domestic and foreign trade, surpassing even the famous port city of Sakai.

Hideyoshi's death in 1598 led to a political crisis within the government. From his deathbed, Hideyoshi appointed five councillors to rule until his son reached maturity. One of these men was Ieyasu Tokugawa (1542–1616), a vassal warlord who controlled the eastern provinces. However, Ieyasu's bid for power was challenged by Mitsunari Ishida, a brilliant general and favorite of Hideyoshi, who sought to remove Ieyasu through military action. Both armies clashed in the famous Battle of Sekigahara to the east of Kyoto. In a fortuitous turn of events, Ieyasu emerged victorious and established the Tokugawa shogunate that would rule Japan for the next 270 years, until the Meiji Restoration in 1868.

Ieyasu quickly established his authority throughout the country. In 1603, after being appointed Shogun by the Emperor, he built the famous Nijō Castle in Kyoto to keep watch over untrustworthy warlords in the western provinces, and moved his capital to Edo (present-day Tokyo) in the east, the stronghold of his military power. Another strategic castle was built on the coast at Shizuoka to control movements on the Tōkaidō road between Kyoto and Edo. To strengthen his naval forces against the Portuguese and Koreans, Ieyasu brought into his court an Englishman by the name of William Adams, the Pilot-Major of the Dutch ship *Liefde* that had run aground during a storm, who taught navigation and shipbuilding to the Tokugawa shogunate. With his flanks thus protected by land and by sea, Ieyasu proceeded to build the

Tokugawa *Baku-han*—a form of government combining the shogunate (*bakufu*) and 250 domains (*han*).

Like his predecessors, Ieyasu used castle towns to punish his enemies and strengthen his vassals. He distributed large fiefs to his most trusted vassals, known as *Fudai*, or hereditary lieges of the Tokugawa house, who were assigned to castles at strategic points from Kyoto eastward along the Tōkaidō road to Edo. Less reliable warlords, known as *Tozama*, or "Outside Lords," were carefully watched and required to build castles at great expense. Ieyasu took steps to prevent uprisings and sabotage by limiting the size of these castles, rotating lords among the provinces (called *kunigae*), and requiring them to spend alternate years in Edo (a practice known as *sankin kōtai*). The policy of allowing only one castle per domain was strictly enforced. Centrally located on plains near transportation lines, these castles were constructed with majestic turrets and sweeping rooflines to impress onlookers with the lord's wealth and power.

With the return to peace, Edo became the primary castle town, as people poured into the capital city under orders of the Tokugawa shogunate. Over 80,000 standard-bearers (*hatamoto*), 300 regional lords living alternately in Edo and their own domains, and hundreds of thousands of samurai, retainers, and their families established residence in the city. Edo Castle was the largest fortress in the country, with farflung battlements and moats designed to protect the residence of the Shogun and his vast assemblage of samurai and retainers. The castle was divided into several sections: the Honmaru for the Shogun's mansion, the Omote for government officials, the Nakaoku for official business, and the Nishimaru for the samurai and high-ranking retainers. Ieyasu's master plan for improving the capital called for laying out city blocks and assigning townspeople to them according to social class. To prepare the site for the capital, Ieyasu organized massive construction projects. Vassal lords were ordered to mobilize laborers from their provinces to dig canals, fill marshes and bogs, and construct roads, bridges, and port facilities. The major national highway, the Tōkaidō, was linked to the city's main thoroughfare that began in the Nihonbashi district. Situated between the castle and the bay, Nihonbashi became the commercial center as traffic increased at the five major seaports and three river ports designated by Ieyasu.

The immense inflow of wealth from the provinces and the busy construction work attracted merchants, masterless samurai, and artisans, creating a gigantic city surrounding the castle on a scale unparalleled in world history. Edo (Tokyo) was not an industrial city, but a government center with a huge population of consumers who demanded the best in quality goods. As a result, wholesale and retail trade expanded to meet the growing demand, creating a hotly competitive environment that exists to the present. Large financial groups, such as the Mitsui and Mitsubishi families, opened lavish stores which drew huge crowds of free-spending customers. Peasants and laborers from the countryside flocked to the city in search of jobs and entertainment. These small shopkeepers and craftsmen formed the basis of the new merchant class (*chōnin*), one of the four classes fixed by Ieyasu. By 1700, the population of Edo reached one million, followed by Osaka and Kyoto with 300,000 and by Kanazawa and Nagoya with 100,000. During the next 200 years, these castle towns developed into major cities, forming the basis for Japan's economic, cultural, and intellectual life during the Tokugawa era and setting the stage for its emergence in the nineteenth century.

FROM CASTLE TOWNS
TO TECHNOPOLIS

Thus we see that the ancient capitals of Nara and Kyoto and the castle towns of Kamakura, Osaka, and Edo embody a legacy of city building that is deeply ingrained in the nation's thinking and way of life. For the Japanese, carefully planning out future cities and regions seems second nature—like laying out one's rock garden. Indeed, when one speaks with government officials and reads the Technopolis plans, references to the past are profuse. Each city proudly displays its castle and cultural heritage alongside its modern R&D institutes and universities, just as the Europeans do. For Americans, this contrast between old and new is startling, but for the Japanese it is commonplace, for one always preserves, and builds the future upon the past.

Indeed, MITI's Technopolis Concept is a modern-day version of castle building, an effort to rally the country under the banner of high technology. The parallels with Japan's ancient capitals and feudal castle towns are striking: the planned development of a research core of universities and R&D labs (castle) designed to trigger a proliferation of high-tech venture businesses (the *chōnin*) who are linked to the Tokyo by national highways (bullet trains and airports). Moreover, the governors and prefectural officials (vassal warlords) are responsible for constructing and maintaining their own technopolises under the guidance of MITI (the Tokugawa shogun). Given Japan's large budget deficits, MITI has little money for the technopolises, which must raise their own armies of developers, financiers, teachers, and researchers.

Although Japanese officials chafe at this comparison, I am convinced that it is the major difference between American and Japanese high-tech regional development. When I visited Kumamoto and Oita on the southern island of Kyushu, Technopolis planners chuckled at my analogy. "We are not like the Shoguns on TV," they insisted. "We are only copying Silicon Valley." I had to remind them that Silicon Valley was never planned; it evolved in a totally spontaneous manner, without much government planning. Its chaotic, leapfrog development reflects the individualistic, money-grubbing legacy of the Gold Rush. In fact, most planning in Silicon Valley occurred after the fact, a decision we are paying dearly for today. Finally, after futilely trying to convince these officials that they were building new castle towns, I pointed out the window of their high-rise government offices. In most Japanese cities, rising majestically out of the crowded mass of office buildings and department stores, is the city's proudest treasure: its castle, surrounded by a public garden and a watery moat. "In America," I explained, "we have no castles—except in Disneyland." There was silence, and then, for the first time, you could see a change in their faces as the realization sank in.

5

TSUKUBA: THE CITY OF BRAINS

Not to mention
The beauty of its snow
Mount Tsukuba shines forth
In its purple robes.

Ransetsu (1654–1707)
Samurai from the Edo period

Viewed from the train window, the sullen gray buildings of the Tsukuba Science City loom high above the rice fields and pine groves of Ibaraki Prefecture, as incongruous in their surroundings as the ancient temples of Hōryūji and Tōdaiji which command the Nara plain. To the casual passerby, these bland concrete-and-steel monuments are unremarkable, aside from their distance from the high-rise housing complexes scattered about the outskirts of Tokyo. Yet against the hazy, blue slopes of Mount Tsukuba they take on a stark, almost ethereal appearance, as though dropped from the heavens by a mad architect. For newcomers, Tsukuba is somewhat of a paradox, a Zen puzzle. Why would anyone want to build this city in the middle of nowhere? The rolling hills seem more suited to bucolic pastures than budding Pasteurs. And why the expensive high-rise buildings? The city defies common sense. But for the Japanese government, which has invested over $5.5 billion in this new high-tech city, the research labs at Tsukuba have taken on an almost religious aura because of their importance for Japan's economic future. These are the new temples of learning and enlightenment, the greenhouses that will spawn the next generation of Japanese scientists and industries.

Since its inception in 1963, the Tsukuba Science City has emerged at the cutting edge of Japanese high technology. Located thirty-five miles northeast of Tokyo and twenty-five miles northwest of Narita International Airport, this "City of Brains," as it is popularly called, boasts over 11,500 researchers and support staff in fifty national research institutes and two universities. The list of research labs in the Science and Technology Agency's handbook reads like a Who's Who of Japanese industry—MITI's Electrotechnical Laboratory and Fermentation Research Institute, the Ministry of Education's High Energy Physics Laboratory, the Tsukuba Space Center, Nippon Telegraph & Telephone's Telecommunications Construction Development Center, the National Research Center for Disaster Prevention, and others (see Appendix J). Tsukuba is the site of Japan's most ambitious experiments in supercomputers, advanced robotics, biotechnology, fine ceramics, and nuclear fusion. Currently, thirty of the top ninety-eight national research laboratories are located at Tsukuba, making it one of the world's leading science cities. The concentration of brainpower is awesome. It would be comparable to the U.S. government concentrating a third of its civilian and military researchers in the city of Bethesda, Maryland. Tsukuba is a young city, but it is rapidly gaining momentum. Already, its daytime population approaches 150,000. By the year 1990, as Japan's national R&D programs pick up speed, Tsukuba and its surrounding industrial parks may well surpass Silicon Valley in basic and applied research.

The train ride to Tsukuba is like entering a time warp. As one leaves Tokyo Station on the Joban Line and weaves through the countryside, new Japan clashes with old. The futuristic vision of Tsukuba painted by the Japanese government seems so distant from the lives of the passengers in the slow-moving train. Across the aisle, seated on the hard wooden benches, are people from a former era—hunchbacked old farmers with gnarled hands, grandmothers wrapped in quilted kimonos, and playful schoolchildren dressed in black, military-style uniforms—who appear totally oblivious to the ambitious experiments being conducted in the faceless research labs only a few blocks away.

As the train pulls to a two-minute stop at Arakawaoki Station, one wonders: How did this brave new world of Tsukuba come to be? What's happening behind the sterile mask of its research labs? And what does Tsukuba portend for Japan's emerging technopolises?

MOVING THE CAPITAL

Ironically, the original idea for building Tsukuba—like the ancient capital of Nara—was not to create a world-class city but to escape pressing problems in the capital. During the 1950s, metropolitan Tokyo grew so rapidly as a result of Japan's economic miracle that it became strangled by overcrowding and pollution. The government tried to rein in the city's runaway growth, but these efforts proved futile in the face of the burgeoning demand for skilled labor. Moreover, preparations for the 1964 Olympic Games, involving massive stadium construction and street-widening projects, accelerated the citywide building boom to a white-hot pace. As the problems intensified, newspapers and government officials began to entertain the idea of moving government offices from downtown Tokyo to the Mt. Fuji area or, more ambitiously, to a floating city in Tokyo Bay. But these ideas gained little political support in an environment heady with the fruits of economic success and mired in a heated debate over the U.S.-Japan Security Treaty. Nevertheless, planners at the Science and Technology Agency (STA)—caretakers for the nation's research institutes—warned that the deteriorating environment in Tokyo would seriously hinder basic research at the government's aging laboratories. They urged Prime Minister Hayato Ikeda to move the labs to prevent Japan from slipping further behind the West in scientific research. The country's future well-being, they argued, was at stake.

Concerned that his high-growth policies might be undone, Prime Minister Ikeda acted with speed. In September 1961, his Cabinet requested the Administrative Agency to study the relocation of government agencies. After meeting with several key ministries, the agency reported back its findings: all government research labs should be moved to an area thirty to forty miles from downtown Tokyo. The Tokyo Regional Development Commission suggested building a new satellite city, but the proposal died for lack of political support.

But Tokyo's accelerating growth worried government research officials, encouraging the Administrative Agency and the Tokyo Regional Development Commission to merge their separate proposals into a single plan. They urged the construction of a world-class research city where scientists could mingle freely and discuss their research unhampered by the headaches of Tokyo life. This new high-tech capital would offer schools, housing, shopping centers, parks, cultural activities, and a relaxed environment deemed conducive to high-level research.

In late 1962 the Regional Development Commission reviewed four candidate sites (Fuji-Roku, Akagi, Nasu, and Tsukuba) and recommended Tsukuba for the new science city. Tsukuba was chosen because of its pleasant environment, good water, stable land, and easy access to Tokyo. A year later, in September 1963, the Cabinet approved the Tsukuba site and authorized the Japan Housing Corporation to acquire the land and develop it.

Despite government support for the plan, Tsukuba got off to a bumpy start. The early Nouvelle-Ville Tsukuba plan triggered strong protests from local residents who opposed the government's plan to acquire 4,700 acres of valuable farmland, redistribute 5,200 acres, and bring in high-density development. They were joined by government workers who were opposed to moving the research labs. Both groups formed an anti-relocation movement and held meetings in Tokyo to question the viability of the Tsukuba plan and the direction of Japan's scientific research policies. Locally, realtors complained that the proposed circular land-use plan would limit the potential for spinoff development. An elongated plan, built along the natural ridges, would use less farmland and permit maximum development. (In rural Japan, housing is usually built along hills and ridges to preserve valuable farmland.) Ibaraki Prefecture officials pointed out that the Nouvelle-Ville Tsukuba Plan failed to take this practice into account and requested that Tsukuba be downsized to lessen its impact on local towns and farmlands. In March 1964 the central government conceded to the various requests. It agreed to preserve 5,300 acres of farmland and provide land-use controls, relocation payments, and a phased ten-year construction program. In the new plan Tsukuba would accommodate forty-two national research institutes and a population of 160,000, but land acquisition would be limited to 2,700 acres.

In 1965 the Japan Housing Corporation drafted the Tsukuba Science City Master Plan, which laid out the land acquisition and development program. Five ministries reviewed the plan—MITI, the Land Agency, the Ministry of Construction, the Ministry of Education, and the Ministry of Agriculture, Forestry, and Fisheries.

A second draft issued in 1966 reduced the site to 3,800 acres, protected more farmland, and promised to compensate affected farmers and towns for disruptions to their livelihood. These revisions were crucial for securing support from the ruling Liberal-Democratic Party (LDP), which derived much of its political support from rural areas. Nevertheless, the new science city carried a hefty price tag of $1.3 billion, of which the central government would pay $1.0 billion.

Despite these revisions, the Japanese government was still unsatisfied with the Tsukuba plan. In March 1966 government officials visited science cities and research parks around the world, including the Stanford Industrial Park, the Research Triangle in North Carolina, Sophia Antipolis and South Ile in France, and Louvain University Science City in Belgium (see Appendix K). The team was greatly impressed—and embarrassed—by the quality of the living environment of foreign science cities, which contrasted sharply with the crowded, unesthetic surroundings of Japanese research labs. Suddenly, Tsukuba became a matter of national pride. If Japan was to catch up with the West, its scientists deserved the very best. The Tsukuba Science City had to be more than just a convenient relocation site; it would be the jewel of the nation, a symbol of Japan's emergence as a technological superpower.

In 1967 land acquisition began in earnest, and ministries developed relocation plans for their research labs. A ten-year construction goal was approved two years later. In May 1970 the Japanese Diet passed the Tsukuba Science City Construction Law, which gave the official go-ahead. In 1972 MITI's Inorganic Materials Research Institute was the first laboratory to open its doors, followed by Tsukuba University in 1973. The Tokyo Teachers' College was scheduled for relocation, but this plan was scotched when several professors resigned in protest rather than move to Tsukuba. Initially, thirty-six labs were scheduled to relocate, but the Cabinet increased this number to forty-three, despite strong opposition from researchers and labor unions. After years of planning, Tsukuba was finally underway, though mired in controversy.

Even with full government support, Tsukuba encountered numerous setbacks. Land prices skyrocketed, partly as a result of farmers participating in the anti-relocation movement's efforts to stop the plan. Early residents complained about high moving costs and the cultural sterility and loneliness of rural Tsukuba. They preferred to be closer to family, friends, shopping, and schools in Tokyo. Indeed, most researchers were reluctant to sacrifice the cultural delights of Tokyo, choosing to commute up to three hours a day rather than live in Tsukuba. In the early days, Tsukuba was such a rustic town that it was mockingly called "the capital of stars and high boots" because residents were often forced to trudge over muddy, unpaved roads by starlight. City services were minimal or nonexistent, dentists were hard to find, and the only entertainment was stargazing and birdwatching. Needless to say, the government quickly learned that it had to provide better services to attract top-flight researchers.

The government responded in several ways. In December 1971 the Diet passed a law authorizing relocation payments equal to 8% of a relocated employee's salary. The Japan Housing Corporation sped up construction of a shopping center, housing, schools, community centers, and parks, while the Ministry of Construction adopted scenic preservation policies and a comprehensive design plan to make the city more attractive. A grants-in-aid subsidy program was created to fund these projects and relieve local towns of the financial burden. The 1973 oil shock temporarily delayed construction at Tsukuba, but relocation picked up in 1975 and continued until 1980, when all forty-five government research institutes were relocated to Tsukuba. In May 1980, after seventeen long years, the "City of Brains" was finally built.

A THIN SLIVER OF LAND

Stepping off the train at Arakawaoki Station, I am greeted by local assemblyman Hiroshi Murakami, who welcomes me with a gracious bow. With neatly-clipped hair and attired in a dark blue suit, he looks like a typical Japanese "salaryman," but he carries himself with a distinctive air of confidence and charisma that hints at his personal success. At 36, he is one of the youngest politicians in Japan, one of a new breed of shakers-and-movers in this land of septuagenarians. Moreover, for a graduate from Tsukuba University with a Ph.D. in agricultural remote-sensing, he is unusual indeed. Recently, he quit a comfortable government research job to open his own public relations firm, the Tsukuba Information Lab, and to pursue a political career. His is the tough job of representing Tsukuba and the surrounding farm towns.

"It's a challenge," he tells me, "because of the sharp contrast between farmers who want to protect their livelihood and high-tech researchers who want better services and cultural amenities. Rarely do they agree on anything. And even among the local farmers there are strong differences of opinion. Some want the amenities so they can sell their land for higher prices, while others just want to stay put. Trying to balance these conflicting interests is a real task."

Driving me through the narrow streets and twisting country roads that lead to Tsukuba, Mr. Murakami points out proposed street-widening projects and industrial parks. Tightly packed with cars and pedestrians, the area looks like any other Japanese town undergoing a face-lift, but in aerial photos Tsukuba stands out like a thin sliver etched into the broad Kanto plain—a compromise with the local protest movement. Encompassing the towns of Kukizaki, Oho, Sakura, Toyosato, Tsukuba, and Yatabe, the new science city covers 110 square miles of gently rolling land northwest of Lake Kasumi-ga-ura, Japan's second-largest lake.

We pass farmers planting a field of rice when, suddenly, the road straightens, widening into a broad boulevard lined with high-rise buildings and ultramodern overpasses. The hustle and bustle of Arakawaoki dissolves into an expanse of manicured lawns and pleasant green gardens. The change is abrupt and startling.

"We've had a lot of problems at this junction," explains Mr. Murakami. "Many freshmen at Tsukuba University get into serious accidents because they speed down these boulevards—right into the fields and walls in the older sections. They're not used to the sudden change. Local residents complain about the noise and the hazards, but it's hard to stop."

The sharp delineation between old and new is a jolting experience for newcomers, like moving from prewar Japan to the 1990s within the space of a few yards. Unlike Tokyo or Yokohama, which churn with people, Tsukuba seems like a lonely, isolated outpost in some distant province. Except for an occasional car or solitary bicycle rider passing by, the city's boulevards and sidewalks remain strangely empty even at noon.

Entering downtown Tsukuba, we pass the main shopping center and high-rise offices clustered around a plaza. Silvery and burnished, the buildings have the look of an architect's fantasy, but they are cool and uninviting. Within the central research district, which measures four miles by eleven, Tsukuba bulges with a daytime population of 150,000 people, of whom 30,000 are researchers, students, administrative staff, and their families. In ten years, Tsukuba's population is expected to grow to 200,000. However, they are nowhere to be seen.

"Our city services are first-class," boasts Mr. Murakami, pointing to the silvery, space-age walls of the Tsukuba Center. "The Japanese government has spent billions of dollars for parks, schools, daycare centers, medical facilities, amusement halls, plazas, shopping malls, and cable TV. We even have the world's largest solar-heated pool and gymnasium complex. But there are drawbacks. We've been criticized for our luxurious facilities, especially since the government is cutting back on services elsewhere. And our maintenance costs are huge. Just taking care of our eighty-nine parks costs us $800,000 a year. To top it off, funding from the national government will be cut off soon, so we've annexed the surrounding towns to organize a city government. But local farmers don't want to pay higher taxes. They refuse to subsidize wealthy newcomers."

Before visiting the research labs, we take a final swing past Tsukuba University, which has 8,500 students enrolled in such fields as biology, electronics, geoscience, linguistics, and public policy. What sets Tsukuba apart is that its 1,500 faculty members work closely with the national laboratories, a point that initially drew much criticism from Japan's rigid educational hierarchy. But the idea is gradually catching on. Since 1984, the Ministry of Education has promoted joint industry-university R&D projects in several of the technopolises.

Nearby are a variety of institutes founded to promote international exchanges and coordination among Tsukuba's research institutes. The Science and Technology Agency (STA) sponsors seminars, symposiums, and training courses for visiting researchers at its Tsukuba Center of Institutes. The Japan Information Center of Science and Technology (JICST) provides online data bases. The Japan International Cooperation Agency (JICA), a branch of the Ministry of Foreign Affairs, runs the Tsukuba International Center to provide training to foreign researchers from developing countries. And the Ministry of Education runs the National Education Center to improve Japan's primary and secondary educational curricula.

Tsukuba is a spacious city. After being in the crowded Tokyo area, it seems almost foreign, with its broad, tree-lined avenues, manicured landscaping, and tranquil atmosphere. Driving through its streets is like navigating through the industrial parks of Silicon Valley at dusk. On the surface, Tsukuba does not seem special; it lacks the color, excitement, and variety that Tokyo has to offer. Yet the peacefulness is only a mask. The real drama lies out of sight, hidden behind the walls of the faceless research institutes that line its boulevards; for deep within these temples are the research projects that will dramatically transform Japan within the next ten years.

THE SEARCH FOR INNOVATION

MELDOG glides along the floor of MITI's Mechanical Engineering Laboratory, sniffing with its ultrasonic sensors to navigate through the clutter of tables and chairs in its path. Stocky and compact, this mechanical guide dog resembles a bulldog with its boxy metallic frame and short pivotal wheels, but it moves with surprising fluidity. Instructed by remote control to find the exit, MELDOG rolls past work counters overflowing with unassembled robots, weaving through the maze of aisles. Its tiny, on-board computer has been programmed to map the shortest route out of the laboratory. Approaching a stool, MELDOG decelerates a moment, its engine whirring quietly, then makes a small detour before heading toward the door. Everything goes smoothly until it bumps into a thin post placed near the doorway. Run experiment again.

Since 1977, MELDOG has been a major attraction at the Mechanical Engineering Laboratory, which is developing guide dog robots for the blind. Although MELDOG is far from commercialization, the basic technology being developed for its on-board computer, ultrasonic sensors, and compact engine is being applied to industrial robots and other medical helpers. Besides

MELDOG, MEL researchers are working on a hospital patient-care robot called MELKONG, capable of carrying up to 200 pounds, and a walking-dog robot with retractable legs for negotiating uneven ground. Within a decade MEL plans to develop home nursing robots designed to help the elderly, handicapped, and infirm with toilet functions, bathing, cooking, washing, cleaning, and other daily activities. As a start, MEL recently chose Mitsubishi Metals, Sumitomo Metals, and Sanyo Electric to design nursing robots for bedridden and handicapped persons, with a target price of $4,300 for home models.

But nursing robots are only part of MEL's overall program. In 1984 MITI launched an eight-year, $80 million Advanced Robotics Technology Project, code-named JUPITER (Juvenescent Pioneering Technology for Robots), to develop third generation robots. First generation robots, now used on factory lines, work by rote, dumbly repeating the same motions. Second generation robots feature sensors and on-board computers, but they are unable to move about. By contrast, third generation robots, with their agile hands, retractable feet, and human-like sensors, will be capable of walking, seeing, manipulating objects, and communicating. Currently, thirty-seven researchers at MEL's Advanced Robot Research Group are working with Japan's top twenty robot makers to develop robots for inspecting and repairing nuclear plants, underwater remote-controlled robots for maintaining marine oil rigs, and emergency robots for rescuing people from fires, earthquakes, and floods.

These robots will be all-round machines, designed to walk over bumpy surfaces, handle dangerous objects, and operate autonomously in hostile environments. They will look like Transformer toy robots, with their multiple wheels, spider legs, hand-like manipulators, and automatic navigation systems. Deepsea robots will be controlled by tele-existence and tele-operation technology using vision, hearing, and tactile sensors that will enable human operators to perform tasks with the sensation that one is actually working in the remote environment. With Komatsu Engineering Company, MEL is building a fifteen-ton walking robot capable of surveying underwater terrain and assisting in bridge construction. These robots will be equipped with high-performance gears, bearings, and new composite materials, and eventually with fifth generation computers.

But all work and no play makes MEL a dull boy. On the lighter side, MEL recently showcased attention-grabbing robots at the Tsukuba Expo 85 world's fair, including a crab-like robot that can climb stairs and a spider-legged robot that clambers up walls with its rubber suction cups. However, Professor Ichiro Kato of Waseda University stole the show with his dancing robot, called WABOT I, that can flex its hips and walk sideways, and organ-playing WABOT II, which has a computer-controlled TV camera "head" that hears requests, then plays the tune from sheet music with its mechanical fingers and legs. Eventually, robots may even invade amusement parks and fitness centers. Matsushita displayed an artistic robot that draws impressionistic sketches of people and objects, and robot maker Fanuc showed off its "Fanuc Man," an ambidextrous robot standing fifteen feet high and weighing twenty-five tons, capable of hoisting barbells up to 500 pounds.

Because of Japan's success at installing robots on the factory line, Japanese technology has become synonymous with robots in the West. But MEL is only one of the forty-five national research labs in the Tsukuba Science City, of which nine are handled by MITI's Agency for Industrial Science and Technology (AIST). Founded in 1948, AIST is a semi-independent organization with the charter of monitoring scientific developments around the world, identifying key technologies for Japanese industry, encouraging patent and licensing agreements, and sponsoring research. It has 2,640 elite researchers nationwide, the cream of the crop, or one-fourth of all Japanese government researchers. About 2,000 work at AIST's Tsukuba Research Center, making it the highest concentration of brainpower in Tsukuba. In 1984 the center spent about $130 million for basic research and joint R&D projects.

Probably the key attraction for visitors from Silicon Valley is AIST's Electrotechnical Laboratory (ETL), the heart of Japan's leading-edge electronics research. In 1984 ETL assigned 525 researchers to work on 150 projects, including supercomputers, biotechnology, semiconductors, new alloys, medical engineering, speech synthesizers, energy conservation, and projects in numerous other fields (see Appendix L). Each year ETL sends fifty researchers overseas to gather information and study the latest developments at MIT, Stanford, the National Bureau of Standards, and the Heinrich Hertz Laboratory in West Germany.

Semiconductors are a hot topic at ETL because they are the basic building blocks for Japan's future supercomputers and fifth generation computers. In the New Semiconductor Functions Project, ETL researchers are working with Japan's major semiconductor companies to develop superlattices (new crystal structures), three-dimensional ICs, and rugged ICs, with the goal of building superfast "high-rise" chips. MITI's Optoelectronics Project, which has developed semiconductor lasers for factory robot "eyes," is now refining them for optical communications. Probably MITI's most low-key but crucial project is the Supercomputer Project, which is exploring ultrafast materials such as gallium arsenide (a metal compound), ballistic transistors, and Josephson junction devices (an electron effect discovered by Brian Josephson of Bell Labs in 1962) to develop circuits thousands of times faster than silicon. By 1990 MITI's goal is to build supercomputers that will outperform America's fastest supercomputer, the Cray 2 by Cray Research of Minnesota. During the early 1990s, MITI plans to merge the new technologies developed by its Fifth Generation Computer Project, such as parallel processing, artificial intelligence, and natural language processing, to develop an ultrafast fifth-and-a-half generation computer that can think.

But according to Shigeru Maekawa, director of ETL's Research Planning Office: "We not only have our eyes set on developing the fifth generation computer, but also the sixth generation computer."

What is a sixth generation computer? According to MITI, the sixth generation computer will be a biocomputer with the memory and logic processing capabilities of the human brain. In July 1985 MITI announced that it will invest $30 million in a ten-year joint R&D project to develop a biocomputer that will mimic human brain functions, such as pattern recognition, reasoning, and learning. The sixth generation computer, which will not appear until the twenty-first century, will utilize biochips capable of storing a billion bits of information, as well as technologies developed for the fifth generation computer, such as artificial intelligence, image processing, and knowledge bases. MITI also plans to explore three new areas: computer architectures based on the human brain, complex neural systems derived from lower animals, and non-harmful methods for measuring human brain activity. These are ambitious goals. Who are the researchers exploring this brave new world of Japanese computing?

Tucked away in the Electrotechnical Laboratory is Gen Matsumoto, director of ETL's Computer Analog Information Research Group, who is studying the nerve cells in squid to develop logic systems for the biocomputer. Recently, Matsumoto announced a new model, based on his findings that nerve cells can be either stimulated or prevented from transmitting electrical signals to the brain, the basic mechanism for developing on/off logic circuits. His discovery is a thin tube on the side of the nerve cell wall that prevents external stimuli from exciting the nerve. By activating this tube, Matsumoto believes he can develop the basic switching mechanism for the biocomputer in ten years. In the meanwhile, he plans to continue a favorite pastime—raising squid in his laboratory tanks.

Michio Sugi, a collegue of Matsumoto's and a researcher at the ETL Basic Products Research Division, is exploring molecular electronics (or bioelectronics) to create new circuits for the biocomputer. In his experiments, he is arranging organic molecules on a liquid surface and stacking molecule layers one at a time to form ultrathin film circuits. His goal is to build a biocomputer using his novel molecular structures, a goal that keeps him in the laboratory long hours. "Since I have to commute three hours a day to Tokyo," he says, "I've decided to stay overnight in my lab twice a week to have more time for research." But his motivation is more pressing; during the last year, many Japanese companies have entered the race to develop biochips, including Asahi Breweries, Asahi Chemical, Hitachi, Matsushita, NEC, Nippon Telegraph and Telephone (NTT), Sharp, Suntory, and Toyobo. They are looking to MITI for technological leadership, as well as to the Science and Technology Agency, which has also jumped into the race.

Biotechnology fever has also struck other laboratories in Tsukuba. Since 1980, when Dr. Stanley Cohen of Stanford University and Dr. Herbert Boyer of the University of California were granted a patent for recombinant DNA technology, the Japanese government has pushed hard into the biotechnology field. In 1980 MITI budgeted over $150 million for the seven-year New Fuel Technology program to produce biomass (organic material used to generate energy). In 1982 MITI initiated the ten-year

Biotechnology Research Project as part of its Next Generation Industries Program. Budgeted at $85 million, this project coordinates fourteen companies with the Fermentation Research Institute, which is applying recombinant DNA, bioreactors, and cell growth culture techniques to mining, industrial processes, environmental protection, and medical care. To coordinate the 150 companies involved in biotechnology research, MITI created the Office of Biotechnology to provide R&D funding and technical information. In addition, a Biotechnology Council has been formed in the Council of Economic Federations (Keidanren) to advise MITI's Industrial Structure Council.

Other ministries have also entered the field. The Ministry of Agriculture, Forests, and Fisheries (MAFF), which is located near the site of Tsukuba Expo 85, has assigned 460 researchers to work on bioreactors to improve plant varieties, cell fusion to produce new agricultural chemicals, and tissue culture to grow seedlings. At its National Institute of Agro-Biological Resources and National Institute of Agro-Environmental Sciences, researchers are working on recombinant DNA, genetic mutations caused by X-rays, and new photosynthetic processes. One of the more interesting developments was recently announced by the Science and Technology Agency (STA), which created a $25 million fund in 1981 to finance recombinant DNA research. STA has developed with Seiko Instruments a novel "biorobot" which automates the tedious task of analyzing DNA specimens. With a push of the button, this robot can perform a hundred complex chemical processes, a task that takes veteran researchers up to a week.

To cope with Japan's never-ending plague of typhoons, floods, and earthquakes, Tsukuba researchers are experimenting with new disaster prevention technologies. The Earthquake Simulator, a giant, hydraulically powered "shaking table" that recreates the movement of the earth's crust, is operated by the Ministry of Construction's Building Research Institute to test new construction methods and materials. A computer control room simulates major earthquakes and records structural damage using videotapes and time-lapse cameras. In 1981 a five-year program was initiated to develop a nationwide earthquake warning system, consisting of a network of seismographs, tide-level and groundwater observatories, and laser range finders.

At the Public Works Institute, a Rainfall Simulator is used for river and highway engineering, flood control, and mudslide prevention. In a cavernous building, researchers can unleash torrents of water to flood a river model with movable locks and dikes. Flooding scenarios, ranging from a short downpour to a major typhoon, can be simulated, with overhead video cameras and computers assessing the potential damage to communities along the river.

At the northern end of Tsukuba is the National Laboratory for High Energy Physics, popularly known as KEK. Created by the Ministry of Education for joint use by national universities, KEK research is focused on elementary particle physics. In March 1982 the world's largest synchrotron radiation research facility was completed, enabling KEK to accelerate electrons up to 2.5 gigavolts (billion volts). This facility has a linear accelerator measuring 400 meters in length (compared to Stanford University's 3,200 meters) and an oval electron beam 68 meters in diameter. Research in ultra-high-speed electrons is being carried on for use in biology, medicine, and IC design. KEK also has a large-scale project called TRISTAN (Transposable Ring Intersecting Storage Accelerators in Nippon), a ring about 960 meters in diameter, to investigate the existence of the top quark, one of the six quark particles said to comprise neutrons or protons. Although smaller than the ring at the Fermi National Accelerator Research Institute, the KEK's ring is the world's largest collision-type synchrotron.

Tsukuba is gradually attracting private research labs. About a kilometer east of Tsukuba University is the Japan Automobile Research Institute (JARI), a nonprofit research institute formed in 1969 by Japan's top automakers to conduct road tests for their new models. The 615-acre site has a 3.4-mile high-speed test track, a full-scale wind tunnel, anechoic chambers (free of echoes and reverberations), impact test equipment, and tire testing machines that are used by customers on a contract basis.

Next to the test track is the Todokai Research Park, a 100-acre industrial park with over twenty-seven private research organizations. Eight of these companies recently formed the Tsukuba Research Consortium, comprising Akashi Works, Hamamatsu Photonics, Japan Metals and Chemicals, Stanley Electric, Teisan, Tokyo Ohka, Ulvac, and Yaskawa Electric. The Consortium conducts joint research and runs a Research Forum to promote the cross-fertilization of ideas among government, industry, and foreign researchers. Its goal is to create an open, informal "clubhouse" environment that is clearly missing in Tsukuba.

For years, Tsukuba has been off limits to private researchers because the Japanese government was worried that private companies would compromise Tsukuba's long-term, basic research orientation and steal ideas for new products. But attitudes are gradually changing. Recently, MITI announced that it will open its laboratories to Japanese companies, allowing them to use its sophisticated equipment and to share patent rights. This change, which represents a major departure from MITI's past "closed door" policies, was made due to growing industry pressure for access to government research. However, Tsukuba is still not an "open city" in the sense that foreign researchers are welcome to its laboratories. Perhaps this will change as foreign companies begin locating in the nearby Tsukuba industrial park. Meanwhile, Tsukuba will continue piling up its bargaining chips for that day.

PROBLEMS IN PARADISE

Tsukuba is a paradoxical city, one that sticks in your mind long after you have left, because it subtly operates at so many levels of consciousness. On the surface, it is an open, reassuring city, with its broad streets, green grass, clean air, and relaxed atmosphere, reminding one of an American suburb or an English garden city. Yet in the course of one's first visit, this superficial openness is quickly dispelled. Because of its high-level research, Tsukuba remains as tightly enshrouded in secrecy as the Pentagon, restricted to visitors and guests with special permission from the government. Casual visits or exchanges, even among government researchers, are not openly encouraged, and the rich cross-fertilization of ideas that occurs in Silicon Valley is noticeably absent. Self-contained and isolated, each laboratory is a world unto itself. One senses the frustration of researchers who must adhere to these strict guidelines, and the social tensions that underlie the sharp dichotomy between scientist and farmer, elite and commoner. Unlike other Japanese cities, Tsukuba is a totally cerebral place, a one-dimensional brain with very little spontaneity or surprise.

"Even among the Japanese," says Tetsuzo Kawamoto, director of the Tsukuba Research Consortium, who has studied science cities around the world, "Tsukuba residents are extremely homogeneous people. They are all highly educated researchers from Japan's top universities who have had very little exposure to people from differing backgrounds. Engrossed in their work, they form an island with almost no contact with the outside world."

As a result, Tsukuba has been criticized by many Japanese as a boring, culturally sterile environment. The science city lacks the variety and stimulation of Japan's major cities. There are no elderly people, poor people, corner grocery stores, street vendors, museums, or hustle and bustle. Everyone is a scientist or related to one, and everything is carefully planned and programmed.

"I feel spiritually disjointed here," says Dr. Shigeru Yamane, a researcher at MITI's Electrotechnical Laboratory. "I just don't feel at home here the way I did in Tokyo. It's hard to explain to a foreigner, but any Japanese understands—we Japanese like being close together."

Lewis Simmons, Tokyo correspondent for the *San Jose Mercury*, puts his finger on the problem: "Many Tsukuba-ites long for nothing more than to be packed together, to swarm in huge crowds down narrow sidewalks, to sit shoulder to shoulder in unimaginably tiny cafes and restaurants, warming belly and spirit with sake and rich brews, burnishing the personal relationships of a lifetime with the butcher, the baker, and the local policeman. And this is what the residents of Tsukuba say they miss in their scientifically engineered environment: it may be a city of brains, but it has no heart or soul."

Kimihisa Murakami, a researcher at the Department of Agriculture, Forestry, and Fisheries' Division of Disaster Prevention, notes that Tsukuba's elitism has its darker side: "About a quarter of the students at Tsukuba's Azuma Primary School have parents with PhDs. They are fervent 'education parents' who pressure their children to excel. They demand the very best for their children, who have gone to elite schools and studied abroad. But several years ago, we had a tragic incident. One of the English teachers committed suicide because many of his students spoke fluent English and corrected him in class. He was so humiliated that he felt that he had failed them as a teacher."

Herein lies the real danger to Tsukuba. In its search for scientific excellence, Tsukuba may become a cold, heartless place where sheer intellect takes precedence over other human values, and where excellence becomes synonymous with elitism and intellectual arrogance. Already one senses a certain smugness among Japanese researchers and businessmen who take great pride in Japan's commercial successes. Perhaps their self-confidence is long overdue, but as Japan becomes a technological superpower, the best and the brightest in this "city of brains" could easily become a hermetically isolated elite without a conscience. It has happened before.

Now that Tsukuba is built, the Japanese government has turned its attention to the Technopolis program. The four ministries that planned Tsukuba—MITI, the Ministry of Construction, the National Land Agency, and the Ministry of Agriculture, Forestry, and Fisheries—are responsible for helping the prefectures plan their technopolises. While these ministries will only play an advisory role, their experience with Tsukuba will be invaluable. What lessons can be drawn from Tsukuba? What are the problems and pitfalls of high-tech development? How can they be avoided? These are questions relevant not only for Japan, but for all countries pursuing high-tech regional development.

Before exploring these questions, it should be emphasized that Tsukuba is *not* part of the Technopolis program. It was built much earlier and serves totally different purposes. What are these differences? First of all, Tsukuba was conceived as a national research center, to be totally built and funded by the central government. By contrast, the Technopolis Concept is a *regional* development program being carried out at the local level. Although the central government offers guidance and tax incentives, the main responsibility for planning and building the technopolises falls on the local prefectures, cities, and towns.

Another difference is that private industry plays a minor role in Tsukuba. By contrast, the technopolises will be industrial cities— new Silicon Valleys—combining private industry (*san*), academic facilities (*gaku*), and government laboratories (*kan*). The commercialization of high technology will be their major goal.

Third, Tsukuba's main focus is basic research, while the technopolises will emphasize applied research. (MITI and other ministries run regional testing laboratories to transfer basic technology
developed at Tsukuba to local industries.)

Finally, Tsukuba benefitted from large construction budgets
which enabled it to build luxurious boulevards, parks, sewers, and
public facilities. In an era of fiscal stringency, the technopolises
will have to maximize the use of their existing infrastructures and
limited resources. In that sense, the Technopolis Concept will be
a much greater challenge than building Tsukuba.

Despite these differences, Tsukuba has become a model for
many technopolises. Hiroshima, Ube, and Kagoshima have
adopted the idea of building an academic city as the focal point
for their technopolises. However, as Tsukuba's past suggests, this
new-town approach entails many problems. Probably the major
challenge is securing political support from local communities,
since farmland acquisition has always been a touchy issue in
Japan. In Tsukuba's early years, the central government selected
large tracts of prime farmland without consulting local farmers. In
land-scarce Japan, where consensus-building is a time-honored
custom, this was a major policy error, as the Tsukuba protest
movement and the violent demonstrations at the Narita International Airport indicate. According to Tetsuzo Kawamoto, political
leaders listened more carefully to Tsukuba residents after the
Narita incident, but even then Ibaraki Prefecture had to intervene
and request payments to displaced farmers. Still, Tsukuba residents face major disruptions to their livelihood, community ties,
and natural environment, which cannot be easily compensated.

The technopolises, which are being planned locally, will hope-
fully avoid many of these problems. But some residents will be
forced to make sacrifices; high-technology development offers
many benefits, but exacts a heavy price. Who will be the winners
and the losers? How will they be treated? In Silicon Valley, it is the
landowners, venture capitalists, financiers, and "yuppies" who
benefit most from high-tech development; and the poor, the aged,
and the shopkeepers who are pushed out by skyrocketing inflation. In Tsukuba, the real estate developers and landowners holding out for higher prices will benefit, while the landless and the
young researchers and their families stand to pay the most. The

price of land alone for the average residential lot in Tsukuba now averages $85,000 to $130,000.

Below the surface, there is simmering conflict between long time residents and the newcomers at Tsukuba. Shunichi Watanabe, Associate Director at the Ministry of Construction's Building Research Institute, says: "Local farmers are land-rich, but cash-poor. They resent having to pay for nice amenities. On the other hand, Tsukuba researchers are the urban rich with little property—the real source of wealth in Japan. Thus, there are sharp inequalities between the two groups. Although the older residents are outnumbered, they turn out in numbers on election day—generally 90% compared to 20% to 50% for Tsukuba residents. So local grower interests often prevail. Recently, we began holding a 'Tsukuba Festival' each April to build a bridge between the two groups, but it takes time."

Finally, there are questions about the impact of Tsukuba on Japanese society. Some critics say Tsukuba is a "white elephant" without cultural and historic roots. Others doubt that it will have much influence in improving the creativity of Japanese industry and education. Except at MITI laboratories, private researchers have not been allowed to enter national research laboratories. Japan's national universities have few ties with Tsukuba University or the research laboratories. If the Japanese government's goal is to accelerate the pace of basic research and to diffuse high technology throughout all sectors of society, its closed door policies at Tsukuba are certainly self-defeating. The new science city threatens to fall into the same trap as American military research—very expensive, good at its main mission, but poor at benefitting industry and society with its advanced technologies. Perhaps this situation will change as Tsukuba lures more foreign researchers and becomes more of an open, international science city. But until then, it runs the risk of becoming an expensive laboratory for industrial secrets—or just another "ivory tower."

PART III: TECHNOPOLIS

Creating a High-Tech Archipelago

技術集積都市

During the past ten years, many Americans have become so awed by Japan that we have lost confidence in our own institutions. We have studied Japanese industrial policies and management techniques for clues to Japan's commercial success. Ironically, while we have tried copying Japan, the Japanese have asked themselves a different set of questions: What makes Silicon Valley tick? How can we clone it? How can we develop a venture capital market? How can we become more creative and entrepreneurial? How can we transform Japan into a high-tech archipelago? They have scoured the United States, not just for new technologies, but also for new ideas to revive their sinking industries and regions.

What is fascinating about Japan's search for new ideas is that it sheds light on our own search for renewed international competitiveness. If America has been Japan's tutor, Japan is America's looking-glass, a mirror to our national psyche. By carefully studying what interests our Pacific partner, we can better understand our own strengths and weaknesses as a nation. Thus, MITI's Technopolis Concept can be viewed as a crystallization of the symbiotic relationship between East and West—a merging of Japan's traditional city-building with American entrepreneurialism and creativity.

6

THE TECHNOPOLIS CONCEPT

Technopolis marks the beginning of
a grassroots technology revolution.

Governor Morihiko Hiramatsu,
Oita Prefecture

In October 1981 a busload of Japanese sightseers ventured southward from Stanford University into the heart of Silicon Valley.
Filled with forty camera-toting businessmen in dark suits, the
chartered bus slowly weaved its way through the maze of industrial parks dotting the valley floor, stopping momentarily in front
of high-tech companies such as IBM, Intel, Zymos, Xerox, Hewlett-Packard, Signetics, and Advanced Micro Devices. "On your
left," announced the female tour guide in polite, high-pitched Japanese, "are the corporate offices of Intel, one of the leading U.S.
semiconductor makers and the inventor of the microprocessor. In
1980, it had revenues of $300 million, making it slightly larger
than Fujitsu's semiconductor division." Suddenly, cameras fired
away and pens flew as the businessmen furiously scribbled in
their notebooks, craning their necks for signs of engineers working inside. Curiously enough, they did not get off the bus to visit,
but contented themselves with taking pictures of Intel's corporate
logo before continuing on their way to the next company. However, their visit did not go unnoticed. Looking out their windows,
Intel engineers nervously joked about these Japanese "tourists"
who had strayed too far south of San Francisco, while others worried that they were spies out to steal industrial secrets, the shock
troops for another invasion of Japanese products. Who were these
people? What were they trying to learn?

Anti-Japanese paranoia was rampant in the valley, especially after
Fortune magazine published a sensational article in 1978 called

115

"The Japanese Spies in Silicon Valley," which claimed that Japanese agents were aggressively gathering information by both overt and covert means. Recalling the "yellow peril" scare tactics used by the Hearst Press during the 1930s and 1940s, the article intoned:

> One engineer with access to the inner workings of the Japanese intelligence-gathering apparatus reports the emergence of a new breed of semiconductor samurai—he calls them "tigers." These young technologists, sent to Silicon Valley expressly to gather information as members of liaison offices, will do anything . . . to get that information. "They'll lie, steal, and cheat."

Many companies were so paranoid about the "Japanese threat" that they refused to let Japanese businessmen into their plants and offices. These fears were inflamed in 1980 when Hitachi and Mitsubishi Electric were caught red-handed trying to buy IBM secrets. Then, in early 1982, Japanese semiconductor makers grabbed over 70% of the world market for 64K dynamic RAM memory chips. After that, Japanophobia ran wild.

What local industry leaders failed to realize, however, was that the Japanese groups touring Silicon Valley in the early 1980s were not out to steal trade secrets. (Indeed, for this bus tours would have been useless.) They were on a totally different mission: to learn what made Silicon Valley tick. The tour group that visited the valley in October 1981 was a planning team of government officials and industry leaders from Hamamatsu City, a middle-sized city 160 miles west of Tokyo and the home of Yamaha, Suzuki Motors, and Kawasaki Motorcycles. Like their European counterparts, the Hamamatsu team was fascinated by the Silicon Valley phenomenon—the incredible outpouring of venture capital, start-up companies, technological innovation, and entrepreneurialism. They were seeking new ideas that could be used to plan high-tech parks and revive their slumping economy, which had been hit hard by the 1979 oil crisis. On their agenda was the layout of research universities and high-tech industrial parks in Silicon Valley, Sacramento, and San Diego. For one week they scoured California for information, returning to Japan with a treasure trove of interviews, notes, and publicly-available documents about regional and local high-tech policies. In March 1982 the group published its findings. Their report is a veritable gold mine of information about California's high-tech regions. Reading it is like viewing the United States through Japanese eyes; it is a study in systematic, collaborative research.

What were its findings? The Hamamatsu team admired Silicon Valley's dynamism, pleasant climate, talented engineers, high educational level, and recreational and cultural activities, but it was highly critical of the exorbitant housing costs, traffic jams, air and water pollution, lack of planning, and worsening living conditions. "Frankly," says Yasuo Mutoh, a planner from Hamamatsu City, "Silicon Valley is not a pretty place. We were more impressed by Boston's Route 128, which we visited earlier, because its dispersed development and beautiful surroundings reminded us of Hamamatsu." Horiuchi Heihachiryo, President of the Hamamatsu Technology Development Association, was equally frank in his assessment: "The United States has had valuable experience with high technology—both good and bad. We must study their lessons to understand the conditions that lead to success and the pitfalls that lead to failure. Despite its phenomenal success, Silicon Valley is not a model that we want to copy."

Similar conclusions were reached by a second study team, the Hamamatsu Advanced Production Machinery Technology Association, that visited Silicon Valley, Boston's Route 128, North Carolina's Research Triangle, and Phoenix's Richfield Park. They thought the Research Triangle was a better model because its careful planning, government-industry cooperation, and university city approach more closely suited Japanese thinking. Moreover, they disliked the ostentatious, get-rich-quick mentality of Silicon Valley, which placed a premium on short-term profits at the expense of long-term growth. The Research Triangle, they felt, showed that a viable high-tech region could be planned, not left to pure chance.

Nevertheless, Silicon Valley's dynamism and creativity appealed to Japanese business leaders and government officials who were desperately searching for ways to keep their local economies afloat. Despite all its failings, Silicon Valley was, in their view, still number one.

CLONING SILICON VALLEY

At the Ministry of International Trade and Industry (MITI), there was keen interest in Silicon Valley's splashy success because of

Japan's troubled economic environment. In the late 1970s, MITI's industrial policies were not working. Heavy industries were sinking fast, forcing MITI into the unpleasant task of forming depression cartels. Pollution had worsened throughout the country, despite the enactment of tough water pollution and smog control laws. Bankruptcies were reaching an all-time high, especially among small- and medium-sized companies that provided 90% of the nation's employment. In 1979 the second oil crisis threatened to derail the economy again, and high-tech companies were ignoring MITI's calls for national unity. Contrary to foreign perceptions about the Japanese economic miracle, "Japan Inc." was in serious trouble.

Among industry and government leaders, there was a growing consensus that something had to be done. But what? In the corridors of MITI, Silicon Valley was revered as the mecca of high technology, a possible solution to Japan's economic stagnation and rising unemployment. MITI was particularly interested in what Dr. Edwin Zschau, the president of a small, high-technology company and a rapidly rising star in the American Electronics Association (AEA), called "the process of innovation." Zschau was considered a key figure to watch because of his growing influence in the valley. In 1978 he successfully spearheaded the AEA's campaign in Congress for a capital gains tax cut and R&D tax credits, which helped trigger a boom in venture capital financing. Thus, while Japan was searching for new sources of technological innovation, Silicon Valley was riding high on a wave of creative start-up companies. In 1980 alone, equity capital offerings in the United States reached $820 million, much of it placed in valley firms.

But there were many obstacles to "cloning" Silicon Valley, which had evolved spontaneously, without direct government planning or guidance. Indeed, many observers concluded that it would be impossible to recreate Silicon Valleys elsewhere— especially in Japan where the central government played such a powerful role. Granted, U.S. defense spending and NASA space programs were crucial in spawning the fledgling electronics industry; but they did not explain Silicon Valley's phenomenal start-up boom. For example, few innovative start-up companies had spun out of the major defense contractors in southern California and Seattle during the 1960s and 1970s, despite the enormous flow of defense contracts. Not until the early 1980s did venture capitalists begin funding start-ups in the two regions. Where government had stepped in, as in Boston's Route 128 and North Carolina's Research Triangle, high-tech growth was more orderly, as Hamamatsu City had observed, but it lacked the vigor and diversity of Silicon Valley's start-up companies and venture capital market. To many observers, Silicon Valley was one of a kind.

MITI officials wondered if they were right. The Japanese government had spent billions of dollars to build the Tsukuba Science City, but had failed to stimulate much industrial development. Most high-tech companies and venture businesses remained in the Tokyo area, where it was easier to recruit top-flight researchers and to cultivate the innumerable personal contacts so important to doing business. Indeed, to MITI officials and businessmen alike, Tokyo remained the ultimate capital of high technology. It had everything—universities, research centers, a huge pool of engineers and college graduates, data banks, rapid transit, communications, and cultural activities. Despite massive funding, Tsukuba remained a rural backwater. The handful of companies that moved into the Tsukuba area were mostly large corporations scattered about the region, not clustered together as in Silicon Valley. Moreover, the government's closed door policy at Tsukuba had stifled spin-off development. There was little sense of professional camaraderie among these firms, and the government did very little to encourage the cross-fertilization of ideas. Networking outside of one's own company was limited to conferences and seminars in Tokyo. Of course, Tsukuba was meant to be a center for national research institutes, not a high-tech industrial park. But for $5.5 billion the Japanese government did not create very many new jobs, only moved existing ones around. Clearly, Tsukuba was not a very good model for high-tech development. Thus, a new approach had to be found quickly. But the questions remained: Could Silicon Valley be cloned? And if so, could it be adapted to Japanese society?

As MITI officials listened to Ed Zschau fervently expound the "process of innovation," they became determined as ever to learn what made the valley tick, for Japan's future depended on their ability to come up with new ideas. They would build their own Silicon Valleys—Japanese-style.

JAPANIZING SILICON VALLEY

In late 1979, MITI began studying the feasibility of recreating Silicon Valley. Professor Takemochi Ishii of Tokyo University's Engineering Department, an influential leader in Japan's electronics industry, formed an informal study group with Hajime Karatsu of the Matsushita Communications Company and Tatsuo Takahashi, an innovative bureaucrat and chief of MITI's Industrial Location Division, to analyze the reasons for Silicon Valley's phenomenal success. Concerned about Japan's lack of creative research, Professor Ishii wanted to create a Japanese-style Silicon Valley where researchers from industry and government could meet on a regular basis to exchange ideas. But he realized that it would be difficult to transfer the valley's informality and lively exchange of ideas that had led to so many discoveries. Although Japan had two high-technology regions, they lacked Silicon Valley's magic. The Tsukuba Science City was strong in basic research, but its researchers were out of touch with industry's needs. Tokyo, on the other hand, was the center of Japan's electronics industry, but its me-too thinking and hyper-competitiveness prevented truly path-breaking inventions. There had to be another way to foster industrial creativity.

The group was casting about for ways to break this technological gridlock when they heard of a new word—*technopolis*—that had been coined by Toshiyuki Chikami, the mayor of Kurume, a small city on the southern island of Kyushu. Mayor Chikami, who became interested in technology while working at the Kyushu Productivity Center, wanted the central government to provide more assistance to middle-sized cities. Using Kurume as an example, he advocated a renaissance of regional cities into new technology centers, or technopolises, which could bridge the gap between major cities and the prefectures. As Japan shifted to high technology, he believed these technopolises could serve as Japan's new information capitals.

The word *technopolis* had nice ring to it, and Mayor Chikami's idea suited the prevailing thinking among government officials in Tokyo. Professor Ishii's study group adopted the word, and in March 1980 MITI's Industrial Structure Council briefly mentioned technopolis in its *Visions for the 1980s*, though without defining it. To develop the idea further, the study group met with

Governor Morihiko Hiramatsu of Oita Prefecture—a neighbor of Mayor Chikami's in Kyushu—who had developed new programs to revive Oita's depressed economy. A former chief of MITI's powerful Electronics Policy Bureau, Governor Hiramatsu emphasized the need to rebuild regional economies with high technology. Japan's competitive advantage, he argued, lay in manufacturing products that were small and light enough to be shipped by air. He pointed to Oita's coastal airport park and surrounding industrial parks as a model for MITI's Technopolis Concept. Professor Ishii's study group recommended the idea to MITI, which announced that two or three model technopolises would be built throughout Japan.

To MITI's surprise, the announcement triggered a stampede; forty of Japan's forty-seven prefectures volunteered to host one of the technopolises. Lobbying was so fierce that MITI formed the Technopolis '90 Construction Committee in July 1980 to flesh out the undeveloped concept. Headed by Professor Ishii, the committee consisted of twenty influential leaders from government, industry, and academia (see Appendix M), who formed three subcommittees to consider long-range industry, R&D, and regional trends. In late 1981 MITI quietly began sending study missions to Silicon Valley and other high-tech regions throughout the world to gather ideas for the Technopolis Concept. Like their counterparts in the commercial arena, the MITI officials used the same painstaking methods of research. They watched, studied, asked questions, and listened—and then came back and asked more questions. Visiting again and again, they dissected the layout of these high-tech regions and analyzed the relationships among universities, industrial parks, high-tech companies, and venture capitalists.

MITI did not try to clone Silicon Valley outright, knowing that the valley's spontaneity and individualism would not fit into Japanese society. Instead, the Technopolis '90 Committee identified the key factors that led to the valley's success—its research universities, industrial parks, large pool of talented engineers, venture capital market, investment banking, management consulting firms, support services, and informal networks—and blended this "process of innovation" with Japanese practices. By focusing on transferable institutions and the *process* of innovation, MITI hoped to avoid the pitfalls of trying to emulate cultural values.

The Technopolis '90 Committee also looked at Japan's major high-tech cities, and concluded that their strength lay in the massive concentration of universities and corporate labs, easy access to technology and market information, highly-qualified labor, airports, highways, telecommunications systems, management networks, and personal ties. The committee took these two models of high-tech development and merged them with existing policies to develop a new approach, the Technopolis Concept. As shown in Figure 6-1, the Technopolis Concept is a synthesis of three streams of thought: MITI's high-tech research strategy, Japan's regional development programs, and Silicon Valley's process of innovation. The first two streams provide the framework for the Technopolis Concept, while Silicon Valley's entrepreneurialism provides the inspiration and drive.

At the core of the Technopolis Concept is MITI's national R&D strategy, which emphasizes the need for Japan to develop creative technologies in order to bolster its bargaining power in the hotly-contested technology race. "In the future," wrote the committee, "we believe technological competition will increase, and it will become difficult to import foreign technology, so we must develop creative technologies which we can trade on a give-and-take basis." MITI was aware that other countries were increasingly wary of the boomerang effect—selling their technology to Japan, only to be inundated by Japanese exports. The Technopolis Concept is seen as a strategic project that will enable Japan to circumvent this problem by generating new technologies to trade. In effect, it will provide bargaining chips for the high-stakes technology game.

But creative technology is a long-term goal; MITI's more immediate concern is to accelerate the transfer of technology from Tokyo and other major cities to regional industries. There are many obstacles to this technology transfer policy. In 1982 almost 80% of all corporate laboratories, 70% of all scientists, and 60% of all university professors were concentrated in the Tokyo, Kanazawa, and Osaka areas. Moreover, there are few ways to transfer basic research from government labs to the private sector. Within industry circles, government and university labs are viewed as ivory towers because of their strict research policies, which require them to remain at arms length from business. Young researchers are discouraged from pursuing their own interests

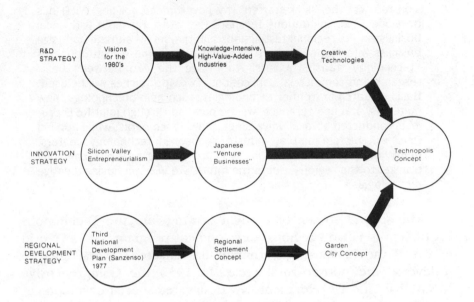

Figure 6-1. MITI's Process of Innovation.

because of the rigid hierarchy in the universities, which gives all power to department chairmen and senior professors. Permanent employment policies and the absence of job-hopping exacerbate this research bottleneck.

To overcome these obstacles, the Technopolis '90 Committee recommended dispersing R&D activities to the prefectures. Each technopolis is responsible for developing a regional R&D strategy based on its strategic industries. This regional R&D strategy consists of various policies: concentrating public and private research institutes in the technopolis zones, promoting hybrid technologies (such as mechatronics), upgrading local university labs, establishing technology centers, forming joint R&D projects, and providing R&D funding.

Professor Kenichi Imai of Hitotsubashi University, chairman of the Technopolis '90 R&D subcommittee, believes MITI can speed up the flow of technology by adopting a technology transfer policy:

Ordinarily, new technologies spread throughout industry and society in a fairly uncontrolled, spontaneous manner. Product improvements and cost reductions follow the typical learning curve. But this diffusion rate can be "kick-started" by government policies. MITI has developed two institutions to share the latest research with local businesses: its regional testing labs and the small- and medium-size business information centers. We plan to use these institutions as "technology transfer agents" to bridge the gap between basic research and commercial applications. Two approaches will be used. Basic research in frontier technologies, such as biotechnology, new materials, and fine ceramics, will be pursued through joint R&D projects conducted at local universities and science parks; while applied R&D will be pursued at industry-sponsored technology centers. Right now, our main headache is improving the rate of technology transfer to the regions. But in the future, we will emphasize creative technologies.

The second stream of thought flowing into the Technopolis Concept is Japan's regional development programs. Since World War II the Japanese government has enacted several laws to develop the poorer rural areas. In 1950 the Comprehensive National Land Development Law designated special development areas for government assistance. In a remarkable parallel to the Technopolis program, nineteen areas covering almost the entire country were selected after fierce lobbying by the prefectures. The resulting program was so diluted that it was unable to overcome the strong pull of Tokyo, Osaka, and Nagoya. Later, the New Industrial City Promotion Law (1962) and the Special Regional Development Promotion Law (1964) were passed to ease crowding in the Tokyo-Osaka regions and decentralize heavy industries to outlying regions. These programs succeeded in accelerating Japan's rapid economic growth, but in the early 1970s industrial pollution undermined their credibility with the public. In the face of public protests and demonstrations, the Japanese government was forced to pass stricter environmental laws.

The Technopolis Concept is not a totally new idea. In 1972 Prime Minister Kakuei Tanaka proposed a costly scheme for remodeling the Japanese archipelago with highways, trains, telecommunications networks, and new cities. At the core of this network would be "quarter-million cities"—cities with a population of 250,000—that would serve as the new capitals for high-growth industries. Although this program offered some novel ideas, it touched off an orgy of land speculation benefitting insiders, and was aborted after the 1973 oil shock derailed Japan's high-growth economy. Tanaka's ideas were thoroughly discredited in the mid-1970s because of political scandals and his arrest in the Lockheed case, but several ideas found their way into the Technopolis Concept, including the model "quarter-million cities" approach, academic new towns in natural settings, computerized agriculture, and the "information archipelago."

In 1979 the Japanese government tried to revive some of the better features of the "Tanaka Plan" in its Third Comprehensive National Development Plan (*Sanzenso*), but it was so unexciting and so filled with compromises that it failed to capture the public's imagination. To many Japanese, regional development was viewed as a bottomless pit, fraught with problems of pollution, corruption, and overcrowding. It meant spending trillions of yen on a lost cause, trying to revive sinking industries.

In 1980, when MITI announced the Technopolis Concept, Japanese were ready for a change. They were tired of hearing about the "sinking of the Japanese economy" (a bestseller title), lowered expectations, and pollution. They were seeking something new and positive that would lift their spirits. According to Dr. Sadakazu Iijima, executive director of the Japan Industrial Location Center, a MITI think-tank set up in 1981: "The Technopolis Concept was the first good news that people had heard in years. After the troubles of the 1970s, it was a light at the end of the tunnel." The Technopolis Concept was a step in a new direction. Instead of reworking tired formulas, it offered a way for prefectures to revitalize their economies with homegrown technologies.

What made the Technopolis Concept different from previous regional development programs was its emphasis on developing the "soft" infrastructure of people, technology, information, and communications. Unlike Silicon Valley, the Technopolis Concept emphasized a more balanced approach to high-technology development. Instead of only focusing on technology, it proposed the creation of totally new cities, complete with research parks, new universities, technology centers, housing, parks, and cultural activities. The goal was to create an environment where people could become creative, well-rounded citizens. By integrating technology with local traditions, MITI hoped to make local agriculture and heavy industries compatible.

The third stream of thought flowing into the Technopolis Concept is Silicon Valley's industrial innovativeness and entrepreneurialism. However, the Technopolis '90 Committee realized that ad hoc, spontaneous industrial development would not work in Japan's depressed regions. Thus, MITI worked with the prefectures to systematically identify and promote strategic regional industries that would form the core of their economies in the twenty-first century. To assist them, MITI compiled market forecasts for key high-tech industries that will play a major role in the Japanese economy. These industries include aerospace, optoelectronics, biotechnology, medical electronics, industrial robots, semiconductors, computers, word processors, software, new alloys, fine ceramics, pharmaceuticals, and flexible manufacturing systems.

To choose strategic industries for accelerated development, MITI suggested that the prefectures analyze their competitive strengths and weaknesses to determine where they had the best chance for success. The local surveys not only focused on strengthening industries through technology transfers, but also on the prospects of attracting high-tech industries from Tokyo and Osaka. MITI required a frank assessment of each prefecture's labor force, transportation and communications networks, plant investment trends, agricultural income, urban services, local R&D and industrial siting incentives, universities, training programs, and environmental controls. By requiring them to look at themselves in the mirror, MITI wanted to separate the dreamers from the hard-headed pragmatists. It was a way to pick the winners in the Technopolis sweepstakes.

PICKING THE WINNERS

MITI's Technopolis selection process began in 1982. Under the leadership of Professor Hisao Nishioka of Aoyama Gakuin University, the Technopolis '90 Regional Committee evaluated the forty regions and narrowed its evaluation to nineteen sites involving twenty prefectures (see Figure 6-2). According to Shuji Kato, former deputy director of MITI's Technopolis Division: "It was a painful process. We had difficulty turning down half the suitors who came into our offices with gifts and greetings from their governors and industry leaders." But MITI officials realized that

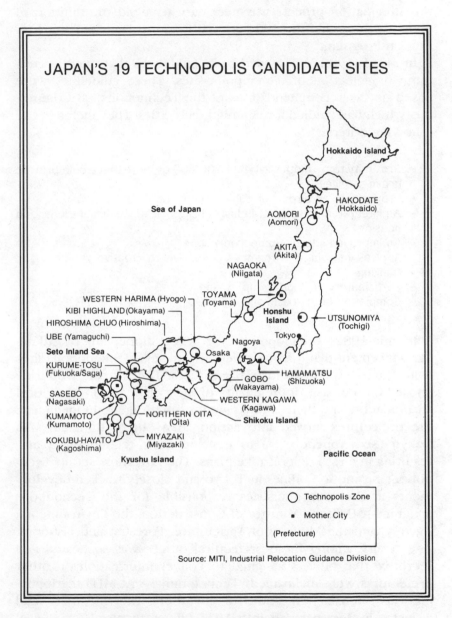

JAPAN'S 19 TECHNOPOLIS CANDIDATE SITES

Hokkaido Island

Sea of Japan

HAKODATE
(Hokkaido)

AOMORI
(Aomori)

AKITA
(Akita)

NAGAOKA
(Niigata)

TOYAMA
(Toyama)

WESTERN HARIMA (Hyogo)
KIBI HIGHLAND (Okayama)
HIROSHIMA CHUO (Hiroshima)
UBE (Yamaguchi)
Seto Inland Sea
KURUME-TOSU
(Fukuoka/Saga)
SASEBO
(Nagasaki)
KUMAMOTO
(Kumamoto)
KOKUBU-HAYATO
(Kagoshima)

Honshu
Island

UTSUNOMIYA
(Tochigi)

Nagoya

Tokyo

Osaka

GOBO
(Wakayama)

HAMAMATSU
(Shizuoka)

WESTERN KAGAWA
(Kagawa)

NORTHERN OITA
(Oita)

Shikoku Island

MIYAZAKI
(Miyazaki)

Kyushu Island

Pacific Ocean

○ Technopolis Zone
▪ Mother City
(Prefecture)

Source: MITI, Industrial Relocation Guidance Division

Figure 6-2. Japan's Technopolis Sites.

this elimination process was necessary to avoid the dilution of effort that crippled the 1964 Special Regional Development Promotion Program.

In March 1982 MITI issued basic guidelines that would determine its selection of technopolis sites. These guidelines were based on the recommendations of the Technopolis '90 Committee, which had studied foreign high-tech cities. They included the following criteria:

- Proximity to a "mother city" of 200,000 or more that would provide urban services
- Proximity to an airport or bullet train station
- An integrated complex of industrial sites, academic institutions, and housing
- An improved information network
- A pleasant living environment conducive to creative research and thinking
- Participatory or "bottom-up" planning
- Completion of the basic plan by 1990

In mid-1982, Technopolis fever was whipped up by MITI's announcement that it would select five to seven Technopolis sites from the nineteen candidate prefectures. The winners would be chosen on the basis of the quality of their plans, the level of local participation, and their enthuasism for the program. Immediately, the prefectures moved into action. Many hired think-tanks in Tokyo (see Appendix N) to develop their technopolis plans, resulting in a rash of look-alike plans. The governors set up Technopolis promotion offices in Tokyo and closely tracked developments at the four ministries responsible for the Technopolis program—MITI, the Ministry of Construction, the Environmental Agency, and the Ministry of Agriculture, Forestry, and Fisheries. The rivalry among these prefectural offices was so heated and secretive that officers assigned to collect information on other prefectures were nicknamed "Techno-ninjas." At MITI the lobbying was intense. Delegations of governors, Diet members, and industry leaders paraded into MITI offices to plead for special consideration, forcing staff members to lock their office doors to get work done.

In preparing their plans, the prefectures called large public hearings (the bigger, the better) and organized industry associations to identify strategic industries and regional R&D strategies. In Yamaguchi Prefecture in western Japan, over a thousand people showed up for a public hearing. Study teams like the one from Hamamatsu City visited Silicon Valley and other high-tech regions in the United States to gather ideas. Borrowing ideas from the twenty-plus American states that had opened trade promotion offices in Tokyo, the prefectures geared up their own industry recruiting campaigns, complete with slick brochures featuring ancient temples and modern IC plants. Politicians jumped on the Technopolis bandwagon in their reelection campaigns. The pressures to be selected as a Technopolis were enormous. Not only were the prefectures desperate for an economic lifesaver, but Technopolis became a matter of local pride. After being ignored for so long, each region in Japan wanted to become known as Japan's Silicon Valley.

During the fall of 1982, the nineteen candidate regions prepared their development plans according to MITI's planning schedule (see Appendix O). Following MITI guidelines, they listed their goals and objectives for upgrading local industries, joint R&D facilities, universities, housing, airports, and highways. MITI called the shots, but the prefectures were responsible for developing their own strategies and plans. Of course, there were occasional conflicts between MITI and the prefectures. For example, MITI opposed Oita Prefecture's plan to scatter new development throughout the region, preferring instead cluster development in a new airport town. The prefecture felt that MITI was out of touch with local residents, and that dispersed development would reduce infrastructure costs, traffic congestion, and environmental impact. After heated debates, Oita finally prevailed—in part because Oita Governor Morihiko Hiramatsu was a former MITI official and had close ties to the prestigious Technopolis '90 Committee. However, Oita Prefecture was the exception, not the rule. Most prefectures lacked political clout and were only too willing to go along with MITI in order to be selected.

In early 1983 the prefectures completed their development concepts, which were evaluated by MITI and the Japan Industrial Location Center, a think-tank set up by MITI to conduct studies for the Technopolis program. In March 1983 MITI refined some of its guidelines for selecting the technopolises: 1) completion of construction by 1990; 2) development areas of less than 500 square miles; 3) within thirty minutes commute from a mother city with at least 150,000 residents. These guidelines were incorporated into the Technopolis Law passed by the Japanese Diet in April 1983. Unlike the United States, where high-tech industries are rushing to the Sunbelt aided by federal tax laws, NASA programs, and defense procurement, the Technopolis Law is aimed at redistributing the population and wealth among Japan's poorer regions. In that sense, the Technopolis program is a form of income redistribution and social welfare, as well as technology development.

The winners of the Technopolis drawing were evaluated in 1984. In November 1983 fourteen regions submitted their final development plans to MITI. During December, MITI held hearings throughout Japan to listen to the governors and planners explain the rationale behind their plans. MITI looked for regional uniqueness and originality in their plans (*chiiki-tokusei*), and for methods of "awakening their towns" (*mura-okoshi*). Finally lobbying pressure reached such a fever pitch that in February 1984 MITI announced it would select all nineteen candidate sites, but only if they resolved problems identified by MITI. This last step was merely a formality, since MITI will eventually approve all of the plans. During 1984 and 1985, MITI designated sixteen areas as technopolis sites, making them eligible for national tax incentives and research subsidies:

- March 1984: Nagaoka, Toyama, Hamamatsu, Hiroshima, Yamaguchi, Kumamoto, Oita, Miyazaki, Kagoshima
- May 1984: Akita, Utsunomiya
- July 1984: Hakodate
- August 1984: Okayama
- September 1984: Kurume-Tosu
- March 1985: Nagasaki
- September 1985: West Harima

Nagasaki was not originally one of the candidate sites, but because of intense lobbying, it was selected in March 1985. The three remaining sites (Aomori, Wakayama, and Kagawa) will be given the go-ahead after revising their plans. By late 1985, all systems were go for the technopolises, which were rapidly building their industrial parks and university research complexes (see Appendix P).

However, the decision to select all nineteen sites drew strong criticism from the press, which accused MITI of caving in to political pressures. Instead of sticking to its original goal of targeting one or two sites, critics charged that MITI had diluted its impact by scattering its limited funding everywhere (*bara-maki*). Some observers wondered whether the whole Technopolis selection process was an empty charade designed to make MITI look good to an increasingly vocal public. They accused MITI of stuntsmanship, calling it *kanban daore* (taking down the billboards after the circus is over), with nothing to show for its elaborate selection process. Others, remembering the backdoor deals and pork barrel politics under Prime Minister Kakuei Tanaka, called it *Seiji-polis* (Politicians' Polis) because of MITI's bending under pressure. "If MITI was going end up like a beauty queen trying to please everyone (*happo-bijin*)," wrote one columnist, "these strict guidelines and the Technopolis Law were totally unnecessary." Perhaps in hindsight the result was not too surprising, given MITI's track record with previous regional development programs. As in 1950, when MITI announced nineteen candidate regions for special development and ended up choosing all of them, MITI again yielded to intense lobbying pressure. History repeats itself.

BUILDING NEW CASTLE TOWNS

Since 1985, Japan's Technopolis regions have been working like people possessed. They are busy building new university complexes, research parks, highways, airports, and information networks, and organizing joint R&D projects and technology centers. Their goal is to beat MITI's 1990 target date for completing construction of the basic infrastructure. However, tight finances will probably delay the program five to ten years. The Ministry of Construction estimates that the construction costs alone for eleven Technopolises will be about $10.4 billion by 1990, or roughly $200 million annually for each Technopolis. For most regions, this is a lot of money. Given their weak financial status and the tight national budget, it is likely that construction will be extended to the year 2000. Even the Tsukuba Science City, which received massive funding from the central government, took seventeen years to build.

When visiting these areas, one is struck by the enormous enthusiasm and energy that the Technopolis program has unleashed—a far cry from the bleak outlook ten years ago. Governors have set up special Technopolis offices to coordinate the efforts of local universities, industry associations, chambers of commerce, and MITI's regional testing labs. Companies are opening Technopolis research centers and staffing software design houses. Universities are inviting top professors from Tokyo to lecture on new technologies, while prefectures are sponsoring Technopolis fairs to drum up interest among local residents. Oita Prefecture, for example, is promoting grassroots technologies through its one-village/one-product campaign. Prefectures from the Kyushu and Tohoku regions sent trade missions to the United States in 1984 to invite companies to their technopolises. For the first time, MITI has turned to local citizens and industries for new ideas to revitalize their economies, and they are responding with vigor to the Technopolis challenge. It is a form of bottom-up industrial planning similar to our own state and local planning efforts. As the Japanese press notes, the era of regionalism has finally arrived.

Of course, all the hoopla over "Technopolis fever" has attracted its share of hype and misunderstanding, just as "Silicon Valley fever" did. In many areas, Technopolis is synonymous with pork-barrel spending for large high-tech companies, construction outfits, and consulting firms, while others view it as a "Yuppie's haven" for Japan's highly-educated elite. In Kyushu, farmers worry that their tax money will end up subsidizing industries. Despite efforts to educate the public, many people still have misconceptions about the program, believing it to be another high-tech Disneyland or high-priced Tsukuba. Katsuji Yuda, the planning director for the Ube Phoenix Technopolis in Yamaguchi Prefecture, recalls: "One mayor from a small village on the island of Shikoku actually went to MITI to plead for a Technopolis because his citizens wanted a technical police station—or techno-police. They thought it was a fancy law enforcement program and wanted one of their own."

Although Tokyoites chuckle over these gaffes, people in Japan's depressed regions are serious about Technopolis. With their traditional industries sinking rapidly, they are desperate for new jobs to keep their children from moving to the major cities. For them, Technopolis is an economic lifesaver; it gives them hope for the future. But what are the goals of Technopolis?

Governor Morihiko Hosokawa of Kumamoto Prefecture probably best enunciates the long-term goals of the Technopolis program: "In the 1990s Japan must pursue creative research in information systems, mechatronics, biotechnology, and new materials. Japan will become a technological leader in the world. . . . I would like Technopolis to create internationally competitive industries, creative technologies, and an attractive urban environment."

For Governor Morihiko Hiramatsu of Oita Prefecture, the Technopolis program is a way to train young people and strengthen local industries with an injection of high technology. "Technopolis is not limited to advanced technology industries," he says. "It is a project to give a vigorous impact to the development of the whole prefectural economy. In the end, industrial and regional development will depend on the people. Students of senior and junior high schools and even pupils of primary schools must be made computer-conscious and trained to meet the trend toward information and internationalization."

To achieve these goals, the prefectures are developing their "hard" infrastructure of roads and airports. Following Oita's lead, many prefectures have expanded their airports to accommodate the jumbo jets required by an increase in electronics trade. New highways are being built to compensate for the delay in bullet train construction due to Japan National Railway's huge budget deficits. Within the Technopolis zones, new "Techno-roads" link research centers to existing towns and cities.

The Technopolis zones consist of three interlocking areas: an industrial zone of factories, distribution centers, and offices; an academic core of universities, government research institutes, and corporate R&D labs; and housing for researchers and their families. Although MITI's guidelines provide the framework for Technopolis planning, each region has its own distinctive approach. Nagaoka City is emulating Silicon Valley by concentrating businesses in a new "Shinano Techno-Valley." Hiroshima, Yamaguchi, and Miyazaki prefectures are building academic new towns patterned after the Tsukuba Science City. Hamamatsu, Toyama, and

Ube are expanding science and engineering departments in their local universities. Most of the technopolises are building "frontier" technology centers and Techno-Centers, which will serve as incubators for joint R&D and venture businesses.

The heart of a Technopolis is the "soft" infrastructure of people, information, financing, and services. A variety of regional strategies are being pursued to develop these resources. To attract companies from the major cities and abroad, the technopolises have developed industry invitation campaigns, complete with brochures describing industrial sites, tax incentives, low-interest loans, and R&D subsidies. These efforts are supported by the Japan Regional Development Corporation (JRDC) and MITI's Industrial Location Guidance Division, which maintain data bases on Japan's 2,200 industrial sites. In 1985 MITI spent about $20 million on plant siting and another $20 million on industrial park construction. For foreign companies wishing to build plants in Japan, MITI provides information about industrial sites through its overseas branch—the Japan External Trade Organization (JETRO)—which has offices in major cities overseas.

Companies investing in the technopolises are eligible for three types of incentives: tax incentives, subsidy incentives, and financial incentives. National tax measures include special depreciation allowances of 30% for machinery (first year only) and 15% for buildings and facilities built within the Technopolis zones. The Japanese government also subsidizes one-third of all capital investments in facilities and equipment for joint R&D projects that are conducted with local industrial research labs. To encourage regional development, local tax incentives are provided and vary by prefecture. They include special depreciation allowances on buildings and equipment, energy conservation, and pollution control, as well as reduced business, fixed assets, real property acquisition, and special land-holding taxes. In depressed regions, special subsidies are offered to promote job creation. In addition, the Japan Development Bank (JDB), Japan Regional Development Corporation (JRDC), and Hokkaido-Tohoku Development Finance Public Corporation (HDFPC) offer low-interest loans for new technology, energy conservation, and pollution control. In 1985 JDB offered $560 million and HDFPC $170 million in low-interest loans at rates shown in Table 6-1:

Table 6-1.
Japan Development Bank Low-Interest Loans
(Effective March 1984).

Loan Program	Interest Rate	Eligible Projects
Foreign Direct Investment	8.2%	Capital investments by firms with 50% foreign ownership
Technopolis	7.3%	Projects in Technopolis areas
Import Promotion	7.6%	Inspection, inventory, after-sales and exhibition facilities
Industrial Technology	7.1%	Research facilities and pilot plants
Electronics & Machinery Industries	7.1%	Joint R&D projects

Source: Japan Development Bank

To promote technology exchanges, the prefectures have formed nonprofit Technology Promotion Associations and Techno-Centers that offer training, information services, industry surveys, counseling, debt guarantees, and low-interest loans. With MITI's Small and Medium Enterprise Agency, they promote joint R&D projects through the Regional Frontier Industries Development Project. Important technologies are funded by MITI's Agency for Industrial Science and Technology (AIST).

The technopolises have also developed innovative ideas of their own. Hamamatsu City, for example, has built a Business House for visiting researchers. Nagaoka City offers a "high-tech striker" (strike force) program in which professors and MITI researchers offer technical assistance to venture businesses. Toyama awards a Novel Prize for the best technology program, and finds talented people for joint R&D projects through its Leadership and Talent Data Bank. And Kumamoto has opened Hometown Counseling Offices to lure homesick professionals back from Tokyo and Osaka! Apparently this program is working, since many young people are getting fed up with big cities.

To link the technopolises to the major cities, Japanese ministries have developed ambitious telecommunications programs.

The core is Nippon Telegraph and Telephone's (NTT) plan to develop its Information Network System (INS), a nationwide network of fiber optic cables and communication satellites. In 1985 NTT completed the main fiber optic trunk cable from northern Hokkaido to southern Kyushu, and will extend branch lines to the prefectural capitals by 1988. Direct broadcast satellites (DBS) and communications satellites will be launched from 1986 to provide backup service.

As part of Japan's efforts to deregulate its telecommunications market, the Japanese Diet passed a law privatizing NTT and opening the market to competition. Since April 1985, private companies have competed against NTT while leasing NTT lines to provide banking, credit, travel, and other business information services through value-added networks. Nomura Research Institute estimates that this market alone will range from $200 to $350 billion over the next twenty years, creating many new market opportunities and jobs throughout Japan.

In addition, MITI recently selected seven regions (including Kumamoto, Oita, and Nagaoka technopolises) out of 135 candidate sites for its New Media Community Concept, which is designed to promote new telecommunications media, such as cable TV, teletext, videotext, value-added networks, satellite broadcasting, and video-conferencing. A two-phase program will introduce new home, office, traffic control, and medical information between 1984 and 1988. According to Professor Kenichi Imai of Hitotsubashi University, a member of the Technopolis '90 Committee, MITI is pursuing this program because it foresees the rapid merging of telecommunications and computers, and believes New Media services will open new markets in the technopolises.

In 1985 MITI introduced the "Techno-Mart Concept" to promote information exchanges and technology transfers. In this program, national universities, research labs, local and foreign businesses, banks, and brokerage houses will be invited to join as supporting members, which will entitle them to exchange information on marketing, distribution, joint venture partners, job offers, and investment opportunities. A model online system will be installed in Tokyo, Osaka, Toyama, Hamamatsu, and Nagoya in 1985, and extended to all the technopolises in 1986.

The Ministry of Posts and Telecommunications (MPT) is not about to be upstaged by MITI. In 1984, after MITI introduced its New Media Community Concept, MPT announced its Teletopia Concept, which will link NTT's Information Network System with ten model cities chosen from forty-five candidate sites. This system will provide cable television, interactive video, and other services to homes and offices. The Industrial Bank of Japan will provide financing for this system to the ten model cities. By 1990, this system will provide the technopolises with improved access to data banks and technical information, and will become the foundation for a "regional new media program" covering a wide variety of telecommunication services.

Thus, Japan's Technopolis program is up and running. Although it will take time for these regions to establish themselves, the prefectures are willing to invest the time and money because they know it took twenty years for Silicon Valley and the Tsukuba Science City to lay their basic foundations. In February 1985, MITI held a symposium called "TECHNOPOLIS: Japan's Super Vision for the Twenty-First Century," which described the "Japan Tech" rapidly coming into focus. Besides the technopolises, other regions are developing their own high-tech cities, including the Chiba New Industrial Triangle Concept, Kawasaki Microcomputer City, the Atsugi Research City, the Future Port Twenty-First Century Concept (Yokohama), the Tokai Techno-Belt (Nagoya), the Kyoto-Osaka-Nara Cultural Research City Concept, Techno-Port Osaka, and others. It appears that Japan is on its way to becoming a high-tech archipelago.

In this chapter we have reviewed the basic outline for the technopolises. Now let's take a look at the leading technopolises to see where they are headed. What does Japan Tech look like at first hand?

7

THE NEW CASTLE TOWNS

> Technopolis is not a place—it is a state of mind.
>
> *Hamamatsu Technopolis Planning Department*

HAMAMATSU: THE CITY OF SOUND AND LIGHT

Ieyasu Tokugawa seethed with rage as, crippled and covered with blood, his men retreated from the Mikatagahara Plain. Many had been cut down at the hands of Shingen Takeda, warlord of the neighboring province. In one stroke, Takeda had shattered young Ieyasu's dream of unifying the country under the banner of his lord and ally, Nobunaga Oda. Now, at the age of thirty-one, Ieyasu had to regroup his men and begin the long task of consolidating his power. His castle, built in the pine forests of Hamamatsu, would be his sustenance and protection. From this fortress, he would expand his military control eastward until he had achieved sovereignty over the Kanto plain (the Tokyo area). Then he would attack Takeda at his doorstep, avenging himself for this humiliating defeat. He would establish the Tokugawa shogunate that would rule Japan for the next 270 years. And Hamamatsu Castle would be his "successful castle," the staging ground for his ambitious campaign.

Four hundred years have passed since Tokugawa built Hamamatsu Castle in his bid to become Japan's third unifier, and time has erased most remnants of his seventeen-year stay there. For most Japanese, Hamamatsu City is just another stop on the Tōkaidō bullet train line between Tokyo and Kyoto, another castle town among the many dotting the countryside. Yet it was

here that Ieyasu Tokugawa began the arduous process of building a network of castle towns that would become Japan's major
cities. Between 1580 and 1610, Japan witnessed a flurry of
urban construction unparalleled in its history. During this
period, Ieyasu ordered the building of over thirty castle towns
that laid the foundation for Japan's emerging merchant class, the
chōnin, who transformed the economy with their entrepreneurial vigor. Under his rule, these castle towns unleashed a wave of
new products and technologies that deeply altered the course of
Japanese history. They were the agents of change that transformed Japan from a peninsula of warring factions to a single,
unified nation.

Today that history is being repeated. Like the Tokugawa
shoguns of the past, MITI has embarked on an ambitious program
to build a nationwide network of technopolises—Japan's new castle towns—that will become the engines for the country's economic growth in the twenty-first century. However, this time the
banner is not national unification and isolationism, but creativity
and internationalism, and the stakes are not military survival, but
Japan's industrial competitiveness. Like the feudal castle towns,
MITI's technopolises will be the vehicles for social and technological change. They will become the focal point for creative
researchers and high-tech entrepreneurs—the new *chōnin*—who
will transform the Japanese economy during the next century.
They will be the new capitals that will enable Japan to make the
leap from "Japan Inc." to "Japan Tech."

Perhaps it is symbolic that Hamamatsu City is one of Japan's
leading technopolises, since it has long stood at the crossroads of
change. Located 160 miles west of Tokyo on the famous Tōkaidō
line, Hamamatsu is in the mainstream of goods and ideas flowing
between the Kanto (Tokyo) and Kansai (Osaka) regions. For centuries, it served as a stopover for messengers, peddlers, and provincial warlords on their way to Edo, Ieyasu Tokugawa's capital.
Today, Hamamatsu is a thriving city of 500,000, the home of such
internationally known manufacturers as Yamaha, Suzuki Motors,
Nippon Automation (robots), Roland (electronic musical instruments), Ando Electric (optical communications), and Hamamatsu
Photonics (optoelectronics). Since World War II, the city has
carved out a comfortable niche in motorcycles, musical instruments, optoelectronics, and home sound systems. In 1984 local

industries shipped over $45 billion in goods, placing it seventh in the nation.

When first viewed from the bullet train, Shizuoka Prefecture casts an alluring spell over the traveler, who is reminded of the moody orange-and-blue woodblock prints of Hiroshige's "53 Stations of the Tōkaidō." The rolling hills and manicured orchards are a pleasant change of pace from the grimy, hectic Tokyo region, and surprises lie at each bend in the track. On a clear day, Mount Fuji rises majestically into the misty sky. Further to the west, near the town of Yui, the hillsides overflow with carefully-tended rows of green tea, melons, tangerines, and strawberries. But around the cities of Shimizu and Shizuoka, industrialization has scarred the land, and high-tech plants are popping up left and right along the shores. For the first-time visitor to Japan, the sharp contrast between old farm houses and modern factories sitting side by side is startling; but after repeated visits it becomes invisible to the eye.

Hamamatsu City sits on the Mikatagahara Plain where Ieyasu Tokugawa once fought for his political life, and reminders of his encampment are clearly visible throughout the city. At the station, one is greeted by a billboard visage of Ieyasu and a large map marking his places of residence. For the thousands of tourists who pass through the city each year, Hamamatsu is one large outdoor museum, its historical monuments and shrines scattered among the pine forests. "If you look over there," says Technopolis planner Yasuo Mutoh, pointing out the window of the prefectural offices, "You can see Hamamatsu Castle, where Tokugawa used to live. Right now, they're fixing up the place for summer." He speaks matter-of-factly, as though Ieyasu Tokugawa had lived there only several years ago.

What are Hamamatsu's plans? As Mr. Mutoh explains, the prefecture is trying to counter the downturn in its existing industries by creating new venture businesses, stimulating high-tech research among small- and medium-sized companies, and luring companies from elsewhere. Its goal is to develop the "Shizuoka Sunbelt Twenty-One," patterned after the Sunbelt region in the United States. The city has chosen a catchy motto: "High-tech/high touch with nature."

Using its automotive, musical instrument, and textile industries as a base, Hamamatsu has targeted four strategic industries for accelerated development: optoelectronics, mechatronics (the merger of mechanical and electronic technology), home sound equipment, and home image information systems. Its goal is to revitalize local industries through a careful process of funding and technical guidance. Motorcycle makers are expanding into computer-aided design and manufacturing equipment (CAD/CAM), flexible manufacturing systems (FMS), and industrial robots. Musical instrument manufacturers such as Yamaha and Roland are moving into the "home sound culture of the future," developing portable electronic pianos and organs, software for composing music on computers, and computerized music education equipment. They are working closely with optoelectronics companies who are developing optical fibers and lasers to link computers and television with telecommunications equipment. The ultimate goal is to develop a total home light-and-sound entertainment and information system that will link stereo equipment, high-resolution digital television, computers, telephones, appliances, home security systems, and musical instruments in an integrated system.

The key to understanding Hamamatsu's strategy can be summed up in one word: teamwork. Since the Technopolis Concept was announced, local business leaders have organized seven industry associations. In 1978 the prefecture formed a Development Enterprise Research Association to provide management training for small businesses. In 1981 the Hamamatsu Technology Development Association was formed to discuss industry trends into the twenty-first century. In 1982 Shizuoka Prefecture Technology Transfer Plaza, the Aircraft Equipment Industry Research Association, and Machinery Technology Research Association began conducting industry surveys, plant tours, and technology exchanges. In 1983 two more groups were formed: the Electronic Machinery Technology Research Association began exchanging ideas on mechatronics, and the Regional Frontier Technology Development Association initiated joint research in lasers, optoelectronics, new materials, fine ceramics, and flexible manufacturing systems. These groups have been instrumental in forging Hamamatsu's Technopolis plans.

According to Takagi Takashi, President of the Hamamatsu Technology Development Association, study groups investigated nine policy areas: urban problems, venture capital and venture businesses, technology transfer, information systems, high-density land use, educational facilities, new agricultural technology systems, life science research, and recreational open space. Their mission was to identify key trends and analyze their impact on Hamamatsu's economic future. In their search, they zeroed in on three questions: What made Silicon Valley tick? How could it be duplicated? And what were the pitfalls—the dark side of the Valley—that they needed to avoid?

In October 1981 the Association sponsored the ten-day study tour of California's top high-tech cities described in Chapter 6. The group had reservations about Silicon Valley, and recommended that other areas be studied in depth in order to get differing ideas and opinions.

In March 1983 another group—the Hamamatsu Advanced Production Machinery Technology Association—conducted its own tour of Silicon Valley, Route 128, North Carolina's Research Triangle, and Phoenix's Richfield Park. This group felt the Research Triangle was a better model because its natural setting, planned development, and government-industry cooperation closely suited prevailing attitudes in Hamamatsu. Their recommendations were submitted to the Hamamatsu Technopolis planning department.

Nevertheless, Boston's Route 128 finally won out. According to Yasuo Mutoh: "We felt Route 128 was a better model for development than Silicon Valley because it is very much like Hamamatsu. It has protected its environment—something we value very much." Hamamatsu has decided to copy Route 128 by scattering development among five areas. It plans to build a "Venture Highland" in the hills to the north of the city. A ring road will connect these high-tech centers. However, land costs are a major problem, forcing the prefecture to rapidly buy up farmland for the Technopolis zones before prices increase. These last-minute acquisitions have triggered land speculation and revisions in the city's plans.

As a result, Hamamatsu is not emphasizing bricks-and-mortar, but institutions. Mr. Mutoh says: "We are are not building a place, but a state of mind. We are trying to raise the technological level of existing industries. In Japanese, we say *level-up.*" To achieve this goal, Hamamatsu has established a $1.7 million Venture Enterprise Promotion Fund to help local companies develop advanced technologies. Small high-tech companies are also offered low-interest loans (5.8%) and loan guarantees for high-risk basic research. Recipients are chosen by a screening committee consisting of local industry, university, and government researchers. If the research is commercially unsuccessful, the recipient is not obligated to repay the loan.

Hamamatsu offers a smorgasbord of financing programs to venture businesses. The Small and Medium-Size Business Technology Development Promotion Fund offers consignment loans (*itakuhi*) and conditional loans (*hōjōkin*). Firms pursuing research in energy, new materials, biotechnology, electronics, and optics can receive up to $30,000 for operating expenses and $20,000 for new product development. The program currently funds research in solid state relays, computerized numerically-controlled (CNC) graphics equipment, and lumber rotary sanders.

Another program is the Frontier Industries Development Association, which spends about $1 million annually on joint research in laser manufacturing technology, fiber optics, optical control systems, and optical "data-highways" for managing production lines, new ceramics, and super-heating technology.

Although Hamamatsu cannot compete with Tokyo or Osaka, local universities and public research labs are making a major effort to revitalize local industries. In 1983 Shizuoka University began research in optoelectronics, new materials, energy, mechatronics, and aircraft design. Toyohashi Science and Technology University is conducting joint R&D with national testing labs and has opened a Business House for visiting researchers. The Hamamatsu Solar Research Laboratory is developing solar batteries and heat-accumulation tanks as well as running a solar equipment efficiency rating program. Hamamatsu Medical School's Medical Equipment Technology Research Lab is developing artificial organs and new applications for electronic devices. The Electronic Machinery Research Lab is studying the use of electronics in automobiles, precision machinery, and manufacturing equipment. Recently, ten companies formed the Shizuoka Prefecture New Materials Research Association.

To tie these research activities together, Shizuoka Prefecture recently built a $3.8 million Western Region Industrial Promotion Center to hold conferences, training programs, and joint research. In November 1984, the prefecture held an International Venture

Business Symposium to discuss future technology trends and venture business opportunities. John Naisbitt, author of *Megatrends*, was the keynote speaker.

Thus, Hamamatsu is pulling together its "soft" infrastructure—the people, research labs, information systems, and funding—that will ultimately drive its Technopolis. Although Hamamatsu has decided not to copy Silicon Valley, it has adopted the valley's approach of building human networks. Indeed, people, not bricks and mortar, are the essence of Hamamatsu's approach. Perhaps it is fitting. Four hundred years ago, Ieyasu Tokugawa used the same approach in his search for national unification. First he built his army—then he built his castle towns.

NAGAOKA: HIGH-TECH SNOW COUNTRY

The Jōetsu bullet train bursts from the ten-mile-long tunnel that drills through the rugged Mikuni Mountains, gliding past the villages of Shiozawa, Muika, and Yamato on its journey northward to the Japan Sea. The river canyon is steep and forested, shaped like a gigantic twisting chute that sends water cascading down the mountainside in white torrents. To the newcomer from Tokyo, the sudden contrast is breathtaking. In little over an hour, the smoggy landscape of the Tokyo metropolis and the lush ricefields of Gumma Prefecture are transformed into snow-covered mountains and rushing streams. One is reminded of Switzerland or Austria, a fact that is not lost on the Japanese who call these mountains the Japanese Alps. Indeed, because of its long, harsh winters and dangerous passes, Niigata Prefecture is known as snow country, a region long overlooked in Japan's rush to prosperity. Local farmers still recall the days when men were forced to head south to the big cities every winter in search of work, leaving women, old people, and small children to fend for themselves in the heavy snows until the spring thaw came. Older children were sent away to school dormitories where they fell melancholy from months of loneliness. Due to blinding snowstorms, infants often died of pneumonia before doctors could reach the isolated hamlets. As in all of rural Japan, life was harsh. In winter the only way to the outside world was a circuitous route via the Aizu Plain.

If Niigata were just another prefecture, its residents might still be trudging through the snow; but they are not, thanks to a local boy who made it big in Tokyo. Nagaoka City is the home district of former Prime Minister Kakuei Tanaka, whose behind-the-scenes arm-twisting (or *kuromaku*, meaning *wire-puller* in traditional Bunraku puppet theater) and "money politics" have benefitted Niigata Prefecture with a shower of bridges, tunnels, highways, sewers, and public buildings. Born and reared in Niigata, Tanaka is a Japanese version of Richard Nixon. Without a college degree, he built a multimillion-dollar construction company and lifted himself to the highest political office, only to resign in disgrace amid allegations of kickbacks and bribery. Despite his conviction in the Lockheed scandal, Tanaka has been a formidable *oyabun*, or political boss, as evidenced by his overwhelming reelection to the Diet in December 1983. His ties to Niigata Prefecture are deep and loyal, and he has brought more than his share of public works projects to the area.

With the backing of his local power base, the Etsuzan Kai, and his political connections in Tokyo, Tanaka masterminded the extension of the Jōetsu Bullet Train Line in November 1982, which cut travel time to Tokyo from four to two hours. In 1985 the Kanetsu Expressway to Tokyo was opened, reducing driving time to four hours. The Hokuriku Expressway, which links Nagaoka City to Niigata International Airport to the east, will be extended west to Osaka in 1988. These high-speed links put the Nagaoka Technopolis on the map, since the region's rugged mountains and heavy snowfall no longer pose barriers to companies wishing to relocate outside of Tokyo. For example, automatic deicing machines keep the tracks of the bullet train snowfree during storms. The train has already triggered commercial development around Nagaoka Station, to the delight of Tanaka's supporters and friends. Once a closed society, Niigata Prefecture is opening up to an influx of people, goods, and new ideas.

However, these developments have not come without their critics. The Jōetsu Line has been sharply attacked by politicians and the press because it is a blatant example of Kakuei Tanaka's pork-barrel politics (or "welfare politics," depending on where you stand). Compared to other rural areas, Niigata Prefecture receives a large share of Japan's $60 billion in annual public works projects. Moreover, Tanaka's wheeling-and-dealing has angered local constituents. In the mid-1960s, farmers asked Tanaka to buy their fields along the Shinano River, which were poor and prone to frequent flooding. Tanaka agreed, directing his family-owned Muromachi Industries to buy the land. Soon thereafter, the national government began building a large bridge and dikes along the river. Tanaka, then Minister of Finance, knew of the plans, but remained silent while buying the land. By 1970, when construction was completed, land prices increased tenfold. This alone would have been enough, but Tanaka approached former Mayor Kohei Kobayashi to lobby the Ministry of Construction for approval to develop the river bottom area. When Tanaka's profiteering came to light, local farmers exploded, sending the "Shinano River Bottom Case" to the district court.

Thus, Kakuei Tanaka played a controversial role in the Nagaoka Technopolis, and his politics can be roundly condemned. But the irony remains that, without his political clout, residents of Niigata Prefecture would not have shared in the benefits of Japan's prosperity, and Nagaoka City would never have become a leading Technopolis.

Situated on the Shinano River, which flows northward to the Japan Sea, Nagaoka City does not look like a promising Technopolis site at first glance. It is located in a sparsely populated area and surrounded by farmland. Situated 125 miles north of Tokyo, Nagaoka is the second largest city in Niigata Prefecture, with a population of 180,000. During the Edo period (1600–1868), it was a minor port town and post station on the Nakasendo route that follows the Japan Sea coastline. With the opening of oil fields in the nineteenth century, it became the site of metals, machinery, and chemical industries, all of which are in serious decline. Currently, auto makers such as Honda, Nissan, and Suzuki produce about 80% of the world's supply of speedometers here. Alps Electric, Lambda Electronics, Matsushita, NEC, Nihon Seiki, and Sanyo have opened plants locally. But the city attracts few experienced engineers; almost 90 percent of all local engineering graduates are siphoned off to Tokyo and other big cities.

Nevertheless, Nagaoka has a headstart because of its advance planning. In 1976, several years before MITI conceived the Technopolis Concept, the city initiated a $425 million urban development project to build a new town of 40,000. The project was the first funded by the Japan Regional Development

Corporation, which was established to coordinate industrial planning. Planners chose the sparsely populated Kawanishi District on the western bank of the Shinano River—Kakuei Tanaka's land—for the Nagaoka New Town. With Tanaka's help, roads, sewers, highways, and a bridge linking the east and west banks were rapidly built.

Not so coincidentally, the new town meets the requirements of MITI's Technopolis Concept, and its 1990 target date coincides with that for the technopolises. Former Mayor Kohei Kobayashi, who proposed the idea after visiting a new town outside of Helsinki, Finland in 1971, says: "I didn't have the slightest intention of remodeling our city into a highly industrialized community. At the time, I was more concerned that the exodus of people and industries from Tokyo would spill over into smaller cities. All we did happened to match what is needed for Technopolis." Perhaps; but on paper the Technopolis Concept looks uncannily similar to Kakuei Tanaka's "quarter-million cities" concept and to Nagaoka City. Is this another case of Liberal Democratic Party politicians leading MITI planners?

Nagaoka has several features that make it a leading Technopolis site: a new technical university, innovative R&D funding, close government-industry-university ties, and an aggressive development plan. In 1978, after heated nationwide competition, the city attracted the government-funded Nagaoka University of Science and Technology (NUST), which now has 1,320 students. Modeled after Britain's Cranfield Technical Institute, NUST has become one of Japan's first experimental universities for basic and applied research in machinery, electronics, construction, and management. The university often holds symposiums and invites prominent guest lecturers, such as Soichiryo Honda (President of Honda Motors) to discuss trends in the metals and machine industries—two of Nagaoka's key industries. Unlike other Japanese universities, Nagaoka University actively cultivates ties with local companies, which provide about 20% of its annual funding. In return, university students are assigned to these companies for five months of on-the-job training.

The Ministry of Education is encouraging this trend toward closer university-industry ties. In an experimental project, the Ministry is sponsoring joint research in blue light-emitting diode (LED) semiconductor technology with Nagaoka University, Nihon

Seiki, and twenty-six local venture businesses. Six other joint R&D projects are being conducted at the University's Technology Development Center. The Small- and Medium-Size Business Association, Nagaoka's Industrial Technology Center, and five local firms are working on industrial robots, while another team is focusing on "'frontier" technologies, such as computerized numerically-controlled (CNC) milling machines, flexible manufacturing systems (FMS), super-precision lathes, cylindrical grinders, and sintered carbide tools. To take advantage of Nagaoka's plentiful snow, another team is experimenting with an air conditioning system that retains snow for cooling in the summer. Recently, IBM, Mitsubishi Trading Company, and Cosmos 80 opened a joint lab to train software programmers for their telecommunications joint venture. In the evenings, these researchers can often be seen talking shop at streetside *aka-chochins* (food stalls decorated with red lanterns).

Since MITI announced the Technopolis Concept in 1980, Nagaoka has refined its plans for a high-tech new town. According to Yoshinori Kameyama, assistant counselor at Niigata Prefecture's planning department: "The Nagaoka New Town has evolved into a broader strategy for revitalizing the prefecture's sagging economy. We hope to create the 'Shinano Techno-Valley,' a Japanese version of Silicon Valley, which will extend fifteen miles along the Shinano River between Nagaoka City and Sanjo to the northeast." The focus of this strategy is twofold: to attract new high-tech companies and to upgrade Nagaoka's traditional metalworking cottage factories and farmlands which have slumped since the 1973 oil shock. Nagaoka has targeted three industries for development: mechatronics (the use of electronics in machinery), business information services, and agribusiness. This reindustrialization program will be phased in over fifteen years.

In Phase I (1983–1987), advanced technologies will be introduced to the region's existing industries. Metal and machinery makers, for example, will be encouraged to automate their plants with computers and robots, and to develop new technologies, such as flexible manufacturing systems (FMS), new metals and alloys, electronic agricultural equipment, and medical electronics. MITI and university researchers will work with rice and sake brewers to develop new food products and liquors. Local farmers will be taught new growing techniques for using their crop roughage to generate power for the city's energy grid. New service industries such as architectural, graphic design, engineering, and software firms will be encouraged to open in the Urban Business Complex.

In Phase 2 (1987–1991), Nagaoka will cultivate these new industries. In the service sector, the Nagaoka Technopolis Foundation will fund new software houses and engineering companies, as well as urban, environmental, and industrial design firms to improve the physical design and public services of the Nagaoka New Town and downtown business center. The textile industry will be encouraged to expand into fashion design, specializing in skiwear, rustic apparel, and cold-weather designs. Sake and rice brewers will work with MITI and university researchers to move beyond new foods and liquors into biochemical fertilizers and industrial resins.

Finally, in Phase 3 (1992–2000), Nagaoka plans to develop "next-generation industries": biotechnology, automated fashion design, new materials industries (new metals, ceramics, and alloys), and agribusiness. In this phase, Nagaoka will be a full-fledged Technopolis, complete with a High-Level System Industry Complex, an Urban Business Complex, and an Agri-Industry Complex. The mechatronics industry—the focus of Nagaoka's reindustrialization program —will produce high-level system equipment utilizing computers, optical fibers, and dedicated software for home security systems, cable TV, satellite broadcasting, local energy generation, and office automation. These manufacturers will be supported by a tier of software design houses, venture capital firms, and consultants. Four high-tech parks are being developed in the Shinano Techno-Valley to accommodate the influx of new venture businesses and companies relocating from Tokyo. By 1995, Nagaoka's population is expected to reach 260,000.

These are ambitious plans; but who would come to Nagaoka? Silicon Valley cannot be recreated merely by building new universities, highways, and industrial parks. Nagaoka still is far behind the valley because it lacks a critical mass of talented engineers and entrepreneurs. It is a small city with a "snow country" image and a new technical university unproven in international competition. Why would researchers come when other cities have more to offer? How can Nagaoka overcome Tokyo's irresistible pull?

Rather than compete with Tokyo, Nagaoka's public relations campaign is designed to take advantage of Tokyo's weaknesses: its overcrowding, pollution, high land prices and rents, long commutes, lack of adequate housing and parks, and impersonality. Unable to match Tokyo's top-flight universities, shopping areas, and cultural activities, Nagaoka is appealing to the growing Japanese hunger for a house of one's own (my-home-ism) and a stronger family life. It is employing tactics used by Silicon Valley's rivals—projecting images of a *Better Homes and Gardens* lifestyle, bucolic surroundings, and happy families to attract harried Tokyoites. This message may work if Nagaoka can create enough jobs for its newcomers.

Rather than wait for people to come, Nagaoka is aggressively creating new institutions to attract and cultivate talented people. In 1981 Niigata Prefecture created an Industrial Relocation Promotion Fund to lure companies into the region. In 1982 the Applied Research Foundation was established at Nagaoka University to coordinate joint industry-university research. In March 1983, the Nagaoka Technopolis Foundation was created to provide loan guarantees, technical guidance, and information to small companies conducting high-risk basic R&D. "Recently," says Hiroyoshi Kamekura, Technopolis planner for Nagaoka City, "the Foundation built a Technology Development Center, complete with a clean room for joint semiconductor research."

Nagaoka offers cheap money at bargain-basement prices. According to Nishikata Shinichi, chief of the Nagaoka Technopolis Foundation, venture businesses conducting high-risk R&D can qualify for loans up to $87,000 at 2% interest for eight years. The company is not required to repay the loan if the research fails. A new Nagaoka Technopolis R&D Promotion Fund will offer 4% loans for up to eight years. "High-tech strikers" (advisors)—professors from Nagaoka University and MITI researchers—will offer technical assistance and advice.

Nagaoka already has the reputation of being "where the action is," due to Kakuei Tanaka and former Mayor Kobayashi. However, Professor Fukuoka Masayuki of Komazawa University notes that Kakuei Tanaka and the Etsuzan Kai are giving way to a new generation of Tanaka-style politicians. Tanaka's recent stroke and guilty verdict in the Lockheed trial, the aging of his Etsuzan Kai supporters, and the completion of the Jōetsu Bullet Train Line are weakening his political influence. Many residents of Nagaoka are looking for new leaders who can make Technopolis a success. Ironically, these young politicians are using the same strongman techniques employed by Tanaka.

Nagaoka has a long way to go to catch up with Silicon Valley, but it has made a fast start. As Kenichi Kajima, Nagaoka Technopolis planner, notes: "We residents of Nagaoka are strong people. We must be—to endure the long winters. We are like leaders in a snowstorm. The pioneering group has the toughest job, but someone must plow through the heavy snow if we are to survive. Once the path is cut, everyone else has an easier time."

TOYAMA: REVIVING THE SNOWBELT

A hundred miles southwest of Nagaoka, on a broad plain gently rising from the Nōtō Peninsula to the snow-covered Tateyama mountain range, is the city of Toyama—Nagaoka's rival for the title of "Technopolis on the Japan Sea." With its dramatic mountain range and bright tulip fields, it is one of most picturesque areas in Japan. Each year thousands of tourists flock to its hot springs and towering ski slopes in search of open spaces. To the visitor, Toyama has an air of expansiveness and freedom from the suffocating crowds of Tokyo. It is open sky country, bounded by mountain and sea. As the local train heads southward, one travels deeper into the old Japan. Thatched farm houses dot the countryside and the rolling hills bordering Nagaoka turn into icy precipices that rise thousands of feet above the city. One is reminded of Denver and the Rocky Mountain National Park. But there the comparison ends, because, unlike Denver, Toyama is cut off from the rest of the country, trapped in its snowy isolation because it lacks the political clout that brought the bullet train to Nagaoka's doorstep. Toyama's leaders are still trying to persuade the Japan National Railway to extend the Hokuriku bullet train line from Osaka. But given JNR's huge budget deficit, this lobbying effort faces an uphill battle. Unlike Nagaoka next door, Toyama will have to rely on pure economic strength and grassroots ingenuity, not wheeling and dealing, to revive its stagnant economy with an injection of high technology.

Established as a castle town during the Edo period (1600–1868), Toyama was famous for its itinerant medicine peddlers, who developed "Toyama medicine" into a thriving pharmaceutical industry. Since the turn of the century, it has been one of the leading manufacturing centers and shipping ports on the Japan Sea coast. Consisting of two major cities (Toyama and Takaoka) and four small towns, Toyama Prefecture has 7,200 companies and a population of 1.1 million. Its industrial base is similar to that of Gary, Indiana. Almost 80% of its shipments are concentrated in heavy industries such as steel, metals, chemicals, textiles, paper, coal, and machinery. As a result, Toyama has declined economically since World War II. In 1942 it ranked ninth in industrial output among Japan's forty-seven prefectures. By 1980 it had fallen to twenty-sixth place. Although Toyama has many internationally known companies, such as YKK (zippers), Suzuki Motors (motorcycles), NEC (electronic circuit boards), Nachi-Fujikoshi ("Uni-man" robots), Fujisawa Pharmaceutical (antibiotics), they are not creating enough new jobs. In 1982 only 40% of the region's college graduates were able to find jobs locally.

To revitalize its slumping economy, Toyama has planned its Technopolis in a business-like manner. In 1981 local industry and government leaders reviewed Toyama's industrial problems so as to chart the region's future. With the help of Tokyo University Professor Ibo Ishii (member of MITI's Technopolis '90 Committee), the prefecture developed an industrial strategy based on three next-generation industries: mechatronics, new materials, and biotechnology. This approach builds upon Toyama's traditional strengths. For example, over 1,100 machinery makers are focusing their research on mechatronics—industrial robots, numerically-controlled machines, medical equipment, computerized machining centers, and flexible manufacturing systems (FMS). In the field of new materials, Toyama's 1,800 mining and metals companies are developing new metals, sophisticated resins, and fine ceramics. In biotechnology, Toyama Medical and Pharmaceutical College and 128 chemical and pharmaceutical companies, such as Nippon Gene and Fujisawa, are conducting joint research at the Biotechnology Research Center. Unlike Nagaoka, which is forced to woo companies from Tokyo to develop its new city, Toyama is pursuing a bootstrap approach. It is encouraging local industries to develop their own grassroots technology.

Toyama has ambitious plans for its five Technopolis development zones. The core of the Technopolis area is the Kureha-Imizu Hills Research Park, which is the site of Toyama University, Toyama Medical School, and the Pharmaceutical Research Institute. This area, which features the Taikoyama New Town, will become the incubator for venture businesses. Currently, major pharmaceutical companies such as Kokando, Toyama Chemicals, Nichiko, and Japan Pharmaceuticals, are conducting biotechnology research with local universities. Several companies have located in the new industrial park built near Toyama Airport, which has daily flights to Tokyo and Seoul. South of the airport is the Toyama-Yatsuo Industrial Park, which has attracted twelve major companies, such as Fujisawa Pharmaceuticals, Hokuriku Electric, Showa Radio, and Toyama Chemicals. This industrial park is served by the Kosugi Distribution Area, a warehousing and transportation point, and the Toyama Airport Industrial Park. The fifth area is the Nishiyama New Town, the site of Takaoka College and the Industrial Technology Center, which is being developed into a research park.

These plans are ambitious, and they carry a high price tag. According to Toyama officials, the Technopolis areas will cost $4 billion, or $200 million a year—two-thirds of the cost for the Tsukuba Science City. By comparison, MITI's entire budget in 1984 for the Technopolis program was a miniscule $6.5 million, of which very little went to Toyama. Thus, the financing will be the major obstacle. Where will Toyama get the funds? About half will come the prefecture, 30% from local cities and towns, 10% from the central government, and the remainder from public corporations, companies, and fundraising activities. Toyama has imposed a regional "Technopolis tax" to finance these projects.

Like Nagaoka, Toyama is also pursuing a "soft" infrastructure strategy that consists of establishing new industry associations, funding high-risk research, expanding academic research facilities, retraining workers, encouraging cooperation among industry, government, and academia, and promoting conferences and plant siting. Toyama is fairly generous with its funding. The Toyama Technology Development Foundation and Venture Enterprise Corporation (VEC) offer three types of R&D financing:

interest-free loans for applied research, loan guarantees for large-scale, high-risk research, and seed financing for basic research. According to Seiji Hamamatsu, a Technopolis planner for Toyama Prefecture: "We've had good luck so far. About $1.7 million has been granted to over seventy-five companies since 1976, but the failure rate has been only 10% because our review committee has done a good job screening applicants and providing management and marketing advice."

These research projects are funneled through a variety of new research associations that have been established recently, as shown in Table 7-1. To encourage innovative research, Toyama Prefecture awards the Toyama Novel Prize each year. Recently, the prefecture also set up four talent data banks to secure top-level researchers for its joint R&D projects: a Leadership Data Bank of potential project managers; an Industrial Technology Data Bank of industrial technologies and patents; a Toyama Researcher Data Bank of Toyama-born researchers; and a Recruiting Data Bank of science or engineering graduates from Toyama. The goal of these programs is to identify and lure homesick researchers back to the fold. Apparently the idea is contagious, since all of the technopolises have established "Come Back Home" offices in the major cities.

Thus, Toyama is making great strides in its Technopolis plans. Despite its heavy snowfall and declining industries, its leaders have adopted a "never-say-die" attitude. They are out to prove that Toyama's former industrial might was not a historical fluke. But what really sets Toyama apart from other Japanese cities is not the close collaboration between government and industry nor its comprehensive planning, but its eye for beauty. When walking through its streets, one is struck by the bronze statues and stone sculptures gracing the landscaped paths that meander along the city's main river. After being in crowded Japanese cities, it is Toyama's small touches—the riverside walkways, the public sculptures, the rolling greenbelts—that stick in one's mind. In the rush to build its Technopolis, it is reassuring to know that Toyama has taken the time to enrich the lives of its people with a top-flight modern art museum, a gymnastics center, and cultural amenities. Perhaps it is the influence of the *Manyō-shū*, a collection of ancient poems, which recalls the "'Manyo spirit" of Sukune Yakamochi, whose poems praised Toyama's spectacular mountain

Table 7-1.
New R&D Associations in the Toyama Technopolis.

1981	Hokuriku Machinery Center
1982	Technology Development Project Research Association
1982	Biotechnology Promotion Association
1983	Food Research Laboratory
1983	Regional Frontier Technology Development Association
1985	New Materials Industrial Technology Center
1985	Pharmaceutical Research Laboratory

Source: Toyama Prefecture

scenery and closeness to nature. In contemporary Japan, with its heated competition and blind materialism, that sense of proportion and balance is refreshing indeed.

OKAYAMA:
THE BIOTECHNOLOGY CAPITAL

In front of Okayama station, which lies an hour and a half west of Kyoto by the bullet train, is a statue of Momotaro the Peach Boy, the hero of one of Japan's most famous folktales. As the story goes, Momotaro pops out of a large peach found floating down the river and grows up to become a strong young man under the care and guidance of a kindly old couple. One day, he goes off to conquer the ogres on Devil Island with the help of a dog, a monkey, a pheasant—and a generous supply of *Kibi dango* (Okayama rice dumplings) made by his stepmother. Like all children's stories, Momotaro teaches a moral. He is held up to Japanese children as a shining example of courage and kindness to elders, a symbol of the relentless striving and fortitude required to overcome life's many obstacles.

Not far from the statue of Momotaro, tucked away among the hotels and warehouses in the Shimoishii district near Okayama station, is a modern-day version of Momotaro: the Hayashibara Biochemical Company. Founded by Katsutaro Hayashibara in 1883 as a small, family-operated rice syrup factory, the Hayashibara Company epitomizes the willingness to take risks in the search for excellence and creativity in biotechnology research. It is the rallying point for the Okayama Technopolis and a classic example of the local Peach Boy who made good.

The Hayashibara Company is one of the largest and most financially secure venture businesses in Japan. With annual sales of 10 billion yen ($50 million), the biochemical company forms the nucleus of the $125 million Hayashibara Group, which plays a major role in the Okayama economy. The company made its start by using barley malt to convert starch into syrup. During the 1930s Ichiro Hayashibara studied starch chemistry under Professor Hitoshi Matsumoto of Kyoto University and expanded the company's product line to acid conversion starch syrups which were sold throughout Asia. Mass production grew steadily, but on June 29, 1945, a B-29 bombing raid reduced the entire city—and Hayashibara's plant—to ashes.

After World War II Hayashibara quickly rebuilt his plant and founded the Kabaya Confectionaries Company, a 100% owned subsidiary, to produce hippopotamus-shaped (*kaba* design) confections that were popular among children. The company grew rapidly, putting it third in market share behind Morinaga and Meiji Seika. He also established an array of diverse companies, including the Japanese Research Institute for Photosensitizing Dyes, Taiyo Estate Company, Showa Transportation and Warehouse Company, and Desaki Development Company. However, before he could consolidate his efforts, Ichiro Hayashibara passed away of cancer in 1961, leaving management of the company to his twenty-year-old son, Ken, who was studying law at Keio University.

True to the Momotaro legend, Ken Hayashibara rose to the occasion and has become somewhat of a folk hero in Japan—ranking with Sony's Akio Morita, Kyocera's Kazuo Inamori, fashion designers Hanae Mori and Issey Miyake, and Sord Computer's Takashi Shiina—as an example of Japan's creative new business leaders. Building upon the company's expertise in fermentation, microorganism culturing, and sugar and starch refining techniques, Hayashibara transformed his traditional starch syrup, candies, and glucose company into a highly diversified, innovative biotechnology research center. The move came when the Japanese government, which had kept starch prices artificially high to protect domestic potato farmers, liberalized its sugar imports in the early 1960s, throwing Hayashibara and other companies into the red and bankrupting farmers. Scrambling for new markets, Hayashibara applied an approach used by oil companies to dissolve crude oil into petrochemical products. The idea was to transform starch into glucose and combine it with other substances to develop new products. Hayashibara pursued a twofold business strategy: he invested profits from the company's large real estate holdings into biotechnology research, and plowed the patent royalties into more R&D.

In 1965 Hayashibara established the Hayashibara Biochemical Laboratories to conduct basic research, using its expertise in enzymes to produce an intravenous, high-purity maltose syrup for diabetics. The laboratory has been highly successful. To date, it has submitted over 4,000 patent applications in thirty-seven countries, and has won numerous awards for its creative new products, including low-calorie sweeteners, starch sugars, and pullulan (a starch-based, edible, water-soluble, and biodegradable plastic material for wrapping food and medical supplies). The company's Japanese Research Institute for Photosensitizing Dyes has developed cyanine dyes used for hair growth stimulants and cell activators in cosmetics. According to Mr. Akaru Mand Yabani, a researcher from Pakistan who graduated from Tokyo University and has lived in Japan for over twenty years, Hayashibara applies for about twenty to twenty-five patents per month. "We are more interested in developing and selling new processes than commercializing them, which larger pharmaceutical companies can do better anyway." To ensure a steady flow of patents, the company invests about 20% of its annual sales in research and development.

Hayashibara's major contribution to the field of biotechnology has been its innovative research into drugs for fighting cancer— the cause of Ichiro Hayashibara's death. In 1975, under the guidance of Professor Yasuichi Nagano of Tokyo University (who discovered interferon in the early 1950s) and Professor Tsunataro Kishida of Kyoto Prefectural University of Medicine, Hayashibara pursued the goal of commercializing interferon for cancer and viral research. At the time, only minute traces of interferon could be produced by extracting it from large quantities of white blood corpuscles or tank-cultured fibroblast. Most pharmaceutical companies had given up the costly search, but the Hayashibara research team persevered, reasoning that the traditional method of transplanting human cells into animals might be used to grow new cells. Their hypothesis was correct. In 1980, after repeated trial and error, Hayashibara developed a method for mass-producing interferon using hamsters, widely known among medical circles as the "Hayashibara Hamster System." According to Dr. Masashi Kurimoto, director of Hayashibara's Fujisaki Institute, the method involves treating newborn hamsters with immune-suppressing agents, then injecting them with human cells. In four week, the lymphoblastoid cells are surgically removed and processed for their interferon. One hamster produces as much interferon as 200 human blood donors, and can give birth to ten babies at a time, offering a cheap method for producing large quantities of interferon quickly. The cost of producing one vial of interferon using this method is only 40 cents, one hundredth the cost of traditional methods. Interferon is used in cancer research, but the primary focus today is its effectiveness against viruses.

Hayashibara has not given up its hunt for a cancer cure. In 1981 the company signed an agreement with Otsuka Pharmaceutical and Mochida Pharmaceutical companies of Tokyo to mass produce interferon and new bioactive agents. In 1982 it expanded the Fujisaki Institute, where the company can breed up to 50,000 hamsters capable of producing 50% of the world's annual supply of interferon. In April 1986 the company began construction of a $40 million interferon production plant and research lab in Okayama's Kibi Highlands Technopolis.

This expansion comes at a crucial time. In 1983 Prime Minister Nakasone announced an all-out "war on cancer," which is a major killer of Japan's aging population. Hayashibara has joined the fight against this modern-day "island of ogres." Currently, it is focusing on a new cancer-killing drug, Carcino-Breaking Factor (CBF), a glycoprotein accidentally discovered by Hayashibara in 1981 from what it thought were impurities from interferon. Mochida Pharmaceutical, its partner, has conducted experiments on leukemic rats demonstrating CBF's antitumor effectiveness. Other potential anticancer agents being researched include Tumor Necrosis Factor (TNE), and Interleukin 2 (IL2), a bioactive substance that strengthens the immune reaction in humans. Hayashibara will need all the hamsters it can raise to conduct cancer research while still meeting the market demand for its interferon.

With Hayashibara as its centerpiece, Okayama officials are planning to transform the city into Japan's biotechnology center, or "Bio Plain," with an emphasis on bioengineering, medical equipment, and physical rehabilitation. The city's nine universities and world-class Okayama University Medical School make it an ideal site for biomedical research. According to Namba Eiji, Technopolis planner for Okayama Prefecture: "We're behind other technopolises, but we're catching up. Recently, Hayashibara and other companies formed an industry association and are working closely with the Okayama Medical School and Okayama University." In 1984 the prefecture established a Science and Technology Forum, and in 1985 the Biotechnology Lab and the Kibi Highland Life Science Hall to promote joint R&D in biotechnology. Hayashibara may be the local Dr. William Shockley that the city needs to achieve its goals.

The collaboration is already beginning to pay off. In June 1984 an Okayama Medical School team headed by Professor Orita Kunzo reported to the Japan Society of Chemotherapy that OH-1, a bioactive substance developed by Hayshibara Biochemical Laboratories using its hamster implantation method, was effective in curing cancer. In the experiment, OH-1 was tested against several other drugs on mice treated with transplanted cancer cells. The medical school team found that, compared with the other drugs, fewer cancer cells spread and weaker side-effects were observed using OH-1. Hayashibara plans to form a link with a pharmaceutical company to commercialize the drug after further trials.

Okayama City is speeding up its Technopolis plans because of the urgency of Hayashibara's cancer research. Traditionally overshadowed by Japan's larger cities, Okayama is a regional castle town known more for its white peaches, Muscat grapes, and *Kibi dango* than the world-class medical research being conducted at the Okayama University Medical School. But this situation is rapidly changing. In 1973 the bullet train was extended to Okayama, bringing it to within four and a half hours of Tokyo and one hour from Osaka. In 1987 the Seto Bridge will be completed to the island of Shikoku, making Okayama a transportation center for western Honshu; and a new Okayama Airport will be built near the Technopolis site in 1988. A new Kibi railway line will link the Technopolis to downtown Okayama.

Okayama City has another ace up its sleeve. Of all the technopolises, it has the best insight into "what makes Silicon Valley
tick" because of its strong Sister City ties with San Jose, California, dating to the early 1960s. During the last twenty years, hundreds of students, professors, researchers, and teachers have
exchanged information at all levels, enabling them to break
down the cultural barriers that often hinder U.S.-Japan relations
at the national level. Indeed, for me, Okayama City is like a
second home. During the mid-1970s I spent two years teaching
and studying at Okayama University as an exchange teacher
from San Jose. I have seen the sister city relationship blossom
into a genuine partnership. In 1985 both cities signed a "Twin
Chamber of Commerce Program" to encourage mutual business
investment and joint research. With biotechnology companies
springing up around Stanford University, Okayama will undoubtedly become a channel for joint U.S.-Japan biotechnology
research in the future. Recently, Hayashibara and consumer
giant Matsushita Electronics teamed up to develop a hot new
field: bioelectronics. They have already announced a method for
using organic materials to develop biosensors for medical testing and polyresists to etch fine-line chip patterns on silicon
wafers. Eventually, we will probably see a similar convergence
of electronics and biotechnology in Silicon Valley, especially
due to the challenge from Japan. Will Silicon Valley become
"Bio Valley" in the twenty-first century?

The Kibi Highland New Town is slowly beginning to take
shape. Located fifteen miles northwest of Okayama City, the new
town will consist of research institutes, a health-rehabilitation
complex, housing areas, a commercial center, and natural recreational parks. The basic infrastructure of roads, water, and utilities
is already in place, but the industrial sites are mostly vacant,
except for Matsushita and Kibi NC, which recently opened
research labs in the complex. Eventually, when the new airport is
built, new companies will be attracted to the Kibi Highland New
Town. As Mr. Yabani of Hayashibara explains: "In Japan, we have
what you call a "master-apprentice" (*banto-dechi*) relationship
between parent companies and their subsidiaries, a custom which
goes back to the Edo period (1600–1868). Unlike Silicon Valley,
where start-up companies often fight with their parent companies, Japanese parent companies usually help establish and train

their subsidiaries. Thus, one parent company may give rise to many smaller subsidiaries."

The ultimate goal of the Okayama Technopolis is to develop a high-tech research town that specializes in biotechnology and health-related areas, including pharmaceuticals, medical instruments, rehabilitation equiment for the mentally and physically retarded, electronic diagnostic equipment, and artificial limbs and organs. In 1986 a rehabilitation center for disabled workers will be built, joining Kibi NC, which is currently using computerized equipment to rehabilitate handicapped people.

Thus, Okayama's Technopolis is growing up, and like the little Peach Boy who once floated down the river, Hayashibara has taken the lead in helping the old, disabled, and handicapped. Perhaps it is symbolic that the Hayashibara Biochemical Company is the focal point for this Technopolis, for its president and staff are quite unlike those of any other company. Today it is one of the most creative companies in Japan. But, in its search for excellence, it has not lost its broader perspective. In front of its Fujisaki Institute stands a cenotaph dedicated to the millions of hamsters that have been sacrificed to save human lives. Once a year, in a short ceremony, Hayashibara and his research team gather around the monument, their heads bowed, to pray for the souls of their little helpers.

HIROSHIMA: A BLOSSOMING OF SOFTWARE HOUSES

"Mamonaku, Hiroshima desu! Next stop, Hiroshima!"

The falsetto voice of the female announcer on the bullet train awakens the slumbering passenger from a daydream. Or is it a dream? From the winter mists, the busy skyline of Hiroshima emerges like a ghost, its seven-fingered alluvial fan reaching out into the steely waters of the Inland Sea. The morning is gray and snowy. It is hard to imagine that this is ground zero, the site of so much suffering and hardship. Like the proverbial phoenix rising from the ashes, the city has undergone a total rebirth. Shiny new high-rises and department stores line the major boulevards, and well-dressed pedestrians stroll through elegant shopping malls overflowing with goods. Everyone appears oblivious of the Atomic Bomb Dome in the distance, which is barely visible behind a forest of office buildings. The pockmarks on the face of the city have been neatly covered over with a veneer of glistening steel and glass.

"Don't be fooled," says the taxicab driver, who hails from Yamaguchi, the prefecture next door. "Hiroshima may look like any other Japanese city, but the people are different—even us newcomers who didn't experience the bombing. We are more melancholy—and yet more adventurous and willing to take risks. Maybe it's because of the hard times we went through. Maybe because we don't know if there will be a tomorrow. I don't know. That's the dark side of the war that nobody likes to talk about."

The dark side of the war—the phrase often pops up in conversations whenever one speaks with Hiroshima residents. Like the Atomic Bomb Dome in Peace Park, the war has left an indelible mark in the minds of the city's residents, a mark that is ignored in everyday life, but one that is not easily forgotten. For years, I have known Japanese-American survivors of the bomb living in San Francisco, and listened to their experiences, but even the most vivid imagination cannot compare with the black-and-white images in the Atomic Bomb Museum. There, pictures speak louder than words. When I meet with Hiroshima residents, I sense a reluctance to speak about the past. Yet it is this very legacy— this struggle for survival and this uncertainty about the future— that has shaped their lives. It must be understood, for it touches the heart of high technology, and gives Hiroshima a special dynamism to create something where nothing existed before.

This latent energy can be seen in the city's push toward high technology. In the last few years there has been a veritable blossoming of computer software houses in Hiroshima. According to MITI, there were thirty-five software houses in 1982; by March 1984 the number had jumped to 81. By early 1986, there were over 120 companies. Why the sudden increase in software companies? And why in Hiroshima, which is better known for shipbuilding and automobiles than high technology? What are the reasons for this sudden blossoming of entrepreneurialism?

For answers to this puzzling situation, I met with Toshiaki Hosoda, President of the Hiroshima Software Industry Association, who observes: "Hiroshima people are adventurous compared to people from other parts of western Japan, especially the young people. Often they're willing to leave a secure job to start up their own company. It's a kind of local custom. These people work for computer makers or banks that have data processing centers. They save enough money to open their own storefront shop, and start doing subcontracting work for banks, insurance companies, or computer makers. Then they quit their jobs. It's fairly easy to find work, since there aren't enough good programmers around. Many companies have computer systems, but they don't have qualified people who can write software. Most of the founders of the software companies in our association are in their late twenties to early forties. The average age is probably around 35."

Japanese entrepreneurs? For years, the American news media have told us that Japanese aren't very entrepreneurial, especially in software. Perhaps the media are asleep: within one mile of Shinjuku station in Tokyo, MITI officials tell me that there are over 2,000 software start-up companies, mostly tiny storefront offices. What is remarkable about the software boom in Hiroshima is its spontaneity and independence from corporate sponsorship—a phenomenon more typical of Silicon Valley start-ups than venture businesses in Tokyo, which are usually subsidiaries of larger companies. MITI and Hiroshima Prefecture, scratching their heads about this rush of entrepreneurialism, commissioned the Nomura Research Institute to conduct a survey of seventy-one software houses. According to the study, most of the companies began within the last few years with minimal capital. About two-thirds started with less than $20,000, and 11% had as little as $10,000. Most work out of small storefront offices in downtown Hiroshima. In general, they are concentrated in computers, office automation, and inspection and measuring equipment. As elsewhere in Japan, the major headache is finding qualified programmers and training facilities.

To meet this demand for programmers, local software firms formed the Hiroshima Software Industry Association in 1984. Consisting of eighty-one software companies and sixteen major computer makers, the Association offers training, low-cost loans, and ideas about commercial applications. In April 1984 the Association opened an office with the Hiroshima Prefecture Small- and Medium-Size Business Information Center and MITI's Japan Information Center Association, a consortium of large computer makers. The goal is to improve the level of software programming among local machinery makers, shipbuilders, and car makers. Major computer firms are rushing to open software development centers to grab a share of the deregulated telecommunications market. NEC plans to increase its staff in Hiroshima from sixty people to 190 by 1986. Fujitsu's team will leap from forty people to 200, and IBM and Mitsubishi are opening a central software school to train programmers for their value-added network system.

This wave of software houses is only part of Hiroshima's larger effort to organize grassroots technologies. In 1983 the Hiroshima Technology Exchange Plaza, a group of small and medium-sized companies, experienced a sudden revival. The group provides advice on marketing, new technologies, management techniques, and product development. It sponsors joint R&D in plastic production robots (Sanyo Industries/Kakihara), printing and adhesives (Dai-Ichi Graphics/Sanwa Industries), and plating factory automation (Fuji Metals/Sanyo Industries). At the same time, Mazda, Matsushita Electronics, and twelve other manufacturers formed an "Innovation Team" to develop advanced manufacturing systems. They are sharing information on totally-automated plants. Another group, the Hiroshima Service Industry Research Association, is advising local shipbuilders and steelmakers on ways to retrain and redeploy their workers in design and maintenance services for industrial robots, office automation, telecommunications, and automated production equipment. A fourth group, the Industrial Technology Center, is exploring "frontier" technologies, such as mechatronics, computer-aided design (CAD), minicomputers, graphic display terminals, fine ceramics, lasers, and fiber optics.

The real heart of Hiroshima's industrial strategy is the Hiroshima Central Technopolis. Located in an undeveloped countryside ten miles east of Hiroshima City, the 260-square-mile area is divided into four Technopolis zones: the Kamo Academic City, a zone with two industrial parks, a new residential town, and the Kure port city. The Kamo Academic City, dubbed "Tsukuba of the West," is the site of a new research complex that includes Hiroshima University's science and engineering departments, an Innovation Park, MITI's testing lab, and a Techno-Center for industrial training programs. From the air the complex looks like a mini-

Tsukuba surrounded by rolling green hills. Research will focus on five "frontier" technologies: electronics, alternative energies, new materials, mechatronics, and biotechnology. According to Nori-yuki Okada, Hiroshima Technopolis planner, Chugoku System Engineering, NEC, Sharp, and twenty-five other private research institutes have already moved to the Kamo Academic City and the nearby industrial parks. In 1982 the Audio Equipment Research Lab was formed. Since 1983 the Hiroshima Innovation Team (HIT) has been investigating commercial uses for carbon fibers. Eventually Hiroshima plans to create an International Materials Research Lab that will become a mecca for car makers, shipbuilders, audio equipment manufacturers, and machine manufacturers.

Surrounding the Kamo Academic City are the support areas. A new town of 15,000 people will be built in Takaya to the east. The western Shiwa/Hachihonmatsu zone will provide housing, shipping, and industrial sites. The Kurose site to the south will be a greenbelt valley of industrial research parks and satellite towns. To the southeast, the towns of Akitsu and Takehara will be the centers for new foods and aquaculture. Hiroshima will be the "father city," and the port city of Kure the "mother city." To improve access, the Trans-Chugoku Freeway linking Hiroshima to Osaka was completed in 1983, and a new bullet train station and airport will be built near the Kamo Academic City.

Because of its prime location, the major problem facing Hiroshima is high land prices. Like Hamamatsu City, Hiroshima has not purchased all of the land required for the Technopolis, a situation that will undoubtedly lead to land speculation and higher project costs. Currently, the budget for the Kamo Academic City and its support zones will be a staggering $1.2 billion for the first phase (1983–1990) alone, or $172 million per year. In an era of fiscal stringency, one must ask whether Hiroshima has the financial resources to build this costly Technopolis. Already the prefecture has delayed its plans beyond MITI's 1990 target date to the year 2000. Even with this delay, there is a possibility that the project could be scaled down.

However, after meeting with local industry leaders and seeing the relentless construction going on throughout the region, one does not worry whether Hiroshima's Technopolis will succeed. Ultimately it will, for Hiroshima residents have been through tougher times since the war. They have shown the world how to build a new life upon the nuclear ashes of the past. Indeed, what they bring to the Technopolis process—and to Japan's search for high technology —is something far more valuable than bricks and mortar, or the software and mechatronics, they will create. It is a vision of the destructive power of technology misused and its potential for building anew that, in the long run, may be its most important contribution.

YAMAGUCHI: THE RISE OF THE PHOENIX

The rivers and mountains glide by as we hurtle westward on the bullet train toward the City of Ogōri. From the window, the beauty of Yamaguchi Prefecture seduces the traveler with its understated charm. The countryside is clean and spacious, a pastel of hazy blue mountains and winding rivers. For the newcomer, accustomed to the hustle and bustle of Japan's larger cities, the change is invigorating. With its stately farmhouses pressed up against a sea of ricefields, the prefecture has a peaceful, almost dreamlike quality.

Located on the western tip of Honshu island, Yamaguchi Prefecture is deceptively humble in appearance. It seems no more than a string of tiny villages and heavy industrial ports going into decline. But behind the facade, hidden from sight, is a powerful legacy that drives its residents with steely resolve; for Yamaguchi was once the stronghold of warlords who challenged Japan's central government. Under the Ōuchi family (1336–1550), Yamaguchi became a political and cultural center for western Japan. Their castle town at Yamaguchi, designed in imitation of Kyoto, was a favorite stopover for traveling noblemen. Later, under the Mōri family (1550–1868), Yamaguchi became the center of the Sengoku warlords who controlled western Honshu. Although dissolved by Ieyasu Tokugawa in the seventeenth century, Yamaguchi (then known as Chōshū) became the base for anti-Shogun forces that eventually overthrew the Tokugawa shogunate in 1868.

The Mōri family left a political legacy that has deeply influenced Japanese society. A breeding ground for strong leaders,

Yamaguchi was the birthplace of Japan's first prime minister, Hirobumi Itō, and two postwar prime ministers: Nobusuke Kishi (1957-1960) and his younger brother, Eisaku Sato (1964–1972). Less known, however, is the profound impact the Mōri family has had on Yamaguchi's cities. As Katsuji Yuda, Ube Technopolis Planning Director, notes: "Unlike other prefectures, Yamaguchi doesn't have one major city, but many small cities. This pattern was caused by the political fortunes of the Mōri family, who moved their castle town to Hagi, but were later forced to retreat by Ieyasu Tokugawa. After the famous Battle of Sekigahara in 1600, their forces were careful not to gather in one location to avoid arousing suspicion. So the population never became concentrated, as in Osaka or Tokyo."

To take advantage of its scattered population and cheap land, Yamaguchi Prefecture is building a multicentered Technopolis that reflects the region's agricultural ethos of local participation and sharing. In a sense, Yamaguchi residents all belong to one family: the legendary Mōri family. This sense of regional kinship was dramatically illustrated in 1980 when local officials called a public hearing to discuss Yamaguchi's Technopolis plans. As Governor Toru Hirai explains: "Over 1,000 residents and industry leaders showed up. Fortunately, we were able to arrive at a consensus about the region's future direction at an early stage." The outcome was a classic example of Japanese collective decision-making. All of the participating groups donated money to prepare the Technopolis plan—private industry contributed $2.6 million, Yamaguchi Prefecture $2.0 million, and local towns and villages $2.0 million. Determined to see Yamaguchi rise again, they chose a slogan that everyone could rally around: the Ube Phoenix Technopolis.

The name dramatizes the urgency of their mission. Until the early 1950s Yamaguchi was a major coal mining center, but gradually shifted to cement, steel, petrochemicals, caustic soda, and other heavy materials. In 1980 these products accounted for two-thirds of the prefecture's industrial output, making it the second highest in Japan. Since the 1979 oil shock, these industries have undergone a serious decline, sending industry leaders scrambling to rebuild the prefecture's sagging economy.

Yamaguchi's industrial strategy is ambitious: to create a local "technology explosion" similar to the one during the Meiji period

(1868–1911) when Japan opened to the West. To achieve this goal, the prefecture is building the Ube Phoenix Technopolis—a new high-tech region centered around Yamaguchi University and consisting of industrial parks, research institutes, housing, and recreational areas. Unlike Hiroshima next door, the Ube Phoenix Technopolis will not be concentrated in one new town, but distributed over a peninsula overlooking the Inland Sea. The Technopolis encompasses the city of Ube, the "mother city," and seven neighboring towns covering an area of 400 square miles. It will be a grid of eight high-tech parks tied together by a network of "Techno-roads." In 1980 there were approximately 408,000 people living within the Technopolis zone, a figure expected to reach 560,000 by the year 2000.

The focal point of the Ube Phoenix Technopolis will be the central development zone, a 7.5-square-mile site where the prefecture will build the Yamaguchi Science City, an international conference hall (Techno-Center), the Sayama and Setobara industrial parks, R&D complexes, and the Obayama New Town housing area. Construction is scheduled to begin in 1985 and will continue to the year 2000. Yamaguchi University, which will form the core of the academic new town, will relocate its medical school and departments of science, engineering, and agriculture to the Ube Technopolis in 1986. The Tokyo Science University will open a electronics production engineering college in 1987. Currently, Yamaguchi University is conducting basic research in lasers, optoelectronics, genetic engineering, ceramic engines, plasma reactors, solar power generation, and robotics. Adjacent to the university is the Yamaguchi Technology Promotion Fund (the project's nerve center) and the Techno-Center, which sponsors symposiums, training programs, trade fairs, and a technology house to promote scientific exchanges with visiting researchers. On hilly sites overlooking the Inland Sea, the Setobara and Sayama industrial parks will be built cluster-style. In these zones priority is given to companies that are conducting research in any of eight target industries: electronics, new materials, software, mechatronics, fine chemicals, biotechnology, energy, and ocean development.

The seven towns surrounding the Central Development Zone serve primarily as support areas, offering "overflow" industrial parks and housing sites. To the south, Ube City is a major transportation and commercial center, with its airport, shopping malls, cultural plaza, parks, and port facilities. Six other industrial parks will be built throughout the Technopolis zone, and telecommunications systems will link the three largest cities in a "Triangle Teletopia Concept."

Although existing infrastructure will be used wherever possible to reduce project costs, the Ube Phoenix Technopolis still has a hefty price tag of $1.3 billion. The science city alone will cost $190 million, and the seven industrial parks $180 million altogether. To reduce this financial burden, Yamaguchi plans to stretch out its plans over an eighteen-year period—ten years past MITI's target goal of 1990. The prefecture will finance 24% of the total amount, local cities and towns 20%, local industry 21%, and the remainder the national government and public corporations.

Like the other technopolises, Yamaguchi lacks a critical mass of top-level researchers and scientists. Although the prefecture has twenty-three government research labs, fifty research companies, and forty-three corporate labs, they are scattered throughout the region. These will be concentrated in the new science city. To lure superior researchers to the Ube Technopolis, Yamaguchi established a "Techno VIP" program in 1983. According to local planner Tsutomu Yoshitomi, the prefecture pays for research facilities, funding, conference fees, and testing labs to promote basic research in the eight target industries. It also offers low-priced land sites to companies for high-quality housing, condominiums, and resort villas as well as golf courses, country clubs, and a marine resort village on the Inland Sea. Yamaguchi's major advantage over other Technopolis sites is its inexpensive land and beautiful surroundings. So far, its industry recruitment campaign is beginning to work. In 1982 Mazda opened an auto plant, and NEC recently invested $150 million in a 256K VLSI chip manufacturing plant. Other new companies include Japan Kanizen and the Yamaguchi Computing Center.

Thus, Yamaguchi Prefecture is making a major effort to bring its heavy industries into the twenty-first century by upgrading their technological base and encouraging them to shift into high-growth markets. Instead of dumping them, Yamaguchi is building on their years of experience. For the Appalachians and the steel-making regions in the Northwest, the "Yamaguchi experiment" is worth watching closely, not only because of its grassroots industrial strategy, but also because of its surprisingly un-Japanese vision of the future:

> The philosophy underlying the Technopolis Concept is essentially one of change and creativity. Japanese society must be reformed. We must respect individual values and those of small, unique groups, but reform only comes from individual action. In order for our Technopolis to succeed, we must develop concrete policies to attract talented people. . . . In short, Technopolis means to create an environment where people can be creative, where business and pleasure are one and the same. For creative business people, business is pleasure.

This chapter has dealt with the leading technopolises on the main island of Honshu. Now let's look at the southern island of Kyushu—Silicon Island—which is Japan's major producer of silicon chips and Silicon Valley's major competitor.

8

S I L I C O N I S L A N D

> Microchips are the rice of industry.
>
> *Governor Morihiko Hiramatsu*
> *of Oita Prefecture*

JAPAN'S SOUTHERN GATE

The bullet train thunders westward past the low-lying hills and coastal waters of Yamaguchi Prefecture, heading toward the Kammon Strait that separates the main island of Honshu from the southern island of Kyushu. As we approach the high suspension bridge at Shimonoseki ("the Southern Gate") the placid waters of the Inland Sea suddenly turn treacherous with riptides, endangering even the heavy freighters and crude oil tankers that lumber through the narrow straits. To foreigners there is nothing special about the bustling port at Shimonoseki, but to Japanese it marks a major turning point in the nation's history. It was here, at the famous Battle of Dan-no-Ura in 1185, that the emerging Minamoto clan defeated the powerful Taira navy, setting the stage for a new feudal regime. Although inferior in numbers and naval strength, the Minamoto forces were rallied by a brilliant strategist, Yoshitsune, whose sharp eye for tactical advantage led to a surprise victory. In the swirling waters of the strait, the Minamoto turned back a savage attack and descended upon the Taira in the turning tide, totally decimating the fleet.

Centuries have passed since that eventful battle, but the lesson of Dan-no-Ura has not been forgotten by the governors and industry leaders of Kyushu, whose heavy industries have been in severe decline since World War II. In industry after industry—coal mining, steel, chemicals, shipbuilding, textiles, and lumber

173

products—Kyushu has been battered by new competitors in international markets. Now, like Yoshitsune, Kyushu's leaders are repositioning their industries by riding the turning tide that is changing the face of Japan. They are luring back talented people from the major cities to inject their sunset industries with a shot of new technologies. Since the early 1970s, when the mass exodus to Tokyo came to a halt, Japanese have begun returning to their home towns. Known as "U-turn" workers, these college graduates and young professionals—Japan's yuppies—as well as retirees and second-career professionals are rejecting the impersonality and rat race of Tokyo and Osaka for the more friendly, leisurely atmosphere of regional cities. They want to pursue their careers while at the same time renewing their ties with family and friends. This desire for a more balanced personal and family life, known as "my-home-ism," is perhaps the major driving force in Japan today, and Kyushu is capitalizing on it.

In the past, local job opportunities were slim. In Kyushu, over half of all high school graduates ended up moving to larger cities on Honshu. However, this situation is rapidly changing. According to MITI's Industrial Location Guidance Division, 10,300 companies have relocated to Japan's outlying regions since 1980, and the pace is picking up. In 1984 alone, regional plant siting throughout Japan jumped 27% as companies sought cheaper land and available labor outside the major industrial centers. Kyushu attracted over a hundred high-tech companies. This trend is being accelerated by the serious overcrowding, pollution, and high housing costs in the major cities, and by the special treatment given less industrialized regions by national tax laws and industrial siting policies.

Kyushu perhaps stands to benefit most from this shift of people and jobs. Located 600 miles from Tokyo, it has all the right ingredients for high-tech expansion—clean water and air, cheap land, strong political leadership, industrial parks, 135 universities and technical schools, eighteen airports, beautiful scenery, and a relaxed lifestyle. Indeed, compared to the congested Tokyo-Osaka-Kobe megapolis, Kyushu is a veritable garden paradise, with plenty of room for industrial growth. It has a total population of thirteen million, but except for the heavily industrialized Kita-Kyushu region in the north, most of Kyushu is sparsely populated (see Figure 8-1).

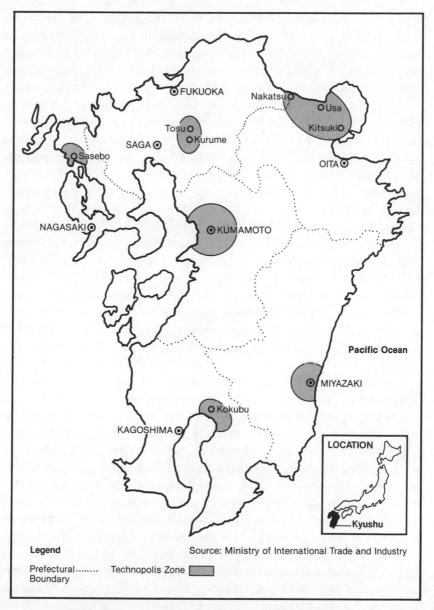

Figure 8-1. Kyushu: Japan's "Silicon Island."

What makes Kyushu unique is the vigor of its electronics industry. Since Texas Instruments built the first integrated circuit plant here in 1968, over 190 electronics companies have set up shop in Kyushu, giving it the title of "Silicon Island." The world's leading semiconductor companies, including Fairchild, NEC, Matsushita, Mitsubishi, Oki, Sony, Texas Instruments, and Toshiba, operate over seventy manufacturing plants here that produced 2.8 billion chips worth $2.7 billion in 1984, or 40% of Japan's total semiconductor output. To put this figure into perspective, Silicon Island produces about 10% of the world's total semiconductor output, compared to 25% for Silicon Valley and 15% for "Silicon Plain" (the Dallas area). But more important than total production figures is its product mix. Kyushu has become the production center for Japan's leading-edge computer chips. NEC's Kumamoto plant and Oki Electric's Miyazaki plant produce the 64K DRAM chip (dynamic random access memory that stores over 65,535 bits of information) which enabled Japan to capture 70% of the world market in 1982. Fujitsu, NEC, Oki Electric, Mitsubishi, and Toshiba now produce the hot-selling 256K DRAM, which stores a quarter-million bits of information, and are already sampling 1-megabit DRAMs (one million bits) which will be mass produced in 1986.

However, this is where the comparison ends. Unlike Silicon Valley, which has over seventy chip plants concentrated within a narrow corridor twenty-five miles long by ten miles wide, Kyushu's seventy integrated circuit (IC) plants are scattered over a 16,000-square-mile area. Moreover, whereas Silicon Valley is an R&D center for America's semiconductor industry, Silicon Island is primarily a manufacturing arm for Japan's electronics industry. Almost all research and product design activities are still conducted in Tokyo and Osaka. Recently, however, major electronics companies have opened large software development centers here. Nevertheless, Silicon Island is more like Oregon, Arizona, and Idaho, which have lured IC production plants from Silicon Valley.

Kyushu's shift from agriculture, coal mining, and heavy industries to high technology is reflected in its changing labor force. Local IC plants have few professionals and are heavily staffed by female assembly line workers. For example, at NEC's Kumamoto plant, one of the largest IC plants in the world, over half of the 2,000 employees are young women fresh out of high school who live in company dormitories. This practice of hiring young women is so common that children often say: "*Ojiichan* (grandfather) works in the fields, *otoochan* (father) in town, and *sanchan* (sister) in a high-tech plant."

Although high-tech plants have created new jobs in Kyushu, they have not developed the critical mass of engineers and researchers necessary for the region's emerging technopolises. Although Silicon Island has 11% of Japan's population, it only has 4.8% of the manufacturing technicians, 3.9% of all private research institutes, 4.2% of the installed computers, and 1.2% of the patent applications. Despite the high visibility of its high-tech plants, electronics provides only 6% of Kyushu's total employment.

To accelerate the shift to high technology, MITI issued an industrial "vision" for Kyushu in the 1980s, which stressed the need for Kyushu to become more internationalized. The report triggered a burst of activity among the island's prefectures to recruit foreign high-tech companies. In 1982 Fairchild announced its plan to invest $87.5 million in an IC plant near Nagasaki. Texas Instruments Japan, the pharmaceutical producer Seale, and Materials Research Corporation set up plants in Oita Prefecture. In early 1983, local governments and MITI formed the Kyushu Trade Mission, which toured the United States to explain investment opportunities, industrial sites, tax incentives, and research subsidies.

Since 1983 the pace has picked up. In May 1983, industry and government leaders issued the Kyushu Area Technology Promotion Plan, which stresses Kyushu's goal of developing creative technologies and a frontier spirit. The plan recommended forming a Kyushu Industrial Technology Center, creating joint research consortiums, accelerating Technopolis construction, and offering technical guidance from national universities and research labs. To explore emerging technologies, the Kyushu Fine Ceramics Techno Forum and the Biotechnology Research Society were formed, and the region's ninety-three technical schools and forty-four technical universities are upgrading their curriculum and linking up with MITI's local testing laboratories.

Silicon Island is working hard to overcome its isolation from Tokyo and Osaka. In 1975 the Tōkaidō bullet train line was extended to northern Kyushu. Currently, the Japan Highway Corporation is completing a highway to link Kyushu with Osaka, and a north-south highway to link Fukuoka in the north with Kumamoto, Kagoshima, and Miyazaki in the south. Kyushu's airports place it within an hour and a half of Tokyo. Thus, a container of microchips worth $600,000 can be shipped to Tokyo for about 0.2% of their selling price. Within the last few years, five prefectures have lengthened their runways to handle the growing trade with southeast Asia. Since it has lower land prices (one-third those of the Tokyo area) and labor costs (20% lower), Silicon Island is a strategic base for IC makers entering Asian markets. Currently, there are 300 industrial parks throughout Silicon Island, which have been developed by the Japan Regional Development Corporation and local prefectures. Information on them is easily accessible from MITI's industrial siting data base.

Now that the technopolis program is underway, rivalry is heating up on Silicon Island for new companies and the best plan. In 1984, the seven prefectures spent $3 million to attract new firms and $6 million in tax incentives and relocation subsidies. They spent another $5 million to build technopolis information centers and research institutes, as shown in Table 8-1. To lure companies, they also maintain PR offices in Tokyo (see Appendix N) staffed with "Techno-ninjas" who report back the latest industry news. Kumamoto has even initiated a "Come Back Home" campaign and operates a "Hometown Counseling Office" to encourage homesick professionals to return to the fold. Although each of these programs has only had a modicum of success, it is still too early to make a final judgment about the ultimate success of the technopolis efforts in Kyushu. To give you flavor of the variety of programs being developed, let's take a closer look at the top four technopolises on Silicon Island—Kumamoto, Oita, Kagoshima, and Miyazaki.

KUMAMOTO: SILICON CASTLE

The castle stands silent and forbidding behind a bulwark of rough-hewn stone walls, commanding Kumamoto City as it has for over 380 years. From its sweeping turrets, one can see as far as the hawk flies, over the broad forested plain from volcanic Mount Aso

Table 8-1.
Technopolis Centers on Silicon Island.

Technopolis	Name of Center	Funding	Research Activities
Kurume-Tosu	Kurume-Tosu Area Technology Promotion Center	$750K $3.6M in 1990	Information system for biotechnology and five other fields
Kumamoto	Kumamoto Technopolis Technology Development Fund	$1.8M $17.5M in 1985	Electronic machinery research laboratory
Kokubu-Hayato (Kagoshima)	Kagoshima Prefecture Industrial Technology Promotion Association	$1.9M	Fine ceramics product development lab & Kagoshima Prefecture Technology Center
Miyazaki	Miyazaki Prefecture Industrial Technology Promotion Association	$190K $875K in 1987	Joint R&D center
Kenhoku-Kunisaki (Oita)	Oita Prefecture Technology Promotion Corporation	$460K $1.9M in 1985	Oita Prefecture High-Tech Research Lab, Oita Prefecture Human Resource Development Center

Source: Japan Industrial Location Center

in the east to Ariake Sea in the west. To the north, Hommyoji Temple rises in the distance. For visitors, Kumamoto Castle is an awe-inspiring place because of its massive, moss-covered walls and dramatic views. Standing on its grassy rampants, it is not difficult to see how the castle shaped Kumamoto City, for everything radiates outward from its protective walls. In the late afternoon sun, the castle casts a long shadow over the surrounding office buildings and stores in downtown Kumamoto.

Since its construction in 1601, Kumamoto Castle has been the geographic and political center of Silicon Island. Under the leadership of Kiyomasa Kato, trusted ally of Ieyasu Tokugawa, Kumamoto served as the military counterbalance to the defiant Shimazu clan in southern Kyushu, and a recruiting ground for Ieyasu's invasions of Korea. For helping Ieyasu in the climactic Battle of Sekigahara, which led to the founding of the Tokugawa shogunate, Kato was rewarded with total control over the Kumamoto region, then known as Higo. Here he built his castle—the linchpin for Tokugawa's southern strategy—from which he launched military campaigns against the Koreans. After his death, Tokugawa placed the castle under the control of the powerful Hosokawa warlords.

Although four centuries have passed, Kumamoto is again being ruled by a Hosokawa—this time Governor Morihiro Hosokawa, a young politician whose star is rising. Elected in 1983, Governor Hosokawa has used Kumamoto's strength in integrated circuit production to rally support for the Kumamoto Technopolis. He is a one-man band, and a good one at that. In the 1970s, thirty-five electronics companies, including Fujitsu, Matsushita, Mitsubishi, NEC, and Tokyo Electron, opened manufacturing plants in Kumamoto. Since 1983 over fifty high-tech companies have moved in, making Kumamoto the hub of Silicon Island. In 1983 Kumamoto shipped $735 million worth of ICs, half of all those shipped from Kyushu, making it the top-producing prefecture in Japan. (It accounted for 12% of Japan's total IC production, or 5% of worldwide production.)

NEC's very large-scale integrated circuit (VLSI) plant in Kagami, a town southwest of Kumamoto City, is one of the largest IC plants in the world. Each morning hundreds of young women in company uniforms enter the plant's main gates to run the older production lines. Most are high school graduates who have been selected by a rigorous screening process. Like most Japanese companies, NEC plays the role of local parent and family, quartering its workers from the countryside in multistoried dormitories. The plant produces 256K DRAMs, but is now shifting to 1-megabit DRAMs. By contrast with its older lines, NEC's latest six-inch silicon wafer line at Plant #7 is heavily automated with state-of-the-art robotics technology. Brightly lit and virtually workerless, the plant is an eerie sight, showing few signs of life except for the occasional movement of robot arms and automated carts that have been installed to reduce the level of wafer defects from human contamination. If this is Technopolis, one wonders where all the young working women will work in the future. Will companies create enough new jobs to replace those lost by automation? Where will everyone go?

According to Osamu Torii, Kumamoto Technopolis planner, Kumamoto is bracing itself for a highly-automated future by moving ahead to new technologies and industries. Four strategic industries, known as "ABCD industries," have been targeted: automation (automated machinery, industrial robots); biotechnology (genetic engineering); computers (semiconductors and hardware); and data processing (software and information systems). "Our goal is to establish research labs, software development centers, information services, venture businesses, and other service-intensive industries. We believe this will provide jobs for people who will be displaced by the shift to automated plants. By developing our 'soft' infrastructure now, we're planting the seeds for the future." These are optimistic words, especially given the volatility of high-tech industries. How will Kumamoto avoid the boom-bust phenomenon that plagues Silicon Valley?

The key is planning. Kumamoto is building a "high-technology forest" based on ideas taken from the Research Triangle Park in North Carolina. Like officials from Hamamatsu City, Governor Hosokawa was impressed with the Research Triangle's planned development and scenic environment, which reminded him of Kumamoto. "You've got to see the Triangle from the air," he says. "It's a fantastic environment for research. We don't want to just attract semiconductor companies, but also build a beautiful living environment with lots of greenery for our research labs and educational facilities. This 'soft' approach is a little different from other Technopolis plans."

Kumamoto's Technopolis is a melange of ideas from several American high-tech regions. Local planners mixed the Triangle's scattered development approach with Oregon's lab-in-the-forest concept, and threw in Boston's Route 128 ring road concept. The resulting Kumamoto Technopolis consists of high-tech "forests" scattered along Route 325, which lies east of Kumamoto City. At the northern end of the ring road is a "Biotechnology Forest," which will eventually accommodate sixty regional makers of sake, soy sauce, soybean paste, and other fermented products. In May 1982 over 260 companies laid the groundwork by forming the Biotechnology Research Association to conduct joint R&D with

Kumamoto University and three other universities. By 1990 the Association plans to build the Kikuchi Laboratory for genetic engineering research, a Food Processing Research Lab, and an Environmental Sanitation Engineering Lab. There are also plans for an International Blood Plasma Center, a Therapeutic Hot Springs Center, and a Local Medical Care Center. The long-term goal is to develop the Biotechnology Forest into an international center for advanced medical and biotechnology research.

Immediately to the south, in a beautifully forested area, is the Takamori Software Forest, where twenty computer companies and software houses have formed an industry association to promote software development. This new complex will eventually have a population of 9,000, and is divided into software, fashion design, architectural design, and cultural zones. A major participant is Yokogawa-HP, a Japanese joint venture involving Hewlett-Packard of Silicon Valley, which is working with the prefecture to develop this area. In the future, the software association plans to organize a Software Plaza, which will provide cheap financing and technical advice to new venture businesses.

Further south on Route 325 is a new airport industrial complex that is becoming a center of electronics research. At its core is Kumamoto International Airport, which was recently expanded to handle jumbo jets. Nearby is the Techno Research Park, the site of the Electronic Machinery Research Lab that is conducting joint research in mechatronics, expert systems, custom ICs, and disaster prevention information systems. Recently, participating companies pitched in $3.1 million to build a Technopolis Center where they can exchange information. In addition, a Venture Business Plaza will be built to promote joint product development among thirty smaller firms. This airport complex has already begun attracting companies. Since 1984 several automated IC plants and research institutes have located in the Kumamoto Research Park to take advantage of the joint R&D programs.

Local universities and junior colleges are also jumping onto the joint R&D bandwagon, and have plans to build their own research complex north of Kumamoto City. Kumamoto University is actively pursuing mechatronics, software, and genetic research. The Kumamoto Industrial College is working with local food processors to develop new biotechnology applications. Kyushu Tokai University is developing new information systems, and the

Kumamoto Electrical Engineering Technical Institute has set up research projects to investigate microcomputer applications. These universities are working closely with the prefecture and MITI's regional testing labs to refine their approach.

Despite its success in attracting high-tech companies, Kumamoto still has an image problem. The area still lacks enough roads, power systems, and industrial sites, and needs a deeper pool of talented engineers and marketing people. So far, most local graduates head for Osaka and Tokyo. The few who return have a difficult time finding singles housing and social activities. A 1982 survey indicated that 60% of all returnees, or "U-turn workers," could not find adequate work.

To resolve these problems, Governor Hosokawa and local leaders have instituted an "image-up" campaign. For returning workers, the prefecture has set up job information centers, a talent bank, and informal networks. For incoming companies, the prefecture has established three financial incentive programs. The Industrial Site Location Promotion Fund offers 6.9% loans with a ten-year repayment period to finance up to two-thirds of plant investments over $400,000. The Software Fund exempts software houses and scientific research centers from property and business taxes. For high-tech companies that hire in rural areas, the Remote Area Site Location Promotion Fund offers subsidies of $1,250 for each employee, up to 100 new employees.

The Kumamoto Technopolis Foundation is an active fundraiser that has raised $20 million for the Technopolis Center near Kumamoto International Airport. In 1983 the Foundation sponsored its first "Shape-Up Technology Symposium," followed by an international symposium with France's Sophia Antipolis science city. It also held a citywide Technopolis Fair to generate local support. With MITI, the Foundation is planning a "Techno-Mart" to promote local products, patent sales, and information exchange. Recently the Foundation opened its offices in the "Techno Communication Plaza" where electronics makers exhibit office automation and teletext products. One novel idea has been the creation of a "Technopolis Account" at a local bank for individuals, groups, and school children interested in contributing to the Technopolis effort.

Governor Hosokawa, who fashions himself after North Carolina's Governor James Martin, has much bigger dreams for Kumamoto than merely building a Technopolis. He has a vision of the future that combines technology with traditional Japanese values and customs. "Technopolis construction is not only a matter of technology and information. We must be proud of our city. We must invest in public services and facilities so that we can have colorful commercial areas, a creative educational system, generous welfare services, and rich cultural and athletic activities. We should not build only fancy facilities to promote national and international events, but also develop people-oriented services."

For someone who has spent a lifetime watching Silicon Valley, this philosophy is a change of pace from the valley's "get-rich-quick/beggar-thy-neighbor" attitude that ignores social services and cultural activities—a point that many outside observers dislike about the valley. John Naisbitt, author of *Megatrends,* calls this return to balance "high-tech/high-touch." Whenever there is high technology, there is a need for the human touch. In Kumamoto, it is called "softnomics"—the development of industries, services, and technologies that cultivate the human spirit and a sense of community.

OITA: SILICON HOT SPRINGS

As the wide-body jet banks into the sunset awaiting final landing instructions, the 3,000-meter runway of Oita International Airport emerges from the shadows below, protruding from the Kunisaki Peninsula like a slender foot. Isolated from urban areas and bordered on the west by farmland and forests, the massive landfilled runway looks strangely out of place against the stretch of blue ocean. The coastal area is sparsely populated; the nearest cities, Oita and Beppu, are over thirty-five miles to the south. The only signs of activity are a few small industrial parks scattered about the town of Aki. To the first-time visitor, Oita's Toyo-no-Kuni Technopolis—considered one of the leading technopolises—is disappointing. From the air it looks more like a California resort town than a future rival to Silicon Valley. Yet it is here, in the orange groves and ricefields of Oita, that some of the most creative ideas for MITI's Technopolis program are being tested. The guru of this bold experiment is Governor Morihiko Hiramatsu, the former chief of MITI's powerful Electronics Policy Bureau and a key strategist on the Technopolis '90 Committee.

Since his election to office in 1979, Governor Hiramatsu has transformed Oita from a depressed rural area into one of the hottest spots for high-tech development on Silicon Island. In late 1982, with Dr. Sheldon Weinig of New York-based Materials Research Corporation (MRC), Governor Hiramatsu announced that MRC would open a semiconductor equipment plant in Oita, only five miles from Texas Instruments' IC production plant. As a result of Governor Hiramatsu's lobbying at MITI, the Japan Development Bank extended a $1.5 million loan to MRC and its Japanese partner, Midoriya Electric, to construct the plant. Since then, there has been a rush of foreign companies to secure JDB's low-interest loans.

Governor Hiramatsu is one of Japan's strongest promoters of foreign investment in Japan; he cuts through red tape and invites foreign executives to Oita, where they are taken on guided tours and royally entertained at Beppu's famous hot springs and inns. He is trying to give Oita a human face. So far, his "high-touch" campaign has paid off handsomely. He has attracted Materials Research Corporation, Sony, Canon, NEC, Toshiba, Dai-Nippon Ink and Chemicals, HOKS Electronics, Kyushu Matsushita Electric, Fujitsu Software Laboratories, TDK, and others.

It is impossible to talk about Technopolis without hearing about Governor Hiramatsu because of his enormous influence in Japan. He is "Mr. Technopolis." Whenever one goes, his name is mentioned. He is the high priest of the new "Japan Tech"—a cross between politician and seer, Congressman Edward Zschau of Silicon Valley and John Naisbitt.

Besides recruiting high-tech firms, Governor Hiramatsu is actively promoting new ideas. His pet project is the "one-village/one-product" campaign, in which each village, town, and city is encouraged to develop at least one product or technology that can compete on a national or international level. Quoting John Naisbitt, Hiramatsu believes that Oita must "act locally with a global perspective." This approach is an integral element of Oita's balanced economic development strategy. The prefecture has formed a "One-Village/One-Product" Council consisting of representatives from farming, forestry, fishing, consumer, retail, educational, and financial sectors to identify unique products and technologies with export potential. To promote the concept, the prefecture sponsored its first high technology fair in October 1984.

Aquaculture is a good example of the creative research being conducted under Governor Hiramatsu's leadership. In 1982 the prefecture organized the Marinopolis Project at the port city of Saiki to develop fish breeding and aquaculture technologies. Located on the Bungo Channel where the waters of the Inland Sea meet the northward-flowing Black Current, the port of Saiki has traditionally been the launching point for trawlers heading to off-shore areas rich in sardine, tuna, and mackerel. However, in recent years, overfishing has taken its toll on local fisheries, and enact-ment of the 200-mile fishing boundary by maritime nations around the world has reduced Japan's access to fishing areas. For Japan, heavily dependent on imported fish, these trends threaten to raise fish prices. In 1976 the Japanese government enacted the Coastal Fishing Ground Improvement Law to promote fish and shellfish farming within Japanese waters. In the early 1980s Oita Prefecture established the Marine Production Engineering Center at Oita Uni-versity, a Fish Disease Research Center at the prefecture's marine test laboratory, and a Fish Breeding Center, where local fisheries are taught fish cultivation and harvesting techniques.

According to Mineo Igarashi, Technopolis planner for Oita Pre-fecture, the project relies on age-old carp breeding techniques mixed with a dash of applied psychology, Buddhist customs, and high technology. Minnows are raised in large saltwater ponds where they are fed near an underwater speaker which emits the sound of religious drumbeats recorded at Oita's Shiyakuma Shrine. By conditioned response the fish gradually become accus-tomed to the drumbeats and gather whenever the speaker is low-ered into the water. When the fish are large enough, they are released into the ocean where they migrate to feeding areas. Then, when the fish reach maturity and return to their breeding grounds, fishermen drop speakers into the area and net the fish which are attracted to the familiar drumbeats! So far, the harvest rate is only 5% of the fish released, but if it can be raised to 10%, fish-breeding will become commercially feasible and Japan may never have to import fish again.

According to Governor Hiramatsu, the Marine Production Engi-neering Center uses computer systems to monitor changes in water temperature, plankton, pollution, and feed to determine the optimal conditions for raising and harvesting different varieties of fish. With the Mitsui Shipbuilding Company, Komatsu Works, and electronics companies, the prefecture is developing underwater robots to build and maintain sea-bottom fish breeding areas, a marine sports park, and recreational fishing areas. Eventually, Oita plans to develop an integrated aquaculture/coastal resort complex with resort hotels, marine research centers, high-tech fisheries, aquariums, and Marineland-type tourist attractions. Trawlers and recreational boaters will be provided with round-the-clock reports on fishing, weather, and tide conditions through the use of satellite broadcasting.

Oita's Toyo-no-Kuni Technopolis program has four other project areas. The Kenhoku-Kunisaki Technopolis zone, located west of Oita International Airport, is a center of Buddhist culture that dates back to the Nara and Kyoto era (794-1185). Traditionally known as *Bungo,* it has numerous temples, shrines, and Buddhist statues carved out of large rocks. To preserve its historic quality and the surrounding farmland, Oita is dispersing high-tech plants throughout five zones (Nakatsu, Usa, Takeda, Kunisaki and Kitsuki). According to Technopolis planner Suenobu Tamada, MITI opposed this plan because it preferred a new town near Oita International Airport. Oita planners argued that dispersed development would reduce infrastructure costs, traffic jams, and pollution. After lengthy negotiations, Oita finally prevailed, but in the words of local planners: "MITI was a real headache because it is out of touch with what people in Oita feel. Farmers want to preserve their lands, and towns want to share the wealth. We don't have money for an expensive new town." So far, Oita's approach is proceeding according to plan. Canon, Sony, and Materials Research Corporation have located north of the airport, while Matsushita, NEC, Searle, and Kanto Seiki are situated among the orange groves. Other companies are locating along the "Techno-Road" running through the prefecture.

To overcome its weakness in research, Oita Prefecture has established R&D programs at Oita University, Oita Medical School, and other local colleges. A team at Oita University is pursuing research in optoelectronics, underwater fiber optic cables, and laser measuring equipment. Oita Medical School is conducting experiments in genetic engineering, inherited cancer cells, and fermentation process equipment, while Oita National Technical College is developing robots, sensors, and numerically-controlled equipment at its Automated Equipment Research Center. Over 260 researchers at fifteen prefectural laboratories are working on high-tech farming, biotechnology, alternative energies, fine ceramics, mechatronics, integrated circuits, and software.

In its quest for creative research, Oita has not forgotten its cultural and agricultural roots. The Ono River Development Area Project is introducing new technologies, such as biomass, solar energy generation, and computerized feed formulation, to reduce farm costs and improve crop yields. In 1983 Kyushu University founded the Highlands Agricultural Experimental Lab to develop large-scale farming techniques. To the west, the Hita-Kusu Model Settlement Area is promoting tourism through a program of historic renovation and local handicrafts. In 1982 a regional arts and crafts center featuring Onda ceramics, *geta* (wooden clogs), and bamboo products was built to display the works of local artists. One interesting spot is the Children's Folk Tale Pavilion, which features a library of 50,000 children's books, and runs puppet theaters, storytelling, children's games, and other educational programs.

Although Oita is far from the powers-that-be in Tokyo, its influence is felt throughout Japan because of its innovative programs. Perhaps this receptiveness to new ideas has its roots in the past. Almost 400 years ago, Oita was the site where William Adams, better known as Miura Anjin (or Anjin-san in the novel *Shogun*) was shipwrecked in a storm. It was on the shores of Toyo-no-Kuni that the value of Anjin-san's shipbuilding and navigation techniques were recognized by the local lord. Instead of killing him on the spot, the lord sent Adams to Ieyasu Tokugawa, who used him to build his navy.

KAGOSHIMA: SILICON VOLCANO

Viewed from downtown Kagoshima, the rugged spine of Sakura-jima thrusts into the sky, spewing clouds of gray ash over the southern tip of Silicon Island. The volcano is awesome and unpredictable. Its last major eruption fused the tiny island in Kagoshima Bay to the Ōsumi Peninsula in 1914. To local residents, the primordial might of Sakurajima (Cherry Blossom Island) symbolizes Kagoshima's fierce pride and independence from Tokyo, a sentiment best captured by the phrase *Satsuma Hayato,* which captures the spirit of the Hayato clan that rebelled against the imperial government and dominated the Kagoshima region until the eighth century.

Kagoshima has traditionally served as the southern gateway to Japan, a role that has made it receptive to new ideas. In the seventh century, Kagoshima was the jumping-off point for Japanese scholars and envoys en route to the T'ang court. In the sixteenth century, Portuguese traders blown off course by a typhoon introduced firearms, known as *Tanegashima,* for the island where they were later mass produced by local craftsmen. Kagoshima was also the point where the Jesuit priest St. Francis Xavier introduced Christianity to Japan. Despite the brutal suppression of Christianity under the Tokugawa shoguns, the Satsuma lords defied the central government by treating the foreign missionaries with respect.

Founded as a castle town by the Shimazu family in 1602, Kagoshima (Fawn Island) was the home of powerful leaders, such as Takamori Saigō, whose military victories forced the Tokugawa shogun to resign, paving the way for the transfer of power to Emperor Meiji in 1868, and Toshimichi Okubo, whose policies laid the groundwork for the Meiji Restoration. Satsuma, as Kagoshima was once called, made its mark on modern Japan as one of the last provinces to defy the authority of the new Meiji state. In 1877, disgruntled samurai under the leadership of Saigō joined forces in the famous Satsuma Rebellion to protest the Meiji reforms. Although the uprising was crushed by the government's conscripted army, Saigō and Okubo are still revered for their strong political leadership.

It is that fierce independence and pride which Kagoshima is trying to revive with its Technopolis plan. "Our goal is a Kagoshima Renaissance," says Governor Kaname Kamada. "Our predecessors led the way in the modernization of Japan with their progressive spirit. The Kagoshima Renaissance means that the people of Kagoshima will emulate their predecessors in heralding the dawn of the twenty-first century in Japan."

This call to battle comes at an important juncture in the region's history. Since World War II, Kagoshima has fared poorly in developing new companies to replace its sinking industries, despite its deepwater port which provides its textile, mining, agriculture, and lumber industries access to major shipping lanes in the Pacific and East China Seas. The region has been overshadowed by Kyushu's heavy industrial centers in the north, such as Fukuoka, Sasebo, Kita-Kyushu, and Nagasaki.

But Kagoshima is making a comeback. Since 1969 over 230 companies have relocated from other areas in Japan, accounting for 37% of the prefecture's total shipment of goods in 1983. Thirty high-tech companies, including Kyocera (Kyoto Ceramics), Fujitsu, Sony, NEC, Yamaha Instruments, Matsushita, and NBK Spark Plug, have opened manufacturing plants in the area, and form the core of Kagoshima's emerging economy.

The Kagoshima Renaissance plan consists of three Technopolis areas, including the Kokubu-Hayato Technopolis, Atompolis, and Biopolis. The Kokubu-Hayato Technopolis, which covers an area of 1,260 square miles and includes thirteen towns, is the focal point for high-technology research. Located at the northern end of Kagoshima Bay, the area has the rural ambience of Silicon Valley twenty years ago and San Diego's relaxed coastal environment. Currently, Kyocera's Central Research Laboratory and Sony's semiconductor plant are located in the zone, and Kyushu Fujitsu, Matsushita, and NGK Spark Plug are located nearby. In the future there will be sixteen new industrial parks, including the central Kokubu Uenohara Techno Park, and the Hayato Garden City, a new residential area for 4,000 people being built atop a hill over looking Kagoshima Bay. Nearby is the recently expanded Kagoshima International Airport, which has daily flights to Tokyo, Bangkok, Singapore, Hong Kong, Nauru, and Guam.

West of Kagoshima City is the Atompolis, where the prefecture's energy supply base is being developed. A 890-megawatt nuclear power plant and a 500-megawatt thermal power plant are now in operation in the town of Sendai, with two identical plants under construction. At the town of Kushikino, underground oil reserves are being tapped. Joint R&D is also being conducted to explore the feasibility of alternative energies.

At Shibushi Bay, east of Kagoshima City, is the Biopolis, the center of biotechnology research, where twenty-six agricultural testing stations are developing new techniques for cultivating silk-worms, tea, fruits, fish, cattle, and poultry. With the Kagoshima Software Promotion Association, research labs are writing software to control the temperature and humidity in greenhouses, run automated tealeaf-picking machines, and forecast "red tides" (excess plankton usually fatal to many forms of marine life) along the coast. Kagoshima University and MITI testing labs are studying fermentation methods used in sake and *shochu* (potato liquor) brewing to develop new industrial alcohols and starches, as well as sugar cane to generate energy (biomass).

Kagoshima is also targeting two other fast-growing technologies for accelerated development: aerospace and new materials. Masaaki Ikoma, Technopolis planner for Kagoshima Prefecture, makes no bones about the prefecture's ambitious goals: "We're pursuing frontier technologies to bring people back from the big cities. It's industrial policy at the grassroots."

Kagoshima is known as Japan's Cape Kennedy because of its two space centers. Tanegashima Space Center, run by the National Space Development Agency (NASDA) of the Science and Technology Agency, launches vehicles for applications satellites from an island south of Kagoshima. The Kagoshima Space Center, operated by the Ministry of Education's Institute of Space and Astronautical Science (ISAS), launches scientific satellites. Since 1970 the two centers have launched over thirty spacecraft. ISAS has Japanese companies develop scientific satellites—NEC (earth observation satellites), Mitsubishi Electric (communications satellites), and Toshiba (broadcast satellites). By contrast, NASDA contracts U.S. companies such as Ford Aerospace and Communications Corporation, Hughes Aircraft, General Electric, McDonnell Douglas, Rockwell International, TRW, and Aerojet Tech Systems, to acquire commercial satellite technology.

The Tanegashima center has recently attracted national attention because of NASDA's ambitious space development program. In 1983 NASDA launched Japan's first communications satellites, Sakura CS-2A and CS-2B, from Tanegashima, followed by the BS-2A direct broadcast satellite in January 1984 (which failed to work when two of the three transponders went out). As part of Nippon Telegraph and Telephone (NTT) and Japan Broadcasting Corporation's plans to develop the nationwide Information Network System (INS), NASDA will launch the BS-3 broadcasting satellite in 1988, which will offer pulse-code modulation stereo music broadcasts, still-image relay, and high-definition television programs directly to households equipped with parabolic antennas. NASDA will spend another $300 million on a seven-year-long earth resources satellite development program, and $870 million to develop the high-thrust H-II rocket to lift 2,000-kilogram payloads into geostationary orbit by 1990.

Technopolis planners hope to trigger spin-off development in electronics from these space programs, as Silicon Valley did. One example is Elm Computer, a start-up company founded in 1980 by 33-year-old Takaharu Miyahara. Typical of Japan's new breed of "U-turn" entrepreneurs, Miyahara left a secure job at a systems computer company in Osaka to develop his own weather-reporting software. Using a personal computer, he developed a program that enables users to receive instant graphic displays of weather reports transmitted by Japan's weather satellite, Himawari (Sunflower). His product costs only $12,000, but has 75% of the capacity of sophisticated $65,000 scientific computers. Miyahara sees a big market for his computers in schools, agriculture, fisheries, transportation, and sports industries, and is hiring local graduates to build up his fledgling company. "This is my mission in life and my destiny," he says: "to challenge new technologies."

Elm Computer is not alone. Since 1982 Japan's major electronics makers have expanded their Kagoshima operations in what local observers call an "IC gold rush." In 1983 Fujitsu opened a semiconductor R&D center with plans to hire 500 researchers. Sony invested over $50 million in its three Kagoshima plants. Kyocera, the world leader in ceramic IC packaging, added 1,500 employees in 1984 to its local staff of 2,360. Hitachi opened a software development plant with plans to have 130 programmers by 1988. In addition, well-known firms such as Tokyo Electronics, Nippon Gakki (Yamaha), and Sumitomo Metals and Mining have opened new plants. So business is booming in "Silicon Volcano."

To promote high-tech research, the Prefecture is acting as a technology transfer agent. Recently, nine research associations involving over 210 companies have been organized. In 1983 the Kagoshima Industrial Technology Association (KITA) was created to provide training and conduct joint R&D. It is working with the Kagoshima Small- and Medium-Sized Industry Development Agency, which promotes technology exchanges in metallurgy, machine tools, and mechatronics. The Metal Tooling Association and Mechatronics Research Association are experimenting with types of mechatronics products and industrial robots in conjunction with MITI's local testing labs. The goal is to encourage the national space agencies and rocket manufacturers, who are located in Tokyo and Osaka, to use local companies as subcontractors and suppliers for ICs, ceramic tiles, alloys, sensors, lasers, and fiber optics.

How will this work? Katsuharu Tokushige, Technopolis planner for Kagoshima Prefecture, points to an old Japanese custom called *noren wake*, meaning to separate the folds of the decorative curtain hanging in the entrance of sushi shops. During the Tokugawa period (1600–1868), sushi apprentices who had mastered their trade would start up their own shop elsewhere with the blessings of the master sushi chef. In the same manner, Kagoshima planners are encouraging large IC and aerospace firms to do likewise in the Kokubu-Hayato Technopolis. "We're hoping to trigger a boom in spinoff companies, as you did in Silicon Valley with your space program."

New materials, especially ceramics, is Kagoshima's second target industry because of the region's plentiful volcanic ash, silica, and rare metals. But ceramics is king because of Kyocera, whose president, Kazuo Inamori, comes from Kagoshima. Kyocera's use of local Satsuma ware is an interesting twist to the age-old problem of finding new uses for old products. Satsuma ware is a major handicraft industry in Kagoshima, handed down through the centuries by families who run the Naeshirogawa, Ryumonji, Tateno, Nishimochida, and Hirasa kilns. Noted for its lustrous black glazes, Satsuma ware is used for the tea ceremony, although polychrome variations using a white marbled base and red, blue, and gold decorations are shipped to the West. In 1979 Kyocera combined its four research labs into the Kyocera Central Research Laboratory in the Kokubu-Hayato Technopolis. The lab is studying Satsuma ceramic firing techniques to develop new ceramics for use in IC packaging, artificial bones and teeth, car engines, and machinery parts. In 1984 Kyocera joined with major car makers, local universities, and Satsuma ceramics firms to create the Fine Ceramics Product R&D Institute—one of the New Frontier Technology Development Programs—which is located at the New Artcraft Village in the Kokubu-Hayato Technopolis.

Thus, Kagoshima's Technopolis has taken off with amazing speed. Within three years it has laid the foundation for its twenty-first century economy. But what is fascinating about its approach to high technology is its use of old technologies. For example, traditional Oshima dyeing methods are being developed to create new industrial chemicals and dyes. Silica, volcanic ash, and Satsuma ceramics are used in new types of industrial concretes and household glassware. Even fashion design has been invaded by computers. Designers now use computer-aided design (CAD) software to draw the intricate flower patterns for the expensive Oshima silk brocade! This recycling of traditional arts is Kagoshima's unique contribution to the Technopolis program. It is a particularly Japanese approach to technology. As novelist Yasunari Kawabata eloquently put it:

> He saw his escape in the Shino jar. He knelt before it and looked at it appraisingly, as one looks at tea vessels.

MIYAZAKI: SILICON COAST

The sleek, cigar-shaped train skims over the elevated concrete guideway at 320 miles per hour, making a hissing sound as it zips past lazy palm trees bordering the oval test track. In the distance, the two-car "maglev" (for magnetic levitation) is no more than a speck as it rounds the curve of the three-mile-long track, but within seconds it whooshes past the observation platform in a blur, only thirty feet away. Then, as quickly as it arrived, the maglev is gone, leaving the startled observer gripping the guardrail. The air is still again, disturbed only by the crickets in the nearby field. Welcome to Miyazaki—home of the Sun Technopolis and test site for Japan National Railway's bold experiment in super bullet trains.

Since the test track was opened in 1977 near the town of Hyuga, north of Miyazaki City, the Japan National Railway (JNR) has made great strides in maglev technology under the leadership of Yoshihiro Kyotani, Director of Technical Development at JNR. In 1978 the Maglev-500 test vehicle reached a speed of 187 miles per hour, surpassing that record in 1979 when it topped 320 mph. In 1981 a redesigned two-car vehicle was tested on a more conventional U-shaped track and reached 155 mph. JNR is testing these two-car trains to determine whether they can be made commercially feasible.

Although unlikely to be used in the immediate future, maglev technology is important because of Japan's heavy reliance on the bullet trains to carry thousands of passengers daily from Tokyo to other major cities. In recent years, these lines have begun to show serious signs of wear from the constant pounding of 130-mph trains. Each night the tracks must be carefully aligned by work crews. Wornout rails must be replaced and slipping concrete stakes shored up. To overcome these hazards, Kyotani has devised dynamic maglev technology using repulsion (as opposed to magnetic attraction) to lift the train cars from the tracks. Based on the theoretical work of G. Powell and J. R. Danby of Brookhaven National Laboratory, the JNR technology achieves magnetic levitation by on-board superconducting magnets that repulse conductive coils embedded in a U-shaped guideway. Liquid-helium refrigeration units on the train supercool the magnets to 4.2 Kelvin, maintaining current within the magnets even when the power is cut off. When the train passes over the guideway coils, a strong magnetic field is generated, repelling the train about four inches off the track. Kyotani believes maglev technology could be a viable alternative if JNR's existing bullet trains become plagued with maintenance problems and accidents.

Japan National Railway's maglev test track is something of an anomaly in Miyazaki Prefecture, which is known more for its sandy white beaches and lush vegetation than for its high technology. Each year thousands of tourists visit the Aoshima Subtropical Botanical Garden, Heiwadai Park, and Udo Shrine which are dedicated to Emperor Jimmu, Japan's first emperor. Until recently, Miyazaki was a favorite spot for honeymooners, but declining overseas airfares have slowed the domestic tourist trade, forcing industry leaders to look elsewhere for new jobs.

To attract new plant investments, Miyazaki is conducting a full-scale public relations campaign. In February 1981 the Technopolis '90 Promotion Alliance announced Miyazaki's Technopolis plans, and Governor Suketaka Matsukata formed a Corporate Location Promotion Headquarters to coordinate plant siting activities. The efforts have been a stunning success. Since 1983, Miyazaki has attracted ninety-six companies, giving it the highest growth rate in Japan. Major companies such as Asahi Electric, Fujitsu, Komatsu, Honda Lock, Matsushita Electric, and Oki Electric have established new plants in the region. Although most Japanese semiconductor makers still locate in Oita, Kumamoto, and Kagoshima, Miyazaki has grabbed its share of IC makers. In 1984 Oki Electric added a production line for the 256K and 1-megabit memory chips. Kyushu Fujitsu Electronics opened a new plant in late 1985. The Miyazaki Electronics Technology Research Association was also formed to promote IC research at Miyazaki University.

Selected by MITI in March 1984, Miyazaki's Sun Technopolis is quickly taking shape. The technopolis region covers an area of 334 square miles and consists of Miyazaki City and six surrounding towns. The prefecture has begun several large-scale projects. The Kyushu Expressway, which runs through western Kyushu from Fukuoka City in the north to Kagoshima and Miyazaki in the south, will be completed in 1985, and an expressway along the eastern coast of Kyushu is being planned. In 1982 Miyazaki Airport was expanded to handle Boeing 767s from Tokyo, and construction began on the Miyakonojo New Town housing area. Work has also begun on the Kirishima Mountains tourism plan and the Nichinan Subtropical Garden Belt to the south.

According to Yoshihiro Sano, local Technopolis planner, Miyazaki has chosen to scatter its industrial parks among the seven technopolis zones. "We wanted to build political support for the Technopolis program by sharing jobs and tax benefits among the towns and villages." Company confidentiality was another reason. In Silicon Valley, high-tech firms are concentrated in one area, making it difficult for companies to maintain total secrecy on new products and designs. To avoid this problem, Miyazaki has planned industrial parks that allow subsidiaries to cluster around their parent companies to accommodate the time-honored practice of just-on-time delivery of parts and materials. Planners also hope to avoid the congestion and traffic jams that afflict Silicon Valley.

The heart of the Miyazaki Sun Technopolis is the Miyazaki Science City, the third university town to be built in Japan based on the Tsukuba Science City (the other two are Hiroshima and Ube). Covering 740 acres, the new town will cost $375 million and accommodate Miyazaki University, Miyazaki Medical School,

Miyazaki Women's Junior college, as well as the IC Technology Research Laboratory, Oki Electric, and Matsushita Electronics. The new town is expected to become one of Japan's leading research centers, and will feature such facilities as cable TV, NTT's Information Network System, and local natural energy. Miyazaki University, which moved to the new town in 1984, is exploring cell fusion, biomass fermentation, solar heating systems, maglev trains, and electronics. Recently, it began joint R&D with local companies in seven fields: silicate porous glass from volcanic ash, biotechnology for agriculture, sanitation, food processing, electronics, new materials, and mechatronics.

Miyazaki Medical University has already made its mark in hormone research with its partner, Suntory Ltd., one of Japan's major distilleries. In 1984 the team announced that it had reproduced a hormone called "h-ANP" (human polypeptide) using recombinant DNA techniques—a historic first. The hormone, a protein located in the heart, was found to be effective in relaxing muscles, lowering blood pressure, and promoting urination. This development makes possible new drugs for the bedridden elderly and patients with high blood pressure and circulatory problems.

Beyond the immediate Technopolis zone, Miyazaki has also developed the Sun Ray Plan to promote economic development throughout the prefecture. The plan involves linking the Miyazaki Sun Technopolis with a "Techno-Plain" in northern Miyazaki, the western Miyakonojo district, and the "Techno-Valley" at the southern city of Nichinan. These three mini-technopolises will form an outer ring of high-tech development.

At first glance, Miyazaki Prefecture seems an unlikely place for high-tech development. It is a subtropical paradise more suited to tourism and agriculture. But geography is not destiny. With strong political and industrial leadership, once sleepy coastal towns such as San Diego and Santa Barbara have been able to make a rapid takeoff. Such is the case with Miyazaki. Within the last five years, it has laid the foundations for frontier technologies that will provide jobs for "U-turn" workers and its economic base for the next century. One senses that, as with the rest of Kyushu, Miyazaki's renaissance is only a matter of time.

9

WILL TECHNOPOLIS WORK?

To learn the basics takes three
years; to achieve anything worthwhile at least ten.

Japanese proverb

CULTIVATING THE TECHNOPOLISES

The Technopolis program is a uniquely Japanese synthesis of East
and West—an eclectic mixture of Silicon Valley's industrial parks,
English garden cities, and Japanese castle towns. Although Japanese officials say they are only copying Silicon Valley, I am not
convinced that the technopolises are just pale imitations of the
valley. When visiting these new cities, one has the impression of
glancing simultaneously into Japan's high-tech future and its feudal past. The two eras are tightly interwoven—the castle town
layout, the high-tech industrial parks, the open-air shops, and the
modern bullet train stations on the old Tōkaidō line—reflecting
the postwar reconstruction of Japanese cities over their prewar
outlines. What strikes the visitor about the technopolises is the
subtle, matter-of-fact blending of Japanese and western cultures.
Silicon Valley-style incubators and research labs sit among care-
fully-manicured ricefields and gardens, reminding one of old temples in Nara and Kyoto. Subsidiaries (*shita-uke*) are located next
to their parent companies to facilitate close cooperation and just-
on-time delivery. Centuries-old pottery families work closely with
high-tech ceramics companies. Even the visual signposts are a
mixture of old and new. In Silicon Valley, one orients oneself
according to the surrounding mountains and highways; in the
technopolises the train station, the castle, and city hall serve as
the major landmarks.

But these are only cultural differences. The real question facing Japan is: will technopolis work? Will the technopolises succeed in stimulating new jobs and creative research? Will they be able to attract and nurture talented people?

Perhaps the key to answering these questions lies in understanding how the Japanese view the technopolis program. During my technopolis visits, I was fascinated by the Japanese penchant for long-term planning. Whereas Silicon Valley residents think in terms of months and quarters, most Japanese businessmen and government officials whom I met speak in terms of years and decades. "We're planning for the twenty-first century," they told me, "so we must begin working now." Of course, their comments are partly boosterism and bravado, but even so, rarely have I heard similar pronouncements from Silicon Valley business leaders or researchers. Our companies are far too busy "fighting fires" and worrying about the next quarter or recession to plan very far in advance—certainly not twenty years. When I mention Japan's technopolis plans, my colleagues usually chuckle, quipping: "We're planning too—for our next shareholders' meeting."

Most Americans are aware of this "I want it all now" attitude that pervades our society, but it distorts our perceptions of Japan in subtle ways. For example, when my editor and I first saw the technopolises, we were extremely disappointed by the apparent lack of progress. We wanted to see bricks and mortar. After reading MITI's glowing publicity, we came to Japan expecting to see fully-built technopolises, complete with futuristic monorails, computerized farms, robot-automated factories, and ultramodern research labs—the typical stereotypes of Japanese high technology painted by the western media. Subconsciously, we were looking for a high-tech Disneyland, another dazzling Tsukuba Expo 85. Instead we found ourselves being chauffeured to empty industrial parks and obscure companies. In most of the technopolises, there is not a soul around. The lots are still vacant, the streets are dusty, and the few technology centers are small and unimpressive. If this is technopolis, we thought, it is a dismal failure.

Asked when technopolis will be built, Seiji Hamamatsu, manager of Toyama's Technopolis planning division, told us: *"Mada, mada* (not yet). The technopolises will take time to root, at least ten to fifteen years—like Silicon Valley and Tsukuba did. They won't take off until the twenty-first century. It's like growing rice.

One must work hard and learn to wait. But you Americans are always in a hurry to see quick results. In Japan, there is a saying: To achieve anything worthwhile takes at least ten years."

But appearances are deceiving, and in Japan one must always be careful to not take things at face value. The Japanese march to a different drummer. On the surface, they appear to be taking no action. They are slow to make decisions, spending much time understanding the problem, building consensus, and ironing out details; but once they act, they move with lightning speed because everyone understands his or her role. The same approach is being used in the technopolises. The regions are building consensus by organizing their "soft" networks of people, joint R&D projects, and industry associations. Little concrete is being poured and there are few tangible results, and as a result, most Americans conclude that nothing is happening. But behind the scenes, the technopolises are moving as quickly as possible; local industry is being mobilized to meet MITI's challenge. In the Japanese industrial press, there are announcements from the nineteen technopolises almost every day, but the foreign press misses them completely because of their focus on the "big story." However, the Japanese prefer to work incrementally, improving things a little at a time (*ippo ippo*). By the time the technopolises surface physically, everything will be in place. Indeed, because of its enormous scope, many Japanese view technopolis as a nationwide experiment in long-term business planning, surpassing the fifth generation computer as the big story for the next century.

HOW DO THE TECHNOPOLISES RATE?

Although the technopolises are still in the early organizing phase, how does one evaluate their chances for success? Indeed, how does one define success? One method, which the Japanese themselves used in planning their technopolises, is to identify the key factors behind the success of Silicon Valley and other U.S. high-tech regions. What are these factors? And how do Japan's technopolises rate? When one looks at Silicon Valley, Boston's Route 128, North Carolina's Research Triangle, and Minneapolis, several factors stand out.

Imaginative Local Leadership

Probably the most important factor is the presence of imaginative, committed leaders at the local level, whether in industry, government, education, or the media. In Silicon Valley, Fred Terman, Lee DeForest, and Dr. William Shockley provided the compelling vision and leadership that shaped the direction of the valley and attracted a critical mass of talented researchers. In North Carolina, Governor Luther Hodges and Romeo Guest provided the spark behind the Research Triangle. And in Minneapolis, William Norris of Control Data and other business leaders have been the driving force behind the city's economic renaissance. In each case, the power of new ideas, enduring foresight, and the ability to mobilize others around a compelling vision have been the distinguishing keys to success.

How do Japan's technopolises compare? Until recently, Japanese governors and local industry leaders have kept a low profile in formulating national industrial policy. Because of Japan's strong central government, they have deferred to MITI bureaucrats in matters of industrial planning and to the Ministry of Home Affairs and the Ministry of Finance regarding local administration and finance. When it comes to forging new ideas or policies, Tokyo-based politicians like former Prime Minister Kakuei Tanaka controlled the agenda. For prefectural leaders, the conventional wisdom has been: "The protruding nail gets beaten down."

But the times are changing, and local Japanese leaders have become more dynamic and outspoken. Perhaps the best example is Governor Morihiko Hiramatsu of Oita Prefecture—formerly the head of MITI's Electronics Policy Bureau and the "father" of the Technopolis program—who is a model for aspiring mayors and governors. By thrusting backward Oita Prefecture into the national limelight, he has created a new image for regional leaders. His protégé, Governor Morihiro Hosokawa from neighboring Kumamoto Prefecture, adds an international flavor to the technopolis program, which appeals to younger executives and voters. These governors are replacing the "money politics" image of older politicians such as Kakuei Tanaka, who funneled enormous funds into Niigata Prefecture, giving the Nagaoka Technopolis a chance. Because of their unorthodox charisma and new ideas, Hiramatsu and Hosokawa have lured many companies into their regions. Other governors are following in their footsteps, pointing to a new era in Japanese politics, a trend that promises to open the technopolises to more international exchanges and cross-fertilization of ideas.

Strong Research Universities

America's leading high-tech regions are noted for their top-flight research universities, such as Boston's MIT, Silicon Valley's Stanford University, and Austin's University of Texas, which have strong ties with local industry. However, in this area, Japan's technopolises are severely handicapped. Japan has strong national universities in Tokyo, Kyoto, Osaka, and other major cities, but its regional universities are weak compared to American state universities. Not only do they lack adequate laboratory facilities and equipment because of insufficient funding, but they receive few donations from Japanese companies, which often hold these universities in low regard. Most Japanese firms train researchers in-house and focus on immediately commercializable research. When they donate money, they often fund chairs in foreign universities to buy goodwill. As a result, there are few technology exchanges with local universities.

Moreover, Japanese universities maintain a strict hierarchy that discourages independent research and outside consulting with industry. Most graduate researchers must conduct their work under the auspices of a department head and cannot claim inventions or patents in their own names. As a result, innovative projects are often stifled and basic research goes ignored. Many technopolises are trying to overcome this bottleneck by strengthening their university science and engineering departments, but major policy changes will be required from the Ministry of Education to free these departments from the existing constraints.

National R&D Projects

Many Americans criticize Japanese industrial policies as unfair because MITI and other government agencies fund national R&D projects. But the United States is itself a major proponent of large-scale R&D through NASA's space shuttle program and the Department of Defense's "Star Wars" program. Although industry leaders are reluctant to admit it, Silicon Valley was spawned by NASA's Apollo Project and the Defense Department's huge procurement contracts. Fairchild, the incubator for many Silicon Valley start-ups, received NASA contracts to develop integrated circuits for the Apollo spacecraft computer. Lockheed, FMC, and other companies received billions of dollars in defense contracts to develop new guidance systems, microwave receivers, and satellite communications.

Using NASA and our Defense Department as a model, Japan has organized over thirty national R&D projects to develop leading-edge technologies. These projects are primarily aimed at commercial markets, but they have military applications. Probably the key project is Nippon Telegraph and Telephone's plan to build the Information Network System, a $120 billion nationwide network of satellites and fiber optic cables that will link the technopolises to Tokyo and create new service jobs. Oita, Kumamoto, and other technopolises are installing INS services that will give them an advantage in attracting new companies.

However, technology transfer from Japan's other national R&D projects to the technopolises will be more difficult because of "big business"-oriented policies. Most national projects only accept major corporations with headquarters in Tokyo, eliminating small innovative companies and regional companies. The ministries run regional testing laboratories, but these "transfer agents" are less effective than actual participation by the companies themselves. To overcome this obstacle, the technopolises are organizing Technology Development Centers and local R&D projects, but this is a wasteful duplication of energy and resources. Unless Japanese ministries invite smaller regional companies into their laboratories in the Tsukuba Science City or, better yet, decentralize their research, it is unlikely that national R&D projects will give the technopolises a significant boost.

Close Industry/Government Ties

At the national level, the close ties between the central government and big business have given Japan the sobriquet "Japan Inc." However, at the local level, this strong interaction has been missing, except in Kyushu, where local industry leaders have played an active role in planning the region's transition from coal mining to manufacturing and high technology. In most regions local industry has not been regularly called upon to participate in joint R&D projects or industrial planning, which has been the responsibility of the central government. Even in the early phases of the Technopolis program, many prefectures second-guessed local industries by hiring Tokyo consulting firms to do their planning. Since 1980, Japanese prefectures have begun forging a working partnership with local industry leaders. They are organizing study missions, industry associations, and joint R&D projects. But it will take time to build a consensus and solidify these relationships, the human network that is crucial for building the technopolises.

A Critical Mass of Talented People

But merely having strong research universities and colleges is not enough to create a high-tech region. As Silicon Valley and Boston's Route 128 learned, it is important to attract fresh new talent and to keep emerging "engineering stars" and entrepreneurs from being lured away to other areas. This is the key problem facing the technopolises. Despite the steady flow of local college graduates, few jobs are available to keep these people from leaving. Moreover, "U-turn" workers returning from Tokyo and other large cities find it difficult to apply their sophisticated skills. Even where there are good jobs, such as in Hiroshima and Hamamatsu, there is often no sense of excitement or challenge for many people—that imaginative "spark," if you will.

Several technopolises are trying to create that critical mass of talented researchers. Toyama has set up a talent bank and instituted a Toyama Novel Prize to encourage creative researchers. Okayama has convinced Hayashibara, a creative biotechnology research firm, to open an R&D and production plant in its technopolis. Kyocera, the world's leader in ceramics, has concentrated its research labs in Kagoshima's Kokubu-Hayato Technopolis. And the prefectures in the northern Tohoku region are rallying around Dr. Junichi Nishizawa, a well-known optoelectronics researcher. Each of these approaches holds great promise, but none of them has yet catalyzed the dynamic synergy found in Silicon Valley.

An Attractive Environment and Adequate Services

One area where the technopolises have a distinct advantage over Silicon Valley is an attractive living environment and adequate public services. Because of poor planning in the past, Silicon Valley lacks adequate housing and parks, our cultural and historic roots have been pulled up, toxic wastes threaten our underground water supplies, and our roads are hopelessly snarled with traffic as commuters try to drive from one end of the valley to the other. By contrast, the technopolises are being systematically planned to avoid the mistakes we have made in the United States. Housing areas are located close to industrial parks, highways and airports are being expanded, strict environmental controls are enforced, and adequate parks and recreational facilities are being built.

Nevertheless, there are several glaring weaknesses in this aspect of the technopolis program. Most obvious is the lack of attention paid to farmland acquisition. Despite the Japanese' emotional ties to their rural origins and strong opposition from farmers near the Tsukuba Science City and Narita International Airport, few of the technopolises have well-conceived land acquisition programs to deal with the inevitable land-use conflicts that will occur between farmers and high-tech industries. How will land be apportioned? Who will be the winners and losers? How will costs and benefits be shared equitably? These are questions that many prefectures are only beginning to ask. Indeed, many officials are coming to Silicon Valley for insights into our loss of valuable farmland.

Another problem area is land speculation and high housing costs. Because Japan is such a small country, land prices are generally higher than in the United States, especially near cities such as Hamamatsu and Hiroshima. Even in rural technopolises, land speculation is becoming a problem, since the technopolis zones are already designated. Few prefectures have the money to acquire the land outright, or well-conceived acquisition plans, so landowners are in a strong position to raise the ante. Moreover, the construction of roads, highways, and airports opens the door to the political payoffs, construction kickbacks, and profiteering that plagued the bullet train project and Kakuei Tanaka's "remodeling plan." This land inflation is likely to scare away young researchers and high-tech companies looking for less expensive land.

Finally, like the Tsukuba Science City, the technopolises run the risk of becoming high-priced showpieces that are expensive to maintain and operate. The Ministry of Construction estimates that each technopolis will spend at least $1 billion for major infrastructure projects, and this is likely to double or triple over time, as Tsukuba did, especially given the political pressures for large pork barrel projects to create jobs. As in the United States, Japanese governors and mayors may fall into the trap of pushing bricks-and-mortar and creating monuments to attract media coverage, but at the expense of funding creative research. While this approach may help blue-collar workers in the short run, it will hurt the technopolises in the long run. Already, many Japanese companies are shying away from the technopolises because of media overexposure, high land prices, and uncertain R&D programs.

Venture Capital

In recent years, venture capitalists have become the media darlings in Silicon Valley. They can literally create companies or shut them down overnight. While this injection of funding has helped many start-up companies secure first-round financing, venture capital is no longer viewed as the panacea to maintaining our long-term industrial competitiveness. Venture capitalists tend to be followers, not leaders. They funded too many lookalike computer companies in the early 1980s, then shut off the spigot during the industry downturn in 1984 and 1985, contributing to the rollercoaster effect in Silicon Valley. By cutting off funding to whole industry sectors, they sent signals to Wall Street that trebled the financial impact. Stock prices tumbled and long-term financing dried up.

Because of this hit-and-run, on-off approach to financing, Japan's technopolises are taking a second look at the role of venture capital in promoting high-tech growth. Many prefectures are forming government-sponsored venture capital consortiums that include representatives from local industries, universities, and banks, to overcome the trendy, short-term orientation that plagues the American venture capital market. While such groups are stopgap measures to compensate for the absence of a strong venture capital market, these efforts deserve close attention from American states because of their novel collaborative approach. Perhaps Japan will discover a new way to channel the dynamism of the venture capital market so as to improve its long-term industrial competitiveness.

Innovative Public Schools

A key consideration for the long-term success of the technopolises is Japan's public school system. Unlike the United States, where educational policies are developed at the local level, Japan's educational system is highly centralized at the Ministry of Education. While this approach has ensured a uniformly high standard of education, it has failed to produce enough of the creative researchers and employees needed for high-tech industries. Japanese students are educated to be obedient followers and meticulous workers, rather than entrepreneurial explorers. For the technopolises to succeed in creating next-generation industries, the Ministry of Education will have to modify its rigid, conservative policies. Currently, the Japanese government is considering plans for educational reform, but the government proposals are rather backward-looking, calling for a return to moral training and more discipline. While self-discipline is required for creative research, these proposals downplay the importance of critical inquiry and individuality. The technopolises will need innovative, independent-minded people who are not afraid to challenge conventions and break taboos.

Where will these people come from? How can Japan's educational system, which forms the bedrock for the emerging technopolises, produce these people? In the next chapter we will examine Japan's search for alternative ways of promoting creativity and educational reform.

PART IV: THE FUTURE

Looking Ahead

During the next fifteen years, Japan will race to complete its technopolises. New universities, research institutes, industrial parks, telecommunications networks, housing, and parks will be built throughout the country. Major high-tech companies have begun moving their research labs, software development centers, and production lines out of the Tokyo-Osaka corridor. The new "Japan Tech" is emerging.

But the real challenge for the technopolises is not bricks and mortar; it is the nurturing of creative people. During the next fifteen years, Japan must develop its own sources of creativity if the technopolises are to succeed. Creativity must become its industrial slogan and rallying cry. Until then, "Japan as Number One" will only remain an empty catchphrase.

For America, the challenge of Technopolis is clear. We must clearly understand the nature of the emerging "Japan Tech." We must study Japan's high-tech research projects and technopolises, and apply their lessons to our own high-tech regions. But we should not try to copy Japan. The United States already has its own national industrial policies; we should seek ways to build on our strengths as a nation to prepare our industries and regions for the twenty-first century. Unlike Japan, our challenge is not a lack of creativity, but a lack of imaginativeness in using our creativity to its fullest potential.

10

JAPAN'S PURSUIT OF CREATIVITY

What kind of school shall we build next?

Tetsuko Kuroyanagi
Totto-Chan: The Little Girl at the Window

THE SEARCH FOR CREATIVE EDUCATION

In 1981 a charming memoir written by Tetsuko Kuroyanagi, one of Japan's most popular TV personalities, appeared in bookstores throughout the country. Entitled *Totto-Chan,* the book recalls her experience of being expelled from school for being too curious and spontaneous. Instead of sitting quietly at her desk, Totto-chan was a maverick who drew pictures differently and stood near an open window where she could chat with passing street musicians and nesting swallows. Embarrassed by her daughter's idiosyncracies, Totto-chan's mother enrolled her in an experimental school run by Sosaku Kobayashi, a headmaster who believed that the innate curiosity of children could be nurtured to produce people with individuality. Sharing with his students the joys of music, reading, nature hikes, and independent study, he took the rejects of Japan's rigid educational system and gave them the freedom to blossom in their own way. His school, Tomoe School, was a tiny haven of creativity in Japan's militaristic prewar years.

Totto-Chan was a runaway success. Within two years it sold over six million copies, making it the bestselling book in Japanese publishing history. Overnight, *Totto-Chan* became a household word. Parents, teachers, and educators rushed to the bookstore to learn about this unconventional school, and numerous articles were written about it. Mothers wanted their children to grow up

211

as creative and original as Tetsuko. Women wanted to fathom the secrets of her success. For the Japanese, who are so obsessed with getting their children into the "right" school, why did this book cause so much excitement? What did Kuroyanagi say that was compelling or new? And what does *Totto-Chan* have to do with MITI's Technopolis Concept?

Totto-Chan's popularity stems in large part from Kuroyanagi herself. An unusually dynamic, articulate woman who shatters traditional stereotypes about Japanese women, she is the host of a popular TV talk show, *Tetsuko's Room*—a Japanese version of the Johnny Carson Show. Because of her lively and stimulating interviews, she has singlehandedly changed Japanese thinking about women at work.

But her popularity also reflects the growing disenchantment with Japan's educational system. Despite glowing reviews from foreign observers, Japanese public schools suffer from numerous weaknesses that make them poorly suited to meet Japan's latest push into high technology. Much has been written about the fierce competition, overemphasis on rote memorization, and the infamous university entrance exams ("exam hell") that determine a person's station in life; but these are only symptoms of a deeper, more serious problem: the lack of educational diversity and individual choice.

Dr. Thomas Rohlen, author of *Japan's High Schools*, observes that the tight educational straitjacket may be contributing to the growing alienation among Japanese youth. "The young Japanese finds one's social status and life opportunities are rapidly being fixed. High school does not represent an opening up of choice, but a narrowing down of focus. The overwhelming reality is not one of growing independence, but of certain inescapable givens . . . It is a tight regime that does not encourage personal dreams, experimentation, individual variety or idealism. These remain largely unexpressed and private." In the past, individual choice was sacrificed for the sake of economic survival and the need to rebuild the nation's war-torn economy; but with growing affluence this necessity no longer exists. For Japan's technopolises and high-tech industries, this suppression of individuality is the nation's major weakness.

In effect, Japanese youth are being robbed of the opportunity to dream, explore, and choose—the very essence of creativity. At an early age they are forced to buckle down to the unhappy task of adapting to a demanding society that does not forgive failures. They are told to sacrifice their dreams for the common good; but now the common good demands just the opposite. The problem is not just the exam hell, but the fact that Japanese have little choice in educational matters. Everyone must study the same material at the same time, an approach that enforces uniformity. Students cannot easily take time off after high school graduation to work, pursue their interests, or travel abroad for a few years, since they are not welcomed back upon their return. Diversity of experience, rather than being viewed as an asset, is suspiciously viewed as anti-social or slacking off. As a result, most Japanese young people hide within the safety of convention. If they could pursue alternative paths without fear of rejection later in life, there would be less stress and anxiety in the schools, and less tendency to be risk-averse—the major obstacle to creativity in Japan today.

Japanese schools are good at picking winners, but they do so at the expense of creating a "nation of losers" who are forever burdened with an inferiority complex because they failed one exam. In Japan there is no such thing as a second chance, different options, or "late bloomers." Everything is fixed at college entrance, even among the elite students of Tokyo University, who cannot change majors or take courses freely in other departments. Creativity does not flourish in this stifling environment.

Thus, it comes as no surprise that many Japanese dislike the country's rigid educational system. Growing alienation among Japanese youth, bullying (*ijime*), and violence in the schools worry parents who believe that the educational methods that once propelled the Japanese economic miracle are now faltering. Although low by U.S. standards, juvenile delinquency and assaults on teachers are on the rise. Frustration and disruptive behavior are becoming serious, especially among students on slower tracks and in technical high schools. The sense of purpose that drove the postwar generation to workaholic excesses is missing. In the United States, such rebellion against regimentation and the desire for more free time, friends, and hobbies is considered a natural reaction to growing prosperity. But in Japan it is ominously viewed as the "English disease" or "American disease." A recent White Paper issued by the Prime Minister's Office concluded of today's youth: "They are devoid of perseverance, dependent upon others, and self-centered." There is a growing consensus that Japan's educational system must be reformed, but talk in official circles focuses on the revival of moral education and increased discipline—the antithesis of Japan's search for more creative education.

Into this confusion, *Totto-Chan* came as a breath of fresh air. Instead of painting a glum view of the world, it described an alternative approach to education in which students are active participants in the learning process, not merely empty receptacles to be stuffed with predigested knowledge. At Tomoe School the students were encouraged to pursue their interests and develop their talents to the fullest. The task of the instructor was to bring out the best in each student, especially the disadvantaged and the handicapped. Instead of being punished for being unruly, non-conforming children were allowed to be different. They were praised for their uniqueness and their education was tailored appropriately.

In the United States, with our long tradition of progressive education, *Totto-Chan* may seem anachronistic. But for many Japanese, *Totto-Chan* is seen as the key to creative education. It offers a positive vision of the future comparable to MITI's *Visions for the 1980s,* a bright picture that contrasts with the dark realities of Japan's educational system. Indeed, because of its emphasis on creativity and innovation, *Totto-Chan* might be considered the educational handmaiden to MITI's Technopolis Concept. Instead of relying on heavy-handed methods of shame and externally-imposed discipline, Tomoe School used the carrot to nurture intellectual curiosity. The basic premise of the Technopolis Concept is that the public schools will provide a steady flow of creative graduates in order for the emerging technopolises to flourish. Without talented people, no amount of government funding will help. So far, little has been done to reform local schools. This is probably the major weakness in the Technopolis program.

Tomoe School could be the model for a nationwide network of innovative public schools located in Japan's technopolises—a "Totto-Chan Concept," if you will. This approach would be beneficial for two reasons: it would provide creative graduates and attract discontented parents from Tokyo and other regions. These schools could form a complex of elementary, secondary, and university "magnet schools" designed to promote creativity in scientific research, the humanities, and the arts. Although many students would still prefer to enter top-ranked high schools and universities in Tokyo, more curious and less status-conscious students might be encouraged to pursue their studies in Technopolis schools under the close guidance of professors and teachers conducting research in grassroots technologies, such as fine ceramics, new materials, and aquaculture. These schools could become the source of Japan's creative new researchers, just as Stanford University became the seedbed for Silicon Valley in the 1950s. Moreover, they would prevent the proliferation of so-called progressive schools that are nothing more than private academies for the rich. This change in the public curriculum would take time, but as top coaches know, one must begin with primary school children in order to train Olympic athletes. To be ready for the technopolises when they take off in ten to fifteen years, the Ministry of Education and the prefectures must begin now.

Tomoe School's small student body demonstrates that a new approach to education could work. Akira Takahashi, a shy, physically-handicapped boy who had floundered in regular schools, is now a personnel manager in an electronics company in Hamamatsu City, one of the technopolises, while Taiji Yamanouchi is the assistant director at the Fermi National Accelerator Laboratory in Illinois, the world's largest. The school's other graduates have entered a variety of trades and professions. However, the real value of Tomoe School is not only measured in job status, but also personal enrichment. Unlike other Japanese students, its graduates did not silently suffer through their education. Like Tetsuko Kuroyanagi, they experienced the joy of learning which they have passed on to others. For that, Japan is all the richer.

ARE THE JAPANESE CREATIVE?

One of the most enduring beliefs in the West today is that the Japanese are "copycats in kimonos"—imitators who lack originality and creative skills. This reputation is largely a western perception based on Japan's zealous borrowing of ideas and technologies from the West since the Meiji period. Few Americans would argue, for example, that Europeans are imitators because they borrowed ideas from ancient Greece or Rome, or that Americans are copycats because we borrowed ideas and customs from England, France, Germany, and a hundred other countries. We proudly label our copying "progress," the "melting pot," or the "brain drain." Nevertheless, the stereotype of Japan-as-copycat still persists. Why is this? How does our copying differ from Japanese copying? Is it because Japan is forced to deliberately import foreign technologies because it lacks a steady stream of immigrants who bring new ideas with them? (In Silicon Valley, for example, a quarter of our engineers are foreign-born.) Or is there perhaps a difference between western and Japanese views of creativity?

Keisuke Yawata, formerly of NEC and now president of LSI Logic K.K., believes Japanese view creativity differently. "It depends on how you define creativity," he says. "Japanese are very good at taking existing ideas and improving on them. We are creative in process engineering and industrial design, but weak in thinking up entirely new ideas, especially in basic sciences. Since we don't emphasize western-style individualism, most Americans believe we are not creative."

Robert Rosenfeld of Kodak's Office of Innovation and Jenny Servo of the Community College of the Finger Lakes articulate the western view of creativity. "Creativity refers to generating new and novel ideas, where innovation refers to the application of an idea, leading ultimately to increased profits or improved services. Although creativity and innovation are intimately related, they are distinct concepts. However, in today's complex society, innovation is almost always a collaborative enterprise, requiring the cooperation of numerous individuals."

Using this definition, Japanese are not considered creative because they are group-oriented and prefer to embellish existing ideas. But is this a valid definition of creativity? Or is it a culturally-biased standard that reflects our myth of the rugged individual—the proverbial Einstein or the inventor-in-the-garage? Can't groups be creative too, as in brainstorming sessions? Aren't there other forms of creativity besides scientific discoveries, inventions, and artistic and literary endeavors? What about creativity in business management and industrial design?

To be sure, the cultural and historical roots that underlie our beliefs about creativity differ greatly from those of Japan. In the West, we value rational, scientific thought. In school we are taught the Socratic method of inquiry that involves a series of rationally-framed questions and answers. This intense cross-examining, combined with public debate, is our tool for logical thinking or scientific exploration. We Americans tend to believe there is always a scientific explanation to a problem.

In Japan, the closest historic parallel to the Socratic method is the *Zen-mondo* (question and answer session) in which a *koan,* or rationally unsolvable riddle, is asked by the Zen priest. Unlike the Socratic method, there is no rational solution, because the goal is enlightenment or intuitive understanding. Zen Buddhist philosophy does not place great value on rational thought alone. Daisetz Suzuki, professor of Buddhist Philosophy at Kyoto's Otani University, explains:

> *Prajna* (intuition) is the self-knowledge of the whole in contrast to *vijnana* (reason), which busies itself with parts. *Prajna* is an integrating principle, while *vijnana* always analyzes. *Vijnana* cannot work without having *prajna* behind it; parts are parts of the whole; parts never exist by themselves, for if they did they would not be parts— they would cease to exist.

Because of this non-rational or intuitive approach, discovery or enlightenment (*Eureka* in the West and *satori* in Japan) had totally different meanings in the two cultures. *Eureka* referred to the discovery of rational scientific principles, while *satori* meant personal enlightenment.

Perhaps this emphasis on intuition explains Japan's traditional weakness in basic scientific research where logical reasoning plays a central role. On the other hand, the Zen heritage might also explain why Japanese are strong in the design arts that require synthesis and holistic (right brain) thinking as opposed to rational (left brain) analysis. During the Ashikaga Period (1338–1573), Zen Buddhism gave rise to a strong cultural tradition that emphasizes form, etiquette, and design. The tea ceremony (*cha-no-yu*), the use of natural woods and settings in architecture, rock gardens, Noh theater, and brush painting (*suiboku*) all reflect the discipline and simplicity of Zen. As Professor John Hall of Yale University, notes:

This syndrome of sensibilities was given expression in an aesthetic vocabulary which has endured to modern times as being particularly Japanese: *yūgen* (the mystery between appearances), *wabi* (the mystery of loneliness), and *sabi* (the mystery of change).

This taste for refined simplicity and quiet (*wabi*), combined with a predilection for visual design, can be discerned in many Japanese products, ranging from televisions and stereos to Fumihiko Maki's sparse architecture and Issey Miyake's draped fashion designs. It may explain why Japanese companies have been strong industrial designers, and even why MITI chose an image-oriented approach to fifth generation computers. Can one argue that this process of visual refinement and synthesis, this pulling together of disparate parts, is any less creative than basic scientific discovery and analysis? And if the Japanese are such strong designers, what does this portend for future electronic, computer, and automotive design using powerful computer-aided design tools? Will the Japanese out-design us in the future?

Oryon Ye, visiting scholar at Tokyo University and instructor at Seoul University, believes there is another reason for the difference between Japanese, who are good at miniaturizing, simplifying, and redesigning existing products such as televisions and cars, and westerners, who excel at pioneering new ideas. Japan, he argues, is a *naruhodo* ("I see" or "indeed") culture that works within its geographic and resource limits, while America has always been a frontier society that has explored beyond the horizon, a legacy of its European founders. Unlike England, Portugal, or Spain, which sought routes to the Orient, Japan never became an adventurous maritime nation, despite being surrounded by water. Its ships stayed close to shore and studied nearby China, the most advanced civilization at the time. During the Tokugawa period, Japan's isolationist policies prohibited the construction of seagoing ships. Thus, for thousands of years, Japan's spirit of exploration and discovery was stifled. Its people became expert at taking their meager resources and maximizing their output. Production, not invention or discovery, was a means of daily survival. Creativity meant shaping existing resources into usable items. Is it any wonder then that Japan is weak at exploring the unknown and strong at improving the known? The question is: does this approach mean they are any less creative?

INDUSTRIAL CREATIVITY

Soozoo—creativity—the elegant flow of kanji characters graces the pages of an industrial newspaper, challenging the reader to become more creative at work. Ten years ago, this word was rarely seen in the Japanese business press, but now it appears almost daily. Creativity is no longer just an empty phrase, but has entered the mainstream. It has become a rallying cry for Japanese business leaders determined to show that Japan is no longer just a second-rate imitator.

NEC President Tadahiro Sekimoto argues: "Japan emphasized collective harmony as a way of catching up with the United States and Europe, but as the world moves into the information age, Japanese managers must stress creativity." Fujitsu President Takuma Yamamoto is even more adamant: "The creativity of the Japanese people will be called into question from the latter half of the 1980s through the 1990s. The whole nation must work like one possessed to meet this great challenge." One Japanese leader who has accepted the challenge is Dr. Kazuhiro Fuchi, manager of the Institute for New Generation Computer Technology (ICOT), who sees his own role as more than just developing new computer technology. "The fifth generation computer is important because Japan is trying to make some contribution to the world. It is important for us to overcome the copycat image. We want to encourage innovation. This project is evidence that Japanese society is going to try new things on its own, and not just follow others." The unspoken message is clear: Japan's national pride is at stake. If the country is to hold its head up in the world, Japanese must become more creative.

Where are we likely to see a blossoming of Japanese creativity? If history is a guide, one would expect Japanese industry to be creative in ideas where it has traditionally been strong: the synthesis of ideas and concepts, design, manufacturing processes, and new commercial applications. If one looks around Japan, there are increasing signs of Japanese creativity. Many electronics companies are developing computer-aided design (CAD) systems and software to speed up the design process. Hitachi recently announced a supercomputer-based system that permits three-dimensional analysis of complex chip designs. In biotechnology, CAD systems are being investigated for use in recombinant DNA and gene splicing. Tokyo University researchers recently announced personal computer software that displays images of nucleic acid structures, while Kureha and Fujitsu introduced CAD tools that feature 3-D molecular displays. In the fashion industry, d'Urban and Mitsubishi are using computerized high-speed lasers to cut clothing patterns. Even traditional textile makers are computerizing their operations. In Kagoshima, one of the technopolises, the famous Oshima pongee brocade makers are using CAD systems to design complex floral patterns, a process that is extremely tedious and time-consuming when done by hand.

Fashion design, architecture, photography, graphic design, and video-imaging are also examples of Japanese creativity at its best. Since Kenzo first displayed his designs in Paris and New York, Japanese fashion designers have captured the imagination of people around the world with their wildly innovative designs. Issey Miyake's sculpted fabrics, Yohji Yamamoto's gingham coats, Hanae Mori's silky elegance, and Mitsuhiro Matsuda's Annie Hall look reflect the variety of experimentation going on in Japan. Under their cosmopolitan air, they are also searching for their roots by using traditional Japanese textiles, such as *sashiko* (quilted material used for workmen's clothes) and *tanzen* (housecoat). The fashion industry has spawned a whole industry of fashion photographers and advertisers who can be seen scurrying through the streets of New York, Tokyo, and Paris. This activity is gradually being felt throughout Japan.

The battle for creativity is also heating up among Japan's more traditional companies. Since 1984, over seventy-five electronics companies have opened laboratories to pursue basic research in next-generation technologies, including biotechnology, bioelectronics, fine ceramics, speech recognition and synthesis, artificial intelligence, automatic translation phones, and other fields. Many of these products will not be commercialized for another ten to fifteen years.

This boom in corporate research spending is paralleled by joint research by universities and companies. In 1984 the Ministry of Education launched a new joint R&D system covering twenty-eight technologies involving twenty-six companies and thirteen national universities. The Science and Technology Agency has also organized the Creative Research and Technology Promotion

System and MITI the Next Generation Industry Basic Technology R&D System.

Despite heavy R&D spending, Japanese face an uphill struggle in their search for creativity for one reason: their hiring policies. As Masahiko Ishizuka of the *Japan Economic Journal* notes: "The excessive public preoccupation with academic careers is a direct outcome of the recruiting and employment policies of leading Japanese companies. First-rate companies like to limit their recruitment to new graduates of a handful of prestigious universities, especially Tokyo University." In effect, Japanese companies created the "exam hell" that has stifled creativity in Japan. Because their recruitment and hiring policies emphasize good grades, attendance at the "right" school, and sociability, they automatically eliminate the protruding nails—the creative people who rebel against conformity and convention. It would be like Apple Computer only hiring students from MIT, Stanford, and Cal Tech.

In Japan brilliant, second-rate students are never allowed into the company. Usually, they show up in Japan's blossoming venture business sector. Japan's most creative ventures are begun by graduates of Japan's second-ranked universities and corporate dropouts, such as Takayoshi Shiina of Sord Computer, Masayoshi Son of Japan Soft Bank, and Ikutaro Kakehashi of Rolland.

Thus, top Japanese companies have been hypocritical in demanding creative students from the educational system when their hiring policies discourage experimentation and creativity in the schools. If they were genuinely interested in creativity, they would hire graduates of second- and third-ranked national universities, junior colleges, and private schools. They would place less emphasis on test scores and grades, and more on extracurricular activities and unique achievements. They would sponsor annual science and technology contests for college students and offer scholarships and jobs to those with the best exhibits and ideas. They would donate money and equipment to financially-strapped Japanese universities, instead of donating only to foreign universities to buy goodwill. They would encourage the Ministry of Education to hire foreign professors at the national universities. They would let line managers interview and hire directly instead of going through personnel divisions. They would hire the 5,000 unemployed Ph.Ds who are considered too old, independent, and individualistic. They would hire more foreigners, both overseas and in Japan, and promote top performers to upper management. They would fund venture subsidiaries and let managers recruit freely, giving successful employees an opportunity to work in the parent company. They would recruit Japanese working and studying abroad.

There are many ways Japanese companies can promote creativity, but the key is management policy. Companies must be willing to encourage innovative education and take risks in hiring and promotion. Until this basic change occurs, Japanese students will not take risks and even massive educational reform will fail. And MITI's technopolises will never really take off.

11

WHITHER AMERICA?

Despite the conceits of New York and Washington, D.C., almost nothing starts there . . . America is a bottom-up society.

John Naisbitt, Megatrends

THE COMING DELUGE

America is a strong nation technologically, but there are dangers in being Number One. We have been at the center of creative research for so long that we have developed blind spots and signs of rigidity. In Silicon Valley, most companies do not bother to closely monitor foreign technology or market trends, an activity which they view as an unnecessary luxury or waste of time. They naively believe that if their product is good, the world will beat a path to their doorstep. Many suffer from the "Not Invented Here" syndrome—if it's not invented in Silicon Valley it can't be very innovative. We are so enraptured with our advanced technologies, venture capital, and start-up companies that we believe that Japan will never touch us. Japan's fifth generation computer program may worry a handful of computer experts, but most Americans believe that the Japanese are weak in software, despite the fact that Japanese companies are investing heavily in software development centers, and are already installing expert systems into their computers, communications links, automated assembly lines, and office products. Over 2,000 software start-ups are located in Tokyo, but this news never reaches our shores. By and large, we believe that if it's "Made in Japan," it can't be very creative. Unfortunately, we said the same thing about Japanese quality twenty years ago, and are now losing jobs and industries

223

as a result. Our lack of vigilance has often misled us. We are like a
ship navigating through icebergs without someone on watch.

As we approach the 1990s, the technology race with Japan will
accelerate. We are already seeing the beginning of a patent deluge
from Japan, which will be followed in the late 1980s by a deluge
of creative new products and companies in a variety of areas,
including ceramics, artificial intelligence, robotics, semiconductors, automatic language translation, biotechnology, lasers, speech
synthesis, solar energy, and supercomputers. Japan has over thirty
national R&D programs scheduled to run until 1990; they are
halfway toward completion and spinning off patents and technical
papers. The initial products from these projects are already landing on our shores.

Japanese society is undergoing major changes that will dramatically alter its character. Its population is aging rapidly, moving to
smaller cities, and seeking more creative outlets. Japanese young
people are more interested in family and friends than in
workaholic excesses, but with the aid of advanced technologies
they will work smarter, not harder, to stay competitive with South
Korea and other emerging industrial powers. Since April 1985,
Japan's telecommunications market has been partially deregulated, and Nippon Telegraph and Telephone and its competitors
are pouring billions of dollars into optical fibers, satellites, and
video communications. This is Japan's "bullet train for the 1980s,"
which some economists believe will create a market of $300 to
$500 billion over the next twenty years. It will be an opportunity
for foreign companies, and a springboard for Japanese electronics
companies. Already Japanese companies are reaping the benefits
of AT&T's divestiture; they are selling fiber optics, mobile phones,
satellite broadcasting receivers, and video communications equipment in the United States. To avoid trade friction, they are also
building new R&D centers and plants in the United States. While
this may reduce the trade imbalance, it will pose a major challenge to American industry.

By 1990, Japan will challenge the United States in most areas
of basic research and advanced technology. The Japanese venture capital market, start-up businesses, and technopolises are
still taking shape, but by the early 1990s new products and
industries will emerge. Entrepreneurs are appearing in Tokyo
and other Japanese cities; by 1990 the "herd mentality" may

well lead to a stampede of start-up companies as Japan's yuppies look for more glamorous and challenging work. Ceramics, new alloys, biotechnology, software, robotics, flexible manufacturing systems (FMS), computer-aided design, instruction, and education (CAD/CAI/CAE) are fields to watch because of Japan's traditional strength in industrial design, process techniques, and video technology. Japan is already being forced by South Korea and other Southeast Asian countries to develop more innovative, high-end products, such as "intelligent" televisions, VCRs, and cars. The technology battle will heat up to a white-hot pace. By the year 2000, MITI's technopolises will be ready; they will become major centers of Japanese science and technology for the next century. These new castle towns will be the incubators not only for new products and technologies, but new ideas, services, and lifestyles as well.

Thus, a deluge of creative Japanese technologies is coming, one which will cause a massive restructuring of the world economy. Will we be ready for this high-tech wave from Japan Tech? Or will we resort to Japan-bashing and protectionism, as we are doing now? These are questions we must address now if we are to avoid a bruising, counterproductive trade war and maintain a viable economy in the 1990s. The choice is ours. Which way will we go?

WHAT CAN WE LEARN FROM TECHNOPOLIS?

In light of this coming deluge from Japan, what can we learn from the Technopolis program that will enable us to protect our industries and maintain our industrial competitiveness?

Probably the most important lesson is that Silicon Valley can and is being repeated elsewhere; it is not a one-of-a-kind historical fluke that just "happened." Government agencies, such as the Department of Defense and NASA, were instrumental in providing the stimulus and funding for our semiconductor and computer industries. Without these programs, Silicon Valley would not have achieved its rapid takeoff. Moreover, without ongoing government support in the form of defense procurement, the space shuttle program, state and local funding of education, tax policies, and industrial park development, Silicon Valley companies would not be able to thrive. MITI's Technopolis program recognizes government's important role, and attempts to coordinate it with private industry, focusing on the link between national R&D projects and regional development.

The Technopolis program also sheds invaluable insight into what makes Silicon Valley and American society tick. When I speak with Japanese business and government leaders, they are fascinated by the Yankee spirit for which this country is known. What are they attracted to? Our optimism and enthusiasm, creativity, individuality and personal freedoms, entrepreneurialism, venture capital, critical and unconventional thinking, openness to new ideas and people, excellent universities and colleges, life-long education, cross-fertilization of ideas between industry and universities, regional diversity, local initiative and grassroots organizing, informal networking, labor mobility, equal opportunity, ethnic and cultural variety, and other features of our open society. Indeed, we are blessed with such a deep reservoir of people and new ideas that we routinely take them for granted. Our problem is not a lack of resources, but our short-sightedness and inability to choose among the many opportunities available to us. The Japanese are trying to create this diversity because they know it is essential for their high-tech industries, but it is difficult to achieve in a racially homogeneous, monocultural society.

For this reason, the Technopolis program is fascinating because it reveals how Japan learns and adapts new ideas from foreign countries to overcome its cultural homogeneity and geographic isolation. We have seen this process of "Japanization" in the past, from quality control techniques to semiconductor technology. Now the Japanese are systematically trying to adapt foreign urban forms. What is valuable about this "Japanizing" of Silicon Valley is that the Japanese have systematically evaluated our strengths and weaknesses, and planned their technopolises to incorporate the lessons they have learned. Now many American regions are looking to Silicon Valley for new ideas; they may gain insights from Japan's systematic approach, which involves long-term business planning, "bottom-up" consensus-making, and broad industry-government cooperation at the regional and local level. Moreover, this process of "Japanization" may offer ideas about "Americanizing" practices from Japan.

When visiting the technopolises, I am constantly struck by the vast difference between how Japanese and Americans view high technology. Because of our massive military spending, many Americans have become disillusioned and openly hostile to math, science, and technology, equating them with bigger bombs, "smarter" missiles, and death rays. Our technology, once a symbol of American ingenuity, has become synonymous with Dr. Strangelove and "Star Wars," the love of technology gone mad. By contrast, the Japanese tend to view technology in a more optimistic, hopeful light because of their focus on commercial applications. They see Technopolis and fifth generation computers as ways to develop better products and improve their standard of living. High technology and culture go hand-in-hand; they are not viewed as adversaries, as in the United States.

The Technopolis program reflects this balanced approach to technology. Instead of focusing only on industrial parks and R&D projects, the prefectural governments also emphasize sports programs, cultural activities, and social programs to develop well-rounded citizens. Japanese industry and government leaders are cautious about becoming too myopic and like to discuss the "big picture," often waxing philosophical about broad issues: Where is Japan headed? Where will our city be in thirty years? What type of people do we want to raise? How can we use technology to solve social and medical problems? How can our Technopolis contribute to reducing the trade conflict? In my years in Silicon Valley, rarely have I met business leaders concerned about the big picture. Most people here are only worried about their personal careers and the "big score"; Silicon Valley's future only interests them to the extent that it affects their bottom line. Few industry leaders bother to form advisory groups to study Japan or plan for the future; that is considered government's role.

Finally, the Technopolis program offers valuable ideas about how Japan's regions are reviving their depressed industries with high technology. Instead of phasing them out and laying off older workers, MITI, business leaders, and local government are devising ways to rejuvenate these industries. Kagoshima's ceramic joint research project involving centuries-old pottery makers, and Yamaguchi's investigation of robotics, new alloys, and marine technology, are examples of Japan's "recycling" approach—a strong contrast with the "let 'em rot" philosophy pervading our federal policies.

These are only some of the lessons we can learn from Japan's Technopolis experiment. The Japanese are by no means perfect in their approach, nor should we try to emulate them. Rather, the Technopolis strategy should be seen for what it is: Japan's attempt to revive its declining industries with high technology. There is much we can learn.

THE GRAYING OF SILICON VALLEY

Throughout the world, Silicon Valley is seen as the mecca of high technology, an inexhaustible source of innovative products and new ideas. It is our eternal fountain of youth, our last bastion of strength against the Japanese onslaught. Despite Japan's high-tech challenge, we believe that Japan will never catch up because it lacks the Valley's creativity, venture capital, and entrepreneurial spirit. In our minds Silicon Valley will always reign supreme in high technology because of our top-flight researchers. Japan may out-produce us, our industrial leaders claim, but they will never out-innovate us.

This situation may have been true in the past, but it is rapidly changing. Japan is no longer just copying the West, but pouring money into basic research and joint R&D programs. It is creating twenty Silicon Valleys of its own; many will take off within the next ten years. Meanwhile, Silicon Valley is quickly maturing. Once the destination for young engineers and their families, the valley has become an enclave of the rich and the established, a mecca of high finance, not high technology. Behind the flash and glitter of Mercedes-Benzes and split-level homes, there are signs that the Valley's fire and innovativeness are ebbing. What are the symptoms of this decline?

Since the early 1980s, Silicon Valley has begun reaching its limits. Constrained by San Francisco Bay and the surrounding foothills, the Valley is running out of space for industrial growth. Once centered in Palo Alto and Sunnyvale, new high-tech firms are now moving into north San Jose's Golden Triangle and into the East Bay cities of Milpitas, Fremont, Livermore, and Pleasanton. With the current downturn, there is still plenty of room for growth, but Silicon Valley will be built to capacity within twenty years. Already many companies are leaving the valley because of massive traffic jams, exorbitant housing prices, high taxes, smog, crime, and lack of open space. Intense competition is making people more harried and less neighborly. Once known as "the Valley of the Heart's Content," Silicon Valley is losing its charm. For many people it is no longer "our city" or "our valley," but "me first."

This trend is being pushed by the shakeout in computers, software, and disk drive makers, who are moving their manufacturing operations out of state and to Southeast Asia. Most of these jobs will never return. Dataquest, a high-tech market research firm in San Jose, estimates that the Japanese market will consume more semiconductors than the United States in 1986; the center of gravity is shifting to Tokyo. Moreover, basic research may soon leave the valley because of the high cost of office space and housing. The recent flight of engineering jobs from San Francisco is a harbinger of things to come. Already some companies are moving researchers to Austin, Texas and the Research Triangle to take advantage of lower costs and joint research projects. For many researchers Silicon Valley is no longer the hotbed of new ideas; it is losing its wild-eyed image and is becoming a financial and administrative headquarters staffed by silver-haired managers. Already the valley attracts more banks, securities firms, law firms, and support services than high-tech start-ups.

Indeed, the heady successes of the technological whiz-kids of the 1960s and 1970s are giving way to the cautiousness of investment managers and financial analysts. The entrepreneurial spirit that made Silicon Valley is alive and kicking, but it is now tempered by shrewd financial calculations. Marketing strategy and return-on-investment, not the hottest new technology, are the name of the game. Massive bankruptcies are just the opening shots in this high-tech marketing shootout. Within the next few years there will be more corporate casualties littering the landscape. The days of the garage inventor making it big are numbered. Venture capital firms and Wall Street investors are scrutinizing their investment portfolios and unloading high-risk accounts to provide second- and third-round financing for sure winners. In many cases Japanese conglomerates, not U.S. venture capitalists, are investing in high-risk research. As a result, many viable start-ups are being ignored in favor of existing stars with proven track records. The financial axe is falling over Silicon Valley.

This sudden flight of venture capital could have been expected in an economic downturn, but it bodes ill because it reduces our technological lead. Valley engineers are discouraged from taking risks because of the growing emphasis on finance and marketing. Engineers who were heroes for designing the most advanced microprocessor or floppy disk drive are now assembly-line designers for bottom-line-conscious managers. They are pushed to fill the gaps in product portfolios instead of pushing the limits of new technologies like gallium arsenide, semiconductor lasers, optoelectronics, bioelectronics, and three-dimensional ICs. The thrill of pursuing creative research is disappearing. High-profit, sure-win technology is in; risky designs are out. Ironically, we are now copying the Japanese, who are trying to become more creative like us. Because of cost pressures from Asia, manufacturing is the latest rage in management circles. But will we chase our creative researchers from the valley? How do we strengthen our manufacturing without shortchanging basic research? These issues are not being adequately addressed by our business leaders, who are worried about short-term profits and goals.

The wild card in Silicon Valley's future is toxic wastes. Since 1981, when underground tanks in south San Jose were discovered to be leaking the solvent trichloroethane, toxic chemicals have been found throughout the valley. In May 1984 state water officials found that toxic leaks had contaminated fifty private and public wells. The San Francisco Bay Area Regional Water Quality Control Board issued a list of 141 high-priority cleanup sites and 391 secondary sites throughout the valley. In October 1984 the Environmental Protection Agency placed nineteen major high-tech companies on the Superfund list of the nation's worst hazardous waste sites—giving Silicon Valley the largest number of identified sites in the entire country. Other high-tech areas have also discovered leaks, but Silicon Valley has uncovered the largest number to date. The Regional Water Quality Control Board estimates that more than 1,200 new leaks may be discovered in the valley as cities implement their hazardous materials programs.

The semiconductor industry has worked to solve the toxic chemical problem, spending about $100 million to identify, track, and clean up their sites. The Semiconductor Industry Association, the American Electronics Association, and the Santa Clara Manufacturing Group have organized the Industry Clean Water Task Force and drafted a Hazardous Materials Model Ordinance and a model building code for semiconductor facilities. Companies and government agencies are developing a monitoring and cleanup program, but these efforts are not foolproof; companies may miss spill sites. Recently, the Silicon Valley Toxics Coalition, a watchdog group, and labor unions have organized to keep up public pressure. They are also publicizing the potential occupational hazards to production-line workers exposed to chemicals. The top forty-two firms collectively use some two million gallons of acid, 500,000 gallons of solvents, and 1.5 million cubic feet of toxic gases annually. Although many of these chemicals have been tested on laboratory animals, their long-term effects on humans are still unknown.

Silicon Valley is not alone in its concern over toxic wastes. Japanese semiconductor makers and MITI are closely watching these developments, because toxic wastes could have an even more crippling impact on valuable farmlands and housing in the technopolises. Recently, NEC agreed to consult with local officials before introducing new chemicals and gases at its Kumamoto plant, the largest in the world. Other companies will probably follow suit before leaks trigger a major public reaction.

Thus, the myth of high technology as a "clean" industry has been thoroughly debunked. Silicon Valley is no longer paradise, but a maturing region faced with growing problems. Local cities and towns are working together to resolve these problems, but our quarterly-bottom line obsession and our fragmented form of local government prevents long-term, broad-based planning and cost-sharing. Nevertheless, if these problems are not resolved soon, Silicon Valley could become a high-tech ghost town, putting an end to California's second gold rush just as Japan's technopolises take off in the twenty-first century.

THE NEW SILICON VALLEYS

If Silicon Valley is reaching its zenith as a center of high technology, how will we compete with Japan's emerging technopolises in the twenty-first century? Where is our technological future?

Although some observers advocate a Japanese-style national industrial policy, John Naisbitt suggests in *Megatrends* that we look closer to home for new ideas: "America is a bottom-up society, that is, one where new trends and ideas begin in cities and local communities—for example, Tampa, Hartford, San Diego, Seattle, Denver, not New York City or Washington, D.C. . . . No longer waiting for federal leadership, the states are initiating local solutions to national problems."

Indeed, regional high-tech strategies, not new national industrial policies, may be our best solution. Within the last five years, many cities and states have jumped onto the high-tech bandwagon and are building their own Silicon Valleys. In 1983 Congress' Office of Technology Assessment reported that 150 state and local governments have launched high-tech industrial development programs. As shown in Figure 11-1, there are over forty major high-tech regions scattered throughout the United States, with names like Silicon Foothills (Sacramento), Silicon Coast (Jacksonville/Daytona), Silicon Ranch (San Antonio), and Silicon Bayou (Louisiana). These areas show a great deal of imagination and variety, but they offer basically four types of programs: technical assistance, such as access to facilities and equipment; manpower assistance, including access to scientific and technical personnel; business assistance, including help with licensing or subsidies for sites and facilities; and financial assistance, particularly access to risk capital, R&D tax credits, technical training credits, grants, and loans.

Of course, the rush to high technology is not without its critics, who call many local initiatives Silicon Valley hype. Ira Magaziner, coauthor of *Minding America's Business*, observes: "A lot of these programs are smoke and mirrors, without much substance. But they are still a lot better than what states used to do—write jingles and slogans and steal each other's companies." Many of these programs are nothing more than faltering economic development programs repackaged as high-tech initiatives. In most areas, competition for high-tech companies has heated up into a war among the states, diverting funds from investments in local infrastructure and other more productive uses. However, there has been a noticeable shift from recruitment to reinvestment and reindustrialization. States are learning that raiding is a high-stakes, zero-sum game that requires deep pockets but does not ensure stable, long-

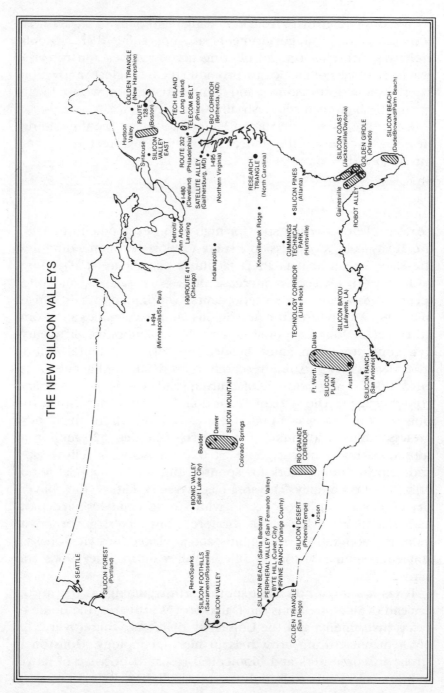

Figure 11-1. The New Silicon Valleys.

term economic growth. Instead of dangling money to attract new-comers, many local governments are upgrading their schools, highways, and airports and offering tax incentives and research grants to local companies to promote technological innovation. After years of disinvestment and deindustrialization, we are finally seeing the high-tech reindustrialization of America.

Where are these new Silicon Valleys and what are they doing? Here are some of the more innovative high-tech programs throughout the country.

Texas

Texas is clearly the hot spot for high-tech development. In 1983 the Texas 2000 Commission issued a report recommending that the state strengthen its R&D facilities, coordinate R&D efforts with the private sector, increase professors' salaries, and offer technical assistance to entrepreneurs. The initiative paid off. In May 1983 Austin lured the prestigious Microelectronics and Computer Technology Corporation, an R&D collaborative of twenty-five computer companies headed by former Admiral Bobby Inman, which is pursuing research in artificial intelligence, computer-aided design and manufacturing (CAD/CAM), software, and chip packaging. The state of Texas donated twenty acres near the University of Texas as a building site, $15 million for thirty new professorships, $20 million for research facilities, $20 million in subsidized home mortgages, $750,000 for graduate fellowships, and help in finding work for spouses. But Austin's appeal is not only Texas oil money. The area has two universities (the University of Texas and Texas A&M) with strong engineering departments, a highly educated labor force, low taxes, government-industry cooperation, rolling hills, and a relaxed lifestyle. It has an ambience similar to that of Silicon Valley during the 1960s and early 1970s.

Texas has three other hot spots worth watching. At the northern end of Silicon Plain is the Dallas-Fort Worth area, the home of Texas Instruments and the University of Texas, where over 20% of all manufacturing growth is in high technology. Houston is strong in computers and biomedical research because of its oil industry and numerous universities, including Rice University, Texas Medical Center, and the University of Houston. To the west is San Antonio, or Silicon Ranch, where Mayor Henry Cisneros is waging an aggressive campaign to attract and develop new high-tech industries. The city is known as Pentagon West because of the presence of Randolph and Lackland Air Force Bases, but high-tech firms are sprouting up along the seventy-mile corridor between San Antonio and Austin. Besides Advanced Micro Devices, Tandy, Control Data, and Sprague Electric, San Antonio has a critical mass of nationally-recognized medical centers that will enable it to become a center of biotechnology and medical electronics (including the South Texas Medical Center, the Southwest Foundation for Research, the University of Texas Health Sciences Center, and the largest Air Force hospital in the country).

Florida

High-tech development is popping up all over Florida. A "Robot Alley" is developing in the northern part of the state between Gainesville and Orlando. On the Atlantic side, between Jacksonville and Daytona Beach, is the Silicon Coast, while Silicon Beach covers Dade, Broward, and Palm Beach counties. The Golden Girdle, also known as the Electronics Belt, runs from Tampa on the gulf coast to Daytona Beach on the Atlantic side. About one-fourth of Florida's manufacturing jobs are in high technology, especially the aerospace industries that surround the Kennedy Space Center. In 1980 the Governor's Task Force targeted five industries for special incentives: defense contracting, communications, electronics, pharmaceuticals, and scientific instruments. To promote these fields, the state has sponsored the private Florida Venture Capital Association, high-tech training programs, and various entrepreneurship promotion programs. Four R&D parks have been set up throughout the state: Tampa Bay Research Park (University of Southern Florida); Central Florida Research Park (University of Central Florida); Florida Research and Technology Campus (University of Florida); and Innovation Park (Florida State University and Florida A&M University).

Southeast

The southeast is rapidly becoming a center of high technology. Since 1960 the Research Triangle in the Raleigh-Durham-Chapel

Hill metropolitan area has been the undisputed leader, but new areas are emerging.

Atlanta's Silicon Pines is a key area to watch. In 1980 Georgia launched its Advanced Technology Development Center (ATDC), jointly run by the state and the Georgia Institute of Technology, to promote high-tech industries. The center provides research advice and low-rent lab space for inventors, and sponsors venture capital conferences to introduce financiers to local start-up firms. In 1983 Georgia Governor Joe Frank Harris established a $30 million Georgia Research Consortium to coordinate research at the state's colleges and universities, half donated by local industry. The goal is to identify high technology growth opportunities and establish centers of excellence at local universities.

Washington, D.C.

The "Beltway Bandits" on the loop which runs around Washington, D.C., long scorned by local politicians and the media, are now worshipped as economic savants on Capitol Hill because of their impressive contributions to the local economy. Over 1,000 companies have set up shop within the last ten years. Interstate 270, which runs through Maryland, is known as Satellite Alley because of its concentration of telecommunications firms. But it is also becoming a Biotech Road as a result of the National Institute of Health (NIH), which has spun off biotechnology firms, including Genex and biochip maker EMV Gentronix. The Maryland High-Technology Roundtable, created in 1982, is advising the legislature on ways to provide financial support, technical education and retraining, and engineering programs. The state already has eight financing programs to promote high-tech start-ups. Recently, the University of Maryland announced plans to build a research park, the Maryland Science and Technology Center, to promote computer science, electronics, and biomedical research.

On the Virginia side, high-tech firms are springing up along I-66, which cuts through Arlington, Fairfax, and Vienna, and I-95, which borders McLean, Tysons Corner, and Alexandria. Many Virginia start-ups are defense contractors working with the Pentagon, although software houses, electronics firms, and Japanese companies can also be found. In 1982 the Governor's Task Force on Science and Technology was formed to recommend strategies for promoting high-tech industries. Unlike Maryland, state officials oppose targeted government loans or special financing, so most efforts are focused on strengthening the state's weak venture capital market. In Fairfax County, businesses are investing money to make George Mason University a top-flight research institute.

Northeast

Route 128 outside of Boston has long been the center of high technology in the Northeast. Since 1979 the Massachusetts Technology Development Corporation (MTDC), a quasi-public agency, has raised over $50 million in private funds and issued public stock offerings to fund local high-tech firms. Companies escaping Massachusetts' high taxes are finding a haven in southern New Hampshire's Golden Triangle. Currently, Massachusetts is planning to develop major research centers in electronics and microbiology.

Under the leadership of Governor Richard Thornburgh, Pennsylvania has developed a high-tech development program in which $100 million in public and private funds has been raised to spur industry/university collaboration. At the heart of the program is the Ben Franklin Partnership Fund, a consortium of business, labor, university, and economic development agencies. Through the Pennsylvania Science and Engineering Foundation, the Partnership provides $1 million in seed money to stimulate joint R&D and training in advanced technologies. Research projects are funneled through one of the four Advanced Technology Centers located at such major universities as Lehigh, Carnegie-Mellon, and the University of Pittsburgh, which offer research help and "incubator" facilities with cheap space and shared services. Funding is raised through a challenge grant program; participating companies must raise matching grants on a one-to-one basis to qualify for state funds. The Ben Franklin Partnership Fund is part of a four-part plan aimed at raising venture capital and the technology level in local industries.

Midwest

Hard-hit by the flight of jobs and people to the Sunbelt, midwestern states have developed innovative programs to revive their sagging economies. In 1984 eight states (Indiana, Illinois, Kansas, Minnesota, Nebraska, Ohio, South Dakota, and Wisconsin) formed the Midwest Technology Development Institute to expand cooperative research at local universities and identify emerging markets. The institute is developing a strategy to promote mutual trade and technology exchanges with foreign countries, especially with Europe and Japan. In addition, each of the states is pursuing its own high-tech strategy.

The twin cities of Minneapolis-St. Paul have dispelled the myth of the declining Snowbelt. Under the leadership of William Norris of Control Data, numerous high-tech promotion groups have sprung up. The Microelectronics Information and Science Center, sponsored by Sperry, Control Data, and 3M, offers advice and technical assistance to high-tech projects. Minnesota Wellspring, chaired by Governor Rudy Perpich, mobilizes support for public policies designed to create new jobs and encourage technological innovation. Other groups include the Minnesota High Technology Advisory Council and the Minnesota Seed Capital Corporation. In 1983, with the support of the 150 medical and biotechnology companies in the state, the Office of Medical Biotechnology and Health Care was established to promote growth and attract venture capital. Recently, the city of Minneapolis has begun working with the University of Minnesota to establish a new high-tech corridor.

Michigan is making a dramatic effort to parlay its strength in heavy manufacturing with its Industrial Technology Institute (ITI), a $255 million R&D center for computer-based manufacturing and robotics systems. Receiving 80% of its funds from the Kellogg Foundation, the Dow Foundation, and other philanthropies, ITI's staff of 300 is developing a vast computerized data base and offering advice to businesses interested in introducing capital-intensive machining and robotics systems. General Motors is a major backer of the project. Michigan is also developing a Center for Robotics Excellence, and its legislature voted in 1982 to allow 5% of its $7.5 billion in retirement funds to be invested in high-tech ventures.

Since 1981, Illinois has targeted four high-tech industries considered central to the local economy: electronics, biotechnology, materials technology, and robotics. A state Commission on Science and Technology is developing long-range economic goals, and working with the federal government to provide disadvantaged students with high-tech skills through its High Technology Training Assistance Program. A biomedical research park featuring a ten-story "incubator" building for start-up firms has been set up in Chicago's West Side Medical Center and a Microelectronics Center has been established at the University of Illinois. City officials are considering a Chicago Science Foundation to fund local research. The University of Illinois offers an online computerized data base of faculty capabilities, called Faculty Research Assistance to the State (FRATS), to businesses interested in specialized research.

Rocky Mountain States

Colorado's Silicon Mountain is shaping up into a major center of high technology, with over 86,000 people working at 350 companies in the corridor stretching from Fort Collins, Boulder, and Denver to Colorado Springs. Home of the National Bureau of Standards, Boulder recently voted down its "no growth" policy, and, like Fort Collins, is nurturing its entrepreneurs. Colorado Springs, center of the North American Air Defense Command and defense industries, is now a free port where high-tech goods can be manufactured without import duties. The rivalry among these four cities is intense, but under the leadership of Governor Richard Lamm, the state established the Colorado Advanced Technology Institute in 1983 to promote research at four local universities. Due to budget constraints, the institute's annual budget of $5 to $8 million is primarily funded by private firms such as Digital Equipment, Ford Aerospace, Hewlett-Packard, Honeywell, Inmos, Martin Marietta, Mostek, Texas Instruments, and TRW, which recruit heavily from these universities.

Utah is rapidly becoming known as Bionic Valley because of its advanced research in biomedical engineering. Under the leadership of Dr. William Kolff, developer of the artificial kidney, the University of Utah has become the leading center of research in artificial organs and the site of several biomedical companies developing artificial hearts and limbs. Dr. Kolff and Dr. Robert Jarvik founded Symbion, which develops artificial ears and hearts, including the heart implanted in Seattle dentist Barney Clark. In 1974 their colleague Stephen Jacobsen founded Motion Control, now the world's leading maker of artificial arms. The Salt Lake City metropolitan area has over 21,000 people working at 200 companies conducting biomedical and electronic research, including Parke Davis, National Semiconductor, Rockwell International, Sperry, and Evans and Sutherland Computer. Thirty-five of these companies are located in the University of Utah Research Park, established in 1970. Since 1978, the University of Utah has run the Utah Innovation Center to promote venture capital financing and advanced research among start-up companies.

Northwest

In an abrupt turnaround from its days as an environmental preserve, Oregon is becoming known as Silicon Forest because of its aggressive recruiting efforts. In 1984 six foreign companies—Epson, Fujitsu, Kyocera, NEC, Seiko, and Wacker Siltronic—decided to open plants in the Portland area as a result of Oregon's decision to repeal its global unitary tax, which taxes companies on the basis of their worldwide revenues. Japanese companies were particularly delighted, because of the state's proximity to Tokyo, availability of engineers, and quality of life. The Portland area has already attracted manufacturing plants of major Silicon Valley firms. Start-up ventures are also popping up, including Metheus Corporation, Sequent Computer Systems, Electro Scientific Industries, Mentor Graphics, Floating Point Systems, and Triquint. To boost its technical base, Tektronix and other companies are supporting the Oregon Graduate Center Science Park project, aimed at building cooperative links between local universities and industry. Governor Victor Atiyeh has also proposed establishing a center for biological and advanced sciences at the University of Oregon, an electrical and computer engineering center at Oregon State University in Corvallis, and an international trade and business center at Portland State University. With attention focusing on the Pacific Basin, these new ideas are falling on receptive ears.

Southern California

Despite its massive aerospace industry and rapid high-tech growth, southern California has long been ignored as a center of high technology. Yet in 1983 its high-tech industries employed 187,000 people who produced $9.6 billion worth of goods, while northern California employed 118,000 and produced less than $6 billion. Moreover, venture capitalists raised $209 million and funded start-ups with $364 million, passing Massachusetts as the second largest venture capital market. From Santa Barbara to San Diego, new Silicon Valleys are blossoming like desert wildflowers. In Santa Barbara, known as Silicon Beach, about 150 high-tech companies employing 15,000 people have set up shop, making the $1 billion industry one of the largest contributors to the local economy. San Fernando Valley, north of Los Angeles, is known as Peripheral Valley because of the numerous companies supplying peripheral equipment to computer makers. In the Los Angeles Basin, the Fox Hills Business Park in Culver City, called Byte Hill, has become the gathering place for the marketing, sales, and distribution operations of over 200 computer firms, including Wang, Apple Computer, Digital Equipment, Prime Computer, Cybertek, and Nixdorf.

The coastal area south of Los Angeles is turning into another biotechnology center. Orange Country, already home to Synbiotex, American Qualex, and a dozen other biotechnology companies, will soon be the site of a 2,000 acre high-tech park with a 225-acre bioscience area and a teaching hospital for the University of California at Irvine. San Diego also has the nucleus for a biotechnology industry, with the University of California at San Diego, Salk Institute, Scripps Clinic and Research Foundation, Hybritech, Molecular Biosystems, and Lee Biomolecular Research Laboratories.

Southwest

Arizona has one of the most aggressive high-tech expansion programs in the country. In 1980 Arizona State University developed a five-year plan that called for investing $32 million to turn the College of Engineering and Applied Sciences into a national center of excellence. In 1981 a Center for Professional Development Program was established to televise live graduate-level engineering courses to high-tech plants. In 1983 ASU opened its Center of Excellence in Engineering in Tempe, with the help of

$13 million in corporate donations. The state also voted to fund fifty-two new faculty positions. The Engineering Excellence plan focuses on six areas of specialization: solid state electronics, computers, computer-aided processes, thermosciences, energy sciences, and transportation. The newly formed Department of Computer Sciences has over 1,000 students. In addition, four new research centers have been created: the Center for Solid State Electronics, the Center for Automated Engineering and Robotics, the Energy Systems Research Center, and the Center for Advanced Research in Transportation. To accommodate the expected rush of high-tech firms, a 320-acre University Research Park is currently being built in Tempe. In Tucson, the University of Arizona is also strengthening its engineering program and building a $13 million facility for its Electrical and Computer Engineering Department. In this way, Arizona is hoping to attract talent for the 200 local high-tech companies, which account for 40% of the state's manufacturing jobs.

As this overview suggests, the states are actively pursuing regional strategies to strengthen their local industries. With very little help from the federal government, they are showing that America can become more competitive. Instead of degenerating into a wasteful battle of the states, the heated rivalry has stimulated many useful programs and ideas for reindustrializing America with high technology. Not all of these programs will succeed, but the lessons learned will benefit everyone. To critics of government intervention, this blossoming of regional initiatives suggests that American business and government can work together at the local level. For those seeking answers to the Japanese challenge, the solutions are all around us.

IMPROVING OUR INTERNATIONAL COMPETITIVENESS

In the face of the growing Japanese challenge, how can we prevent Silicon Valley from becoming another Detroit? How can we help our industries from falling into bankruptcy? What can we do to improve our competitiveness as a nation?

Many business consultants and scholars, awed by Japan's phenomenal successes, advocate that we emulate Japanese-style management practices and national industrial policies. They propose that we target strategic national industries, organize national R&D projects, create a Department of International Trade and Industry, and fund industrial development banks. They believe that by "out-Japaning Japan" we can become more competitive. What they fail to understand is that Japanese industrial policies represent a broad, generalized consensus that has emerged after heated debate over many conflicting ideas. As a spokesperson, MITI only articulates what industry leaders already believe.

Other observers, believing Japan to be the root cause of our trade deficits and industrial woes, want to slap tariffs and quotas on Japanese imports to protect our ailing industries and to save jobs temporarily. They want to retreat behind a wall of protectionism and isolationism. By sticking their heads in the sand, they hope the problems will disappear. Unfortunately, this approach will only exacerbate our problems, which will then haunt our children. We will not become more competitive by bashing Japan or copying Japan, but by correcting our weaknesses and building on our strengths. How can we best achieve this?

First, we must acknowledge that, unlike Japan, a single, unified, national industrial strategy may not be possible or desirable. Despite years of debate over national industrial policies, we are as far away from a consensus as ever. Our primarily advantage as a nation lies in our regional, corporate, and cultural diversity. We should not put all of our eggs in one basket, but promote a variety of industrial strategies.

Second, we should not wait for politicians and bureaucrats in Washington, D.C. to propose an answer, but pursue a "bottom-up" approach to industrial planning that involves a broad spectrum of people. We should encourage companies to work with state and local governments in developing their own tailored responses to the Japanese challenge. Only after feasible ideas have emerged at the local and regional level should the federal government intervene as a policymaking coordinator.

These are the broad parameters of a viable American response. Specificially, how can we improve our competitiveness at the corporate, regional, and national levels?

Corporate Strategies

Our companies should improve their capabilities to monitor and respond quickly to social, economic, and technological changes in Japan. Such policies might include the following:

1. Better Monitoring Systems. Every U.S. company with Japanese competitors, suppliers, or customers should hire full-time Japan watchers to evaluate trends that could affect the company's performance during the next ten years. These researchers should include Japanese nationals, Japanese-speaking Americans trained in science, engineering, business, economics, or law, and Americans with work experience in Japan. Larger companies (over 500 people) should establish offices in Tokyo to gather information, even though they have no immediate plans to enter the Japanese market. These offices should provide online patent, market, and technical information to key divisions within the company.

2. Long-Term Planning and Investment. U.S. companies should develop five-year business plans for hiring, marketing, investment, and fundraising purposes. These plans should anticipate normal business cycles, unexpected events, and the entry of Japanese and other foreign competitors. Although strategic planning has lost credibility in recent years, a longer planning horizon is essential. Corporate investments in R&D and plant capacity should match those of their Japanese competitors.

3. Automated Factories and Offices. To compete with low-cost, high-quality Japanese products, American companies must automate their plants with assembly robots, computerized inventory systems, and flexible manufacturing systems. Offices should be equipped with computer-aided design (CAD) tools and local area network (LAN) communications. To reduce costs, flexible hours, equipment time-sharing, and employee suggestions should be encouraged. Japanese companies are heavily automating their plants to compete with low-cost South Korean products.

4. Retain and Retrain Employees. Rather than laying off employees during downturns, U.S. companies should begin retaining their workers and retraining them for new positions. Besides improving company morale and loyalty, this approach enables companies to bounce back quickly during a recovery. In Silicon Valley, Advanced Micro Devices (AMD), Hewlett-Packard, and IBM have pioneered this approach. Although labor costs are initially higher, retraining increases labor productivity and decreases hiring costs in the long run.

5. Manufacturing Plants in Japan. Companies planning to enter the Japanese market should seriously consider the idea of building a manufacturing base in Japan for several reasons: to tap into cheaper capital, establish credibility among Japanese customers, and learn about automated manufacturing techniques. Although the Tokyo region is popular, the technopolis sites offer low-interest loans, a dedicated work force, and cheaper land. Several U.S. companies have made the move: Fairchild (Nagasaki), Monsanto (Utsunomiya), and Materials Research Corporation (Oita).

6. Strategic Alliances. Since 1980, when MITI lost its legal powers over joint ventures and foreign exchange control, Japanese companies have entered numerous joint ventures and licensing agreements with U.S. companies. For companies looking for market access or new technologies, strategic alliances may save millions of dollars in research and marketing expenses, and provide an "inside view" of the Japanese market. However, companies should be careful of "giving away the store" and viewing these alliances as solutions to poor planning and product development.

State, Local, and Regional Strategies

Instead of looking to Washington, D.C., we should explore ways to harness the boom in entrepreneurialism and regional high-tech initiatives. Our entrepreneurs and state and local governments have demonstrated great creativity in dealing with the problems of unemployment, educational standards, and declining industries.

1. Regional Industrial Strategies. State and local governments should work with businesses, labor unions, consumer groups, and educators to develop short- (five years) to long-term (twenty years) regional industrial goals and strategies. Where does the region want to be in the future? Silicon Valley leaders, for example, should consider the long-term direction and viability of its electronics, biotechnology, financial services, aerospace, and software industries. Are there opportunities for new hybrid industries, such as bioelectronics? University research centers could be funded to analyze these trends.

2. Bilateral Technopolis Program. Over thirty U.S. states have business development offices in Tokyo, and many cities have Japanese sister cities. The U.S. Conference of Mayors and Governors should consider the potential for a U.S.-Japan Bilateral Technopolis Program to promote cultural, academic, and business exchanges. The San Jose-Okayama Chamber of Commerce Sister City Program and the state of Georgia-Kagoshima programs are examples of existing programs. College students and corporate researchers should be encouraged to study in Japanese universities and research centers.

3. Regional Investment Pool. Many states have instituted lotteries and other revenue-generating activities. Besides upgrading local schools, some of this funding should be invested on a competitive, matching-grant basis in long-term research consortiums aimed at upgrading the information and technical levels of local industries.

4. Retraining Centers. Most states operate job training centers to assist displaced workers shift from declining to sunrise industries. Using state funds from the regional investment pool, these centers should identify transferable skills and knowledge that these workers have that can be applied to emerging companies. In Japan, for example, former shipbuiding construction workers are being trained in heavy robotics and new alloy production.

5. Asian Business Libraries. State and local governments should work with the Library of Congress, the U.S. Department of Commerce, and MITI's Japan External Trade Organization (JETRO) to establish Japanese science and business libraries in major cities and high-tech centers. These libraries should offer translation services, Japanese language courses, cultural and business programs, focused study groups, and English- and Japanese-language business and technical journals. Eventually, these should be expanded into Asian Business Libraries to include all Pacific Rim nations.

6. Pacific Rim Networks. Many American companies have a significant number of engineers and managers of Korean, Taiwanese, Japanese, and other Asian ancestry, as well as non-Asian employees, who have experience working in Asia and can give us invaluable insight into these markets. Local chambers of commerce and corporations should establish Pacific Rim Networks to tap into this knowledge pool and offer practical "how to" business programs on doing business in the Pacific Rim.

National Strategies

At the national level, the federal government can pursue several strategies to improve its coordination capabilities, without targeting strategic industries or establishing industrial development banks. These strategies should include:

1. Evaluation of Government Programs. The U.S. government has de facto national industrial policies supporting defense, aerospace, energy, housing, agriculture, and the environment. The White House should issue an annual "State of U.S. Competitiveness" report detailing the impact of various funding, procurement, trade, and tax policies on our international competitiveness, and its recommendations for action by Congress. Unless competitiveness remains highly visible, it is likely to remain forgotten in our list of national priorities.

2. Commercialization of Military Research. The U.S. Department of Defense spends over $26 billion annually on electronics research and $90 billion on electronics procurement, an amount that will rapidly increase under the Strategic Defense Initiative (SDI), or "Star Wars" program. Not only does military research absorb many of our top researchers, but very little research filters down to the commercial sector, opening the door to Japanese companies. The Congress should request the Pentagon to develop a commercialization program to release unclassified research to U.S. companies. Revenues from licensing fees should be reported and reinvested in military programs to reduce spending increases.

3. Permanent R&D Tax Credit. Since 1981 American companies have benefited from tax credits for their research and development investments. This tax provision should be made a permanent part of our tax code, with provisions for an accelerated depreciation life for leading-edge equipment.

4. Regional Information Sharing. The Department of Commerce and other federal agencies should investigate programs to increase the exchange of information on local industrial strategies of cities, states, and regions, as well as Japan and other countries. Online data bases, monthly publications, and conferences are potential vehicles for this information sharing.

5. Patent and Technical Libraries. The U.S. Patent Office and the National Technical Business Service (NTBS) are currently working with the Japanese government to exchange patent and technical journals, and to translate them into English. The U.S. government should investigate the possibility of using computerized language translators and offer low-cost translation services to businesses and universities.

THE NEW YANKEE SPIRIT

In this book, we have reviewed the coming Japanese challenge in high technology and examined some of the possible responses that our companies, cities, states, and federal government can take to maintain our international competitiveness. The strategies proposed here are relatively modest, but compare favorably with the Technopolis program in scope. Nevertheless, I believe these steps are critical for our economic survival during the next fifteen years. During the twenty-first century, we will require a massive groundswell of imaginative corporate and regional strategies comparable to the space shuttle program or "Star Wars" if we are to maintain technological parity with Japan in commercial fields.

As the twenty-first century approaches, the question remains: whither America?—where are we going? And how will we get there? Although some say we are headed down the road to decline, I am not convinced our days as a major industrial power are over; I see too many signs of hope in our entrepreneurialism, massive immigration, and new Silicon Valleys. We are a country always on the move. Indeed, my Japanese friends constantly marvel at Silicon Valley's ebullient start-up companies, which remind them of the Yankee clipper ships that once graced the seas and made America a great trading power. Perhaps, in looking to the future, we should, like Japan, look to our past for inspiration and ideas.

A P P E N D I C E S

Appendix A.
VLSI Research Project (1976–1980).

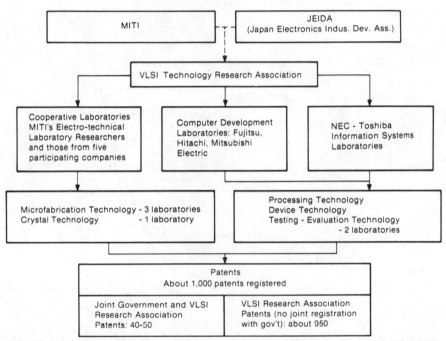

Source: Daniel Okimoto, "Pioneer and Pursuer: The Role of the State in the Evolution of the Japanese and American Semiconductor Industries," Working Paper, 1983. See D. Okimoto et al. *Competitive Edge: The Semiconductor Industry in the U.S. and Japan.* Stanford, CA: Stanford University Press, 1984.

Appendix B.
"The Investment War": Capital Spending for Plant and Equipment by Japanese Semiconductor Firms.

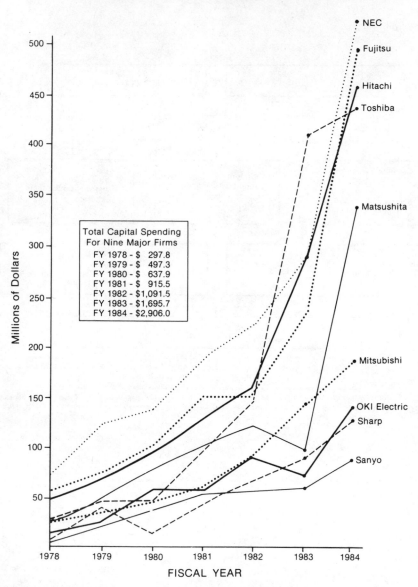

Total Capital Spending
For Nine Major Firms
FY 1978 - $ 297.8
FY 1979 - $ 497.3
FY 1980 - $ 637.9
FY 1981 - $ 915.5
FY 1982 - $1,091.5
FY 1983 - $1,695.7
FY 1984 - $2,906.0

FISCAL YEAR

Millions of Dollars

Source: Dataquest, Inc.

Appendix C.
Joint Ventures and Licensing Agreements between U.S. and Japanese Semiconductor Makers

Japanese Company	Foreign Company	Year	Technology
Aizu-Toko	Motorola	1980	NMOS & CMOS joint venture
	Motorola	1981	Motorola takes over plant
Asahi Chemical	AMI	1982	Custom CMOS ICs
Fujitsu	Intel	1981	16-bit microprocessor
	Standard Microsystems	1982	Coplamos process
	Ungermann-Bass	1982	Ethernet chips
	Texas Instruments	1984	Bipolar & CMOS gate arrays
	Monolithic Memories	1984	Gate arrays
	Intel	1984	16-/32-bit MPU, EPROMs
Hitachi	Motorola	1981	High-speed CMOS process
	Standard Microsystems	1981	Coplamos process
	Fairchild	1982	Communications controllers
	Hewlett-Packard	1982	64K dynamic RAM
	Motorola	1983	Computer-aided design (CAD)
	AMI	1984	Codecs
Mitsubishi Electric	Intel	1981	16-bit microprocessor
	Sperry	1982	64K dynamic RAMs, gate arrays
NEC	Intel	1980	Floppy disk controller chip
	Intel	1982	8-bit microcontroller
	Standard Microsystems	1983	Microcomputer peripheral controllers; Coplamos process
	Tektronix	1983	8-bit microprocessor
	AMI	1983	Microprocessors
	Zilog	1984	32-bit microprocessor
	Yokogawa H-P	1984	V Series MPU support
	Digital Research	1984	V Series MPU support
	Tektronix	1984	V Series MPU support
Nippon Denso	RCA	1983	Computer-aided design for ICs

Appendix C (continued).
Joint Ventures and Licensing Agreements between U.S. and Japanese Semiconductor Makers

Japanese Company	Foreign Company	Year	Technology
Oki	National Semi	1983	64K dynamic RAM
	Standard Microsystems	1984	Coplamos process
	Intel	1984	Microprocessors
	Thomson CSF	1984	CMOS gate arrays
Ricoh	Rockwell	1984	CMOS 64K EPROMs
	Panatec R&D	1984	256K dynamic RAMs
Sanyo	Intel	1983	8- & 16-bit microprocessors
	Intel	1983	16-bit microprocessor
Sharp	Rockwell	1981	CMOS process
	Zilog	1983	Microprocessors
	RCA	1984	Chip design center
	Samsung	1984	4-bit microcontrollers
Toshiba	RCA	1980	1K and 4K dynamic RAMs
	LSI Logic	1981	CMOS gate arrays
	Zilog	1982	CMOS process, micro-processor
	Zilog	1984	8-bit MPU
	Motorola	1984	16-bit MPU

Source: Dataquest, Inc.

Appendix D.
U.S. Defense R&D and Procurement in Fiscal 1984 ($ Billions).

	Research & Development		Procurement	
	Total	Electronics Part	Total	Electronics Part
Aircraft	$ 4.0	$ 1.6	$34.8	$ 8.8
Missiles	6.3	2.9	11.4	5.0
Space	2.8	1.9	3.3	1.7
Ships	1.5	0.3	11.0	2.3
Ordinance & Vehicles	1.6	0.5	11.0	2.8
Electronics & Communications	4.8	4.3	6.0	5.3
Other	5.5	0.6	9.5	0.9
TOTAL	$26.5	$12.1	$87.0	$26.8

Source: *Electronic News*

Appendix E.
Japan's 1985 National R&D Budget ($ Millions).

Ministry	FY1984	FY1985
Science and Technology Agency (STA)	$1,134	$1,202
Space and aeronautics	38	39
Metals	14	15
Radiation medical therapy	23	21
Disaster prevention	8	8
Inorganic materials	6	6
Creative technologies	9	10
Ocean resources development	20	26
Nuclear power & ships	347	383
Power Reactor & Nuclear Fuel Corp.	245	253
Japan Research & Development Corp. (JRDC)	7	6
National Space Development Agency	324	342
Others	93	93
Ministry of International Trade and Industry	249	251
Large-scale industries	35	30
Next-generation industries	23	25
New energy sources (Sunshine Project)	14	12
Energy conservation (Moonlight Project)	6	5
Electronics	18	19
Machinery	7	8
Chemicals	10	10
Others	136	142
Ministry of Agriculture, Forestry & Fisheries	225	229
Ministry of Posts & Telecommunications	17	16
Ministry of Construction	18	19
Ministry of Education	213	215
Ministry of Health & Welfare	96	101
Ministry of Transportation	57	44
Other ministries	60	61
TOTAL	$2,069	$2,138

Source: Science and Technology Agency (STA)

Appendix F.
Joint R&D Projects Sponsored by the Japan Research and Development Corporation's (JRDC) Exploratory Research for Advanced Technology Organization (ERATO).

Project	Duration	$Million	Theme
Ultrafine particles	1981-86	$8.0	Particles for use in recording media, light absorbers, catalysts & fibers
Amorphous & intercalation compounds	1981-86	8.0	New organic materials for industrial use
Fine polymers	1981-86	7.2	New synthetic polymers modeled after living organisms
Perfect crystals	1981-86	8.0	Perfect gallium arsenide (GaAs) crystals for ultrafast digital circuits
Bioholonics	1982-87	7.2	Holonic systems in living organisms
Bioinformation transfer	1983-88	7.2	Mechanism of neuroactive substances for medical uses
Superbugs	1984-89	7.2	Microorganisms grown under high acidity, temperature,salinity, and pressure
Nanomechanism	1985-90	2.0	Ultra-fast mechanisms
Solid State Surfaces	1985-90	2.3	New surface materials

Source: National Science Foundation, Tokyo Office

Appendix G.
MITI's Joint R&D Projects (1966-2000).

Project	Duration	Budget ($ Million)
NATIONAL PROJECTS		
Fourth generation computer	1979-83	$ 93.8
Fifth generation computer	1979-91	250.0
Automated software development (SIGMA)	1985-89	104.2
Water desalination system	1985-89	0.8
LARGE-SCALE PROJECTS		
Super high-performance computer system	1966-71	41.6
Desulfurization process	1966-71	10.8
Olefin production	1967-72	4.6
Undersea remote-controlled oil drilling	1970-75	18.8
Seawater desalination	1969-77	27.9
Electric vehicles	1971-77	23.8
Pattern information processing system (PIPS)	1971-80	91.7
Aircraft jet engines	1971-81	82.9
Automobile control technology	1973-77	30.4
Solid urban waste resource recycling	1973-82	52.6
High-temperature steelmaking processes	1973-80	58.1
Alternative energy sources (Sunshine Project)	1974-2000	1,145.8
Asphalt-based olefin production	1975-81	57.6
Flexible manufacturing systems (FMS)	1977-84	54.2
Undersea oil production system	1978-84	62.5
Large-scale energy conservation (Moonlight)	1978-	257.6
Optical measurement & control system	1979-88	75.0
Monocarbon (C1) chemical technology	1980-87	62.5
Manganese nodule mining system	1981-89	83.3
Scientific supercomputing system	1981-89	95.8
Next-generation basic technologies	1981-90	433.0
Automated sewing system	1982-89	54.2
Advanced robotics (JUPITER)	1983-90	83.3
Resource exploitation observation system	1985-90	95.8
Aqua Renaissance 90	1985-91	54.2
Interoperable data bases	1985-92	83.3

Source: Ministry of International Trade and Industry
Note: Y240 = $1

Appendix H.
The Boom in U.S.-Japan Semiconductor Joint Ventures and Licensing Agreements.

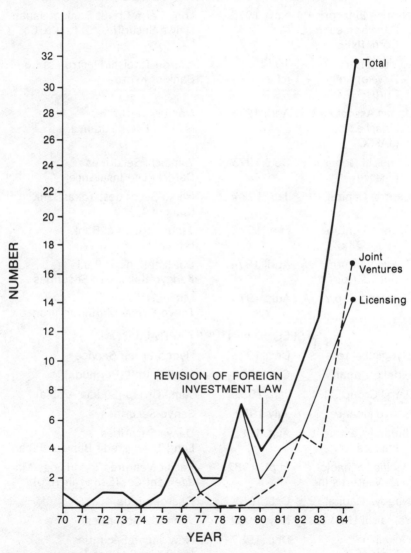

*Excludes semiconductor equipment makers

Source: Dataquest, Inc.

Appendix I.
Japanese Venture Capital Companies.

Company	Founded	Major Shareholders
FIRST VENTURE CAPITAL BOOM		
Nippon Enterprise Development Corp. (NED)	Nov. 1972	Long Term Credit Bank of Japan Daiwa Securities, C. Itoh & Co.
Kyoto Enterprise Development Corp.	1972 (closed 1979)	Omron Tateishi Electronics Co. Bank of Kyoto
Japan Associated Finance Co. (JAFCO)	April 1973	Nomura Securities Nippon Life Insurance
Yamaichi General Finance	Dec. 1973	Yamaichi Securities Dai-Ichi Life Insurance
Central Capital	Jan. 1974	Nikko Securities, Tokai Bank Bank of Tokyo
Techno-Venture	Feb. 1974	Japan Industrial Bank Hitachi Works
Tokyo Venture Capital Co.	April 1974	Dai-Ichi Kangyo Bank Kangyo Kakumaru Securities
Diamond Capital	Aug. 1974	Mitsubishi Bank Tokyo Fire & Marine Insurance
SECOND VENTURE CAPITAL BOOM		
Hyogin Factors	Dec. 1979	Hyogo Credit Service
Fidelity Japan	Oct. 1980	Fidelity Int'l (Bermuda)
Jamil Group S.I.	Jan. 1982	Jamil Group (Saudia Arabia)
Sanyo Finance	July 1982	Sanyo Securities
Japan Investment Finance	Aug. 1982	Daiwa Securities Long Term Credit Bank of Japan
Pacific Technology Ventures Inc.	Sept. 1982	Pacific Ventures Technology Management Co. (San Francisco)
Nagoya Capital	Oct. 1982	Okatoku Bldg.
Yamaichi Uni-Ven.	Nov. 1982	Yamaichi Securities
New Japan Finance	Dec. 1982	New Japan Securities Industrial Bank of Japan
Wako Finance	Dec. 1982	Wako Securities Industrial Bank of Japan
Marusan Finance	March 1983	Marusan Securities

Appendix I (continued).
Japanese Venture Capital Companies.

Company	Founded	Major Shareholders
Okasan Finance	April 1983	Okasan Securities Industrial Bank of Japan
Kansai Venture Capital	May 1983	Osakaya Securities Daiwa Bank
Maruman Finance	June 1983	Maruman Securities Tokai Bank
Nikko Venture Capital	July 1983	Nikko Securities
Fuji Investment	July 1983	Fuji and Yasuda Banks
National Kogyo	Aug. 1983	National Securities
Fidelity Japan	Aug. 1983	Fidelity Venture Associates (U.S.)
CFB Venture Capital Corp.	Sept. 1983	California 1st Bank (Bank of Tokyo)
Kyushu Capital	Sept. 1983	Fukuoka Sogo Bank
Orient Capital	Oct. 1983	Orient Leasing Co. (Tokyo) Baring Brothers (London) Hambrecht & Quist (San Francisco)
Toyo Finance	Oct. 1983	Toyo Securities
Dai-Ichi Capital	Oct. 1983	Dai-Ichi Securities
Micro Technology Corp.	Nov. 1983	Pacific Capital Fund (California) Global Commercial (Tokyo) S.G. Inc. (Tokyo)
Sanwa Capital	Dec. 1983	Sanwa Bank
Alta Jami N.V.	May 1984	Marubeni Corp. Burr, Egan, Deleage & Co. (US)

Source: MITI, Venture Business Research Group, June 1984

Appendix J.
Research Institutes at Tsukuba Science City.

Government Institutes	Staff Researchers	Total
MINISTRY OF EDUCATION	1,565	3,753
1. Tsukuba University	1,307	3,146
2. Library & Information Science University	50	126
3. High Energy Physics National Laboratory	196	423
4. National Education Center Annex	0	34
5. Tsukuba Botanical Garden/National Science Museum	12	24
AGENCY FOR SCIENCE AND TECHNOLOGY	326	536
6. National Metals Research Institute	64	78
7. National Research Center for Disaster Prevention	58	94
8. National Institute for Inorganic Materials Research	108	169
9. Research Exchange Center	0	5
10. Tsukuba Space Center	96	190
ENVIRONMENTAL AGENCY		
11. National Environmental Studies Center	160	239
MINISTRY OF FOREIGN AFFAIRS	0	35
12. Tsukuba International Center	0	14
13. Tsukuba International Agricultural Training Center	0	21
MINISTRY OF SOCIAL WELFARE	10	20
14. Tsukuba Primate Center for Medicinal Science (National Institute of Health)	7	10
15. Tsukuba Medical Plant Research Station (National Institute of Hygienic Science)	3	10
MINISTRY OF AGRICULTURE, FORESTRY & FISHERIES	1,229	2,053
16. Agricultural Research Center	194	282
17. National Institute of Agricultural Sciences	103	175
18. National Institute of Animal Husbandry	120	226
19. Fruit Tree Research Station	47	93
20. Agricultural Engineering Research Institute	68	109
21. Sericultural Experiment Station	99	162
22. National Institute of Animal Health	99	194

Appendix J (continued).
Research Institutes at Tsukuba Science City.

Government Institutes	Staff Researchers	Total
23. National Food Research Institute	104	131
24. Plant Virus Research Institute	35	52
25. Tropical Agricultural Research Center	65	88
26. Forestry & Forest Products Research Institute	287	426
27. Tsukuba Seed Testing Laboratory	8	15
28. Agriculture, Forestry & Fisheries Research Council	0	100
MINISTRY OF INTERNATIONAL TRADE & INDUSTRY (MITI)	*1,855*	*2,542*
29. Agency of Industrial Science & Technology (AIST) General Coordination Department	–	63
30. National Metrology Research Laboratory	137	179
31. Mechanical Engineering Laboratory	213	289
32. Chemical Engineering Laboratory	289	381
33. Fermentation Research Institute	61	80
34. Polymer & Textiles Research Institute	100	125
35. Geological Survey of Japan	218	341
36. Electrotechnical Laboratory	525	664
37. Industrial Products Research Institute	103	134
38. Pollution & Resources Research Institute	209	286
MINISTRY OF TRANSPORTATION	*147*	*241*
39. Meteorological Research Institute	140	180
40. Aerological Observatory	7	39
41. Meteorological Instruments Plant	–	22
MINISTRY OF POSTS & TELECOMMUNICATIONS		
42. Nippon Telegraph & Telephone (NTT) – Tsukuba Telecommunication Construction Development Center	131	197
MINISTRY OF CONSTRUCTION	*492*	*1,336*
43. Geographical Survey Institute	36	643
44. Public Works Research Institute	341	466
45. Building Research Institute	115	175
46. Tsukuba Facility Management	0	52
TOTAL GOVERNMENT	5,915	10,952

Appendix J (continued).
Research Institutes at Tsukuba Science City.

Private Institutes	Staff Researchers	Total
Private Institutes	*205*	*342*
47. Japan Information Center of Science & Technology	0	5
48. Oil Spill Prevention Institute	8	14
49. Testing Laboratory of the Center for Better Living	4	6
50. Japan Construction Mechanization Association	6	9
51. Foundation for Advancement of International Science	11	21
52. Japan Agricultural Research Institute	9	9
53. Japan Automobile Research Institute (JARI)	167	278
TOTAL GOVERNMENT & PRIVATE	6,120	11,294

Sources: Science & Technology Agency, 1983; Japan Housing Corporation, April 1984 Survey

Appendix K.
World's Principal Science Cities.

Name	Designed Scale Area (Hectares)	Population	Objectives	Core Institutions	Number Employees	Family	Distance from Large City
Tsukuba Science City (Japan)	2,700	136,000	Alleviate overcrowding in Tokyo and create a "brain city"	50 institutes 2 universities	11,500	31,000	60 km from Tokyo
Research Triangle Park (U.S.)	2,300	50,000	Foster high-tech industries and create jobs	Over 40 research institutes	Over 8,000	n/a	11 km from Raleigh, North Carolina
Novosibirsk Science City (U.S.S.R.)	1,300	50,000	Foster basic and applied research to develop Siberian natural resources	20 research institutes & universities	18,000	45,000	25 km from Novosibirsk (1,000,000 pop.)
South Ile de France Science City (France)	3,500	112,000	Concentrate research institutes and private sector in a science city	26 institutes & universities	13,000	n/a	15 km from Paris
Sophia Antipolis Science City (France)	2,400	n/a	Construct international science & technology city by 1990s	49 institutes & universities	2,800	n/a	22 km from Nice
Louvain University Science City (Belgium)	900	50,000	Develop multi-lingual research city to reduce cultural disputes between countries	Catholic U. of Louvain, IBM Research Institute	500	n/a	10 km from Brussels

Source: *Science and Technology in Japan*

Appendix L.
MITI Research Laboratories in the Tsukuba Science City.

Laboratories	1984 Research Staff	FY83 Budget	Research Themes
National Metrology Research Laboratory	137	$8.2M	Measurement standards, lasers, X-rays
Mechanical Engineering Laboratory	213	12.8	Robotics, bionics, medical & biological engineering, optical measuring, wind-energy conversion, high-precision controls, energy storage, undersea production, aids for the physically handicapped
National Chemical Laboratory for Industry	289	18.0	Coal liquefaction, aluminum smelting, superconductive materials, hydrogen energy, fine chemicals, heat storage, gene technology, pollution prevention, synthetic membranes
Fermentation Research Institute	61	3.8	New enzymes, recombinant DNA, bioreactors, microorganism industrial processes, industrial waste water treatment, cell fusion, biomass energy generation, photosynthesis hydrogen production
Polymer & Textiles Research Institute	100	5.7	Computer-designed apparel, new plastics and polymers, 3-D fabrics, bioreactors, artificial kidneys, bioengineering, chemical absorbents, synthetic fibers, IC lithography

Appendix L (continued).
MITI Research Laboratories in the Tsukuba Science City.

Laboratories	1984 Research Staff	FY83 Budget	Research Themes
Geological Survey of Japan	218	19.7	Energy & mineral surveys, earthquake prediction, undersea development, geothermal energy, deepsea mining, industrial pollution
Electrotechnical Laboratory	525	39.6	Supercomputers, optoelectronics, microelectronics, intelligent robots, speech processing, energy conservation, new materials, space development, nuclear power, pollution control, superconducting magnets, lasers
Industrial Products Research Institute	103	5.1	Sensors, speech synthesizers, visual aids for the blind, computer-aided design (CAD), ergonomics, bionics, carbon fibers, composite materials
Pollution & Resources Research Institute	209	17.4	New mining & mineral process technologies, coal liquefaction, geothermal energy, energy conservation, pollution control, industrial safety
TOTAL	1,855	$130.3 Million	

Source: MITI, Agency for Industrial Science and Technology; Japan Housing Corporation, April 1984 Survey

Appendix M.
MITI's Technopolis '90 Committee Members.

Member	Representing
Sadakazu Shindo (Chair)	Mitsubishi Electric, Chairman
Sadakazu Iijima	Japan Industrial Location Center, Director
Kazuo Inamori	Kyocera, President
Takemochi Ishii	Tokyo University, Professor
Kenichi Imai	Hitotsubashi University, Professor
Michiyuki Uenohara	NEC, Executive Vice-President
Iwao Kanazawa	Samu Electronic Machines, President
Isao Kamata	*Japan Economic Journal,* Editorial writer
Kimito Kusaka	Japan Long-Term Industrial Bank, Executive Vice-President
Nobuaki Kunimura	Mitsubishi Heavy Industries, Vice-President
Kisho Kurokawa	Architect
Mitsuo Kohno	*Yomiuri Newspaper,* Editorial writer
Takeshi Saito	Fuji Bank, Research Director
Hitoshi Sasao (Industrial Complex Subcommittee Chairman)	Nippon University, Professor
Toshio Doi	Hitachi Maxell, Executive Vice-President
Hisao Nishioka (Regional Subcommittee Chairman)	Aoyama University, Professor
Nagaharu Hayafusa	*Asahi Newspaper,* Editorial writer
Soichi Miyoshi	Sophia University, Professor
Masaaki Yanagisawa	Kureha Chemical Industries, Executive Vice-President
Mitsuru Yamazaki (Regional Development Committee Chairman)	Regional Industrial Economics Research, Director

Source: Ministry of International Trade and Industry

Appendix N.
Addresses of the Technopolis Coordinators.

Administrative Offices of Technopolis-Hosting Prefectures

Hokkaido : Kita 3, Nishi 6, Chuo-ku, Sapporo City, Hokkaido
060
Tel. 011-231-4111

Aomori : 1-1-1, Nagashima, Aomori City, Aomori 030
Tel. 0177-22-1111

Akita : 4-1-1, Sanno, Akita City, Akita 010
Tel. 0188-60-2211

Niigata : 1, Gakkochodori, Niigata City, Niigata 951
Tel. 0252-23-5511

Tochigi : 1-1-20, Hanawada-cho, Utsunomiya City, Tochigi
320
Tel. 0286-23-3198

Shizuoka : 5-1, Ottemachi, Shizuoka City, Shizuoka 420
Tel. 0542-54-2111

Toyama : 1-7, Shinsogawa, Toyama City, Toyama 930
Tel. 0764-31-4111

Wakayama : 1-1, Komatsubaradori, Wakayama City, Wakayama
640
Tel. 0734-32-4111

Hyogo : 5-10-1, Shimoyamatedori, Chuo-ku, Kobe City,
Hyogo 065
Tel. 078-341-7711

Okayama : 2-4-6, Uchisange, Okayama City, Okayama 700
Tel. 0862-24-1111

Hiroshima : 10-52, Motomachi, Hiroshima City, Hiroshima 730
Tel. 082-228-2111

Yamaguchi : 1-1, Takimachi, Yamaguchi City, Yamaguchi 753
Tel. 08392-2-3111

Kagawa : 4-1-10, Bancho, Takamatsu City, Kagawa 760
Tel. 0878-31-1111

Fukuoka : 7-7, Higashi Koen, Hakata-ku, Fukuoka City, Fukuoka
812
Tel. 092-651-1111

Saga : 1-1-59, Jonai, Saga City, Saga 840
Tel. 0952-24-2111

Nagasaki : 2-13, Edo-machi, Nagasaki City, Nagasaki 850
Tel. 0958-24-1111

Appendix N (continued).
Addresses of the Technopolis Coordinators.

Administrative Offices of Technopolis-Hosting Prefectures

Oita	:	3-1-1, Otemachi, Oita City, Oita 870 Tel. 0975-36-1111
Kumamoto	:	6-18-1, Suizenji, Kumamoto City, Kumamoto 862 Tel. 0963-83-1111
Miyazaki	:	2-10-1, Tachibanadori Higashi, Miyazaki City, Miyazaki 880 Tel. 0985-24-1111
Kagoshima	:	14-50, Yamashita-cho, Kagoshima City, Kagoshima 892 Tel. 0992-26-8111

The Tokyo Offices of Technopolis-Hosting Prefectures

Hokkaido	:	2-17-17, Nagata-cho, Chiyoda-ku, Tokyo 100 Tel. 03-581-3411
Aomori	:	Todofuken Kaikan, 2-6-3, Hirakawa-cho, Chiyoda-ku, Tokyo 102 Tel. 03-265-6411
Akita	:	" " "
Niigata	:	" " "
Tochigi	:	" " "
Shizuoka	:	" " "
Toyama	:	" " "
Wakayama	:	" " "
Hyogo	:	" " "
Okayama	:	" " "
Hiroshima	:	Tokyo Gorakubu Bldg., 3-2-6, Kasumigaseki, Chiyoda-ku, Tokyo 100 Tel. 03-580-0851
Yamaguchi	:	3-3-2, Kasumigaseki, Chiyoda-ku, Tokyo 100 Tel. 03-581-2266
Kagawa	:	Todofuken Kaikan, 2-6-3, Hirakawa-cho, Chiyoda-ku, Tokyo 102 Tel. 03-265-6411
Fukuoka	:	1-12, Kojimachi, Chiyoda-ku, Tokyo 102 Tel. 03-261-9861

Appendix N (continued).
Addresses of the Technopolis Coordinators.

The Tokyo Offices of Technopolis-Hosting Prefectures

Saga	:	Todofuken Kaikan Annex, 2-6-3, Hirakawa-cho, Chiyoda-ku, Tokyo 102 Tel. 03-265-6411
Nagasaki	:	Todofuken Kaikan, 2-6-3, Hirakawa-cho, Chiyoda-ku, Tokyo 102 Tel. 03-265-6411
Oita	:	3-3-3, Kasumigaseki, Chiyoda-ku, Tokyo 100 Tel. 03-581-3453
Kumamoto	:	Todofuken Kaikan Annex, 2-6-3, Hirakawa-cho, Chiyoda-ku, Tokyo 102 Tel. 03-265-6411
Miyazaki	:	" " "
Kagoshima	:	Todofuken Kaikan, 2-6-3, Hirakawa-cho, Chiyoda-ku, Tokyo 102 Tel. 03-265-6411

Overall Liaison Office

Industrial Location Guidance Division,
Ministry of International Trade and Industry
1-3-1, Kasumigaseki, Chiyoda-ku, Tokyo 100
Tel. 03-501-1511

Appendix O.
Technopolis Construction Schedule.

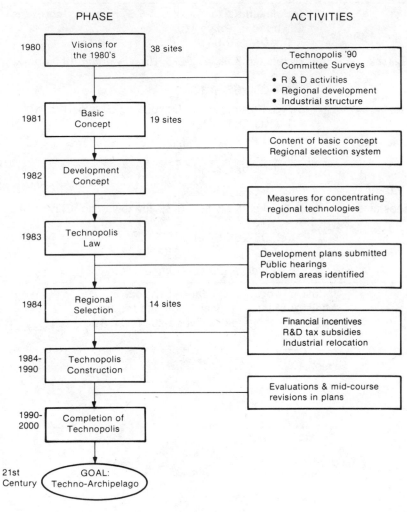

PHASE   ACTIVITIES

1980   Visions for   38 sites
        the 1980's
                                         Technopolis '90
                                         Committee Surveys
                                         • R & D activities
                                         • Regional development
                                         • Industrial structure

1981   Basic   19 sites
        Concept
                                         Content of basic concept
                                         Regional selection system

1982   Development
        Concept
                                         Measures for concentrating
                                         regional technologies

1983   Technopolis
        Law
                                         Development plans submitted
                                         Public hearings
                                         Problem areas identified

1984   Regional   14 sites
        Selection
                                         Financial incentives
                                         R&D tax subsidies
                                         Industrial relocation

1984-   Technopolis
1990   Construction
                                         Evaluations & mid-course
                                         revisions in plans

1990-   Completion of
2000   Technopolis

21st   GOAL:
Century   Techno-Archipelago

Source: Ministry of International Trade & Industry

Appendix P.
Features of Japan's Top 15 Technopolis Regions.

Prefecture	Technopolis Region Name of Region	Principal Universities	Target Industrial Sectors	R & D Facilities
Hokkaido	Hakodate	Hokkaido University	Marine-related industries and making use of natural resources (electronics, mechatronics, biotechnology, etc.)	Hakodate Industrial Research Institute; Hokkaido Prefectural Center of Industrial Technology
Akita	Akita	Akita University	Electronics, mechatronics, new materials, natural resources, energy biotechnology	Akita Prefectural Institute of Industrial Technology
Niigata	Nagaoka	Nagaoka College of Science and Technology	Higher systems & urban industries (design, fashion), industries utilizing local natural resources	Nagaoka Center for the Promotion of Regional Technological Development; Nagaoka Center for Information Studies
Tochigi	Utsunomiya	Utsunomiya University	Electronics, mechatronics, fine chemicals, new materials, software	Utsunomiya Technopolis Information Center

Appendix P (continued).
Features of Japan's Top 15 Technopolis Regions.

Prefecture	Technopolis Region		Target Industrial Sectors	R & D Facilities
	Name of Region	Principal Universities		
Shizuoka	Hamamatsu	Shizuoka University/ Hamamatsu College of Medicine	Optoelectronics industries, advanced mechatronics, home sound culture (electronic musical instruments), etc.	Institute for Research on Electronic Machine Technology; Institute for Research on Medical Appliance Technology; Shizuoka Pref. Industrial Research Institute
Toyama	Toyama	Toyama Univ/Toyama College of Medicine and Pharmacology/ Others	Mechatronics, new materials, biotechnology. Research on Life Sciences and Advanced Technology	Toyama Prefectural Institute of Industrial Technology; Center for Exchange in Advanced Technology
Okayama	Kibi-Kogen	Okayama University/ Okayama College of Science	Biotechnology, electronics, mechatronics (medical and pharmaceutical industries, etc.)	Okayama Prefectural Institute of Industrial Technology; Center for Research on Biotechnology
Hiroshima	Hiroshima Chuo	Hiroshima University	Electronics, mechatronics, new materials, biotechnology, etc.	Center for Research on Frontier Technologies; Hiroshima Prefectural Industrial Research Institute

Appendix P (continued).
Features of Japan's Top 15 Technopolis Regions.

Prefecture	Technopolis Region Name of Region	Principal Universities	Target Industrial Sectors	R & D Facilities
Yamaguchi	Ube	Yamaguchi Univ.	Electronics, mechatronics, new materials ocean development, biotechnology, etc.	Yamaguchi Pref. Industrial Research Institute; Yamaguchi Prefectural Institute of Industrial Technology; Institute for Research on New Materials
Fukuoka-Saga	Kurume-Tosu	Kurume College of Engineering/Kurume University	Mechatronics, fine chemicals, fashion, next generation (bio) industries, etc.	Information Center for the Promotion of Local Industry
Oita	Kenhoku-Kunizaki	Oita Univ/Oita College of Medicine/Others	Electronics, mechatronics, bioindustry, software	High Technology Research Institute and Training Center; Oita Prefectural Industrial Research Institute
Kumamoto	Kumamoto	Kumamoto Univ/Kumamoto College of Engineering/Others	Applied machinery industry, biotechnology, electronic equipment information systems industry	Center for Research on Applied Electronics Machinery Technology; Kumamoto Prefectural Industrial Research Institute

Appendix P (continued).
Features of Japan's Top 15 Technopolis Regions.

Prefecture	Technopolis Region		Target Industrial Sectors	R & D Facilities
	Name of Region	Principal Universities		
Miyazaki	Miyazaki	Miyazaki Univ/ Miyazaki College of Medicine	Local-oriented (bio), introduction-oriented (electronics, etc.), & urban oriented (urban systems) industry	The Joint Research and Development Center; The Miyazaki Prefectural Industrial Research Institute
Kagoshima	Kokubu-Hayato	Kagoshima Univ/ Kyushu Gakuin Univ.	Electronics, mechatronics, new materials, biotechnology, etc.	Center for Research on the Development of Fine Ceramics Products; Kagoshima Pref. General Institute of Industrial Technology
Nagasaki	Nagasaki	Nagasaki University	Electronics, undersea development	Industrial Technology Center

Source: Japan Industrial Location Center

BIBLIOGRAPHY

Chapter 1. Catching Up with the West

Baranson, Jack. *The Japanese Challenge to U.S. Industry*. Lexington, Massachusetts: Lexington Books, 1981.

Borrus, Michael, with James Millstein and John Zysman. *Berkeley Roundtable for the International Economy. International Competition in Advanced Industrial Sectors: Trade and Development in the Semiconductor Industry*. Report to the Joint Economic Committee, U.S. Congress, February 18, 1982.

Gresser, Julian. *Partners in Prosperity: Strategic Industries for the U.S. and Japan*. New York: McGraw-Hill Book Company, 1984.

Hamakawa, Yoshihiro and Yumi Murakami. "Japanese Electronics Industry," in *Kodansha Encyclopedia of Japan*, Vol. 2. Tokyo: Kodansha International, 1983.

Johnson, Chalmers. *MITI and the Japanese Miracle*. Stanford, California: Stanford University Press, 1982.

Johnson, Chalmers. "MITI and Japanese International Economic Policy," in Robert Scalapino (Ed.), *The Foreign Policy of Japan*. Berkeley: Univ. of California Press, 1977.

Kaplan, Eugene. *Japan: The Government–Business Relationship*. Washington, D.C.: U.S. Department of Commerce, Bureau of International Commerce, 1972.

Lyons, Nick. *The Sony Vision*. New York: Crown Publishers, Inc., 1976.

Nakagawa, Yasuzo. *The Development of the Japanese Semiconductor Industry (Nihon no Handotai Kaihatsu)*. Tokyo: Diamond Press, 1981.

Okimoto, Daniel I., with Takuo Sugano and Franklin B. Weinstein. *Competitive Edge: The Semiconductor Industry in the U.S. and Japan*. Stanford, California: Stanford University Press, 1984.

Ouchi, William. *The M-Form Society: How American Teamwork Can Recapture the Competitive Edge*. Reading, Massachusetts: Addison-Wesley Publishing Company, 1984.

Semiconductor Industry Association (SIA). *The Effect of Government Targeting on World Semiconductor Competition: A Case History of Japanese Industrial Strategy and Its Costs for America*. San Jose: 1983.

Sobel, Robert. *IBM: Colossus in Transition*. New York: Bantam Books, 1981.

Takeda, Yukimatsu. "Computer Technology," in *Kodansha Encyclopedia of Japan*, Vol. 1. Tokyo: Kodansha International, 1983.

Tilton, John. *International Diffusion of Technology: The Case of Semiconductors*. Washington, D.C.: Brookings Institute, 1971.

U.S. General Accounting Office. *Industrial Policy: Case Studies in the Japanese Experience*. Report to the Chairman, Joint Economic Committee, U.S. Congress, GAO/ID-83-11, October 20, 1982.

Chapter 2. From Japan Inc. to Japan Tech

Bownas, Geoffrey. "MITI's Underwriting and Vision Determine Direction," *News from Hotel Okura* (Tokyo), June 1981.

Gresser, Julian. *Partners in Prosperity: Strategic Industries for the U.S. and Japan.* New York: McGraw-Hill Book Company, 1984.

Ishii, Ibo. "The Activization of University Research Facilities and Industrial Exchange" (Daigaku Kenkyu Kikan no Kasseika to Sangyo to no Koryu), *Sangyo Ritchi,* April 1985.

Johnson, Chalmers. *MITI and the Japanese Miracle.* Stanford: Stanford University Press, 1982.

Johnson, Chalmers. "MITI and Japanese International Economic Policy," in Robert Scalapino (Ed.), *The Foreign Policy of Japan* Berkeley: Univ. of California Press, 1977.

Johnson, Chalmers (Ed.). *The Industrial Policy Debate.* San Francisco: Institute for Contemporary Studies, 1984.

Konaga, Keiichi. "Industrial Policy: The Japanese Version of a Universal Trend," *Journal of Japanese Trade and Industry,* July/August 1983.

Konaga, Keiichi. "Prospects and Industrial Policies for the 21st Century Economic Society" (21 Seiki e no Keizai Shakai no Tenbo to Seisaku), *Sangyo Ritchi,* March 1985.

Magaziner, Ira C., and Thomas M. Hout. *Japanese Industrial Policy.* London: Policy Studies Institute, 1980.

Nakasone, Yasuhiro. "Prospects and Guidelines for the Economic Society in the 1980s," in *Japan Economic Journal,* August 16, 1983.

Rapp, William V. "Japan's Industrial Policy," in Isaiah Frank (Ed.), *The Japanese Economy in International Perspective.* Baltimore: Johns Hopkins University Press, 1975.

Tajima, Kazuo. "Building the Foundations for the 21st Century" (21 Seiki ni Mukete no Kiban-Zukuri), *Sangyo Ritchi,* March 1984.

Tatsuno, Sheridan M. "MITI's Take-Lead Strategy Shifts into High Gear," *Dataquest Research Newsletter,* October 16, 1984.

Tharp, Mike. "Japan's Industrial Policy is the Latest Target of U.S. Criticism," *Far Eastern Economic Review,* June 2, 1983.

Tsukamoto, Yoshiaki. "21st Century Vision: Prospects for Japan in the 21st Century" (21 Seiki Vision: Nihon no 21 Seiki e no Tembo), *Sangyo Ritchi,* March 1985.

Tucker, Jonathan B. "Managing the Industrial Miracle," *High Technology,* August 1985.

U.S. General Accounting Office. *Industrial Policy: Case Studies in the Japanese Experience.* Report to the Chairman, Joint Economic Committee, U.S. Congress, GAO/IK-83-11, October 20, 1982.

Ueno, Hiroya. "Conception and Evaluation of Japanese Industrial Policy," *Japanese Economic Studies,* Winter 1976/1977.

"Vision for the 1980s: Basic Course of MITI's Trade Industrial Policy," *The Oriental Economist,* November 1979.

Vogel, Ezra. *Comeback: Rebuilding the Resurgence of American Business.* New York: Simon & Schuster, 1985.

Wanner, Barbara. "Washington Grapples with Japan's Industrial Policy," Japan Economic Institute (JEI) Report, April 22, 1983.

Chapter 3. Japan's Take-Lead Strategies

Strategy 1: Parallel R&D Projects

Denshi Kogyo Geppo. "Summary of Fiscal 1985 Electronics and Information-Related Policies" (Showa 60-Nendo Denshi/Joohoo Kanren Shisaku no Gaiyo), Vol. 27, No. 2, 1985.

Gonda, Kinji. "Catching Up on R&D," *Journal of Japanese Trade and Industry,* No. 1, 1985.

Industrial Review of Japan 1984. "Government Boosts Defense Budget by 6.5% for Fiscal 1983."

Japan Economic Journal. "Next-Generation Fundamental Technology R&D Program: Patent Applications Reach 435," March 20, 1984.

Kikai Shinko. "Fiscal 1983 MITI R&D Policies" (Showa 58-Nendo Tsusansho Gijutsu Kaihatsu Kanren Shisaku), April 1983.

Namiki, Toru. "The Mechanics of Large-Scale Projects and Their Current Status," MITI Agency of Industrial Science and Technology, *Japanese Semiconductor Technology,* Vol. 2, No. 1, February 1983.

Nikkei Electronics. "Fiscal 1983 Budget for Electronics Related Projects—No. 1," April 25, 1983.

Sangyo Ritchi. "Summary of Basic Technology Development Harmonization Law" (Kiban Gijutsu Kenryo Enkatsuka-Ho no Gaiyo), June 1985.

Tanaka, Hisayasu. "Technological Demand Spurs Large-Scale Projects," *Look Japan,* May 10, 1984.

Tucker, Jonathan. "Managing the Industrial Miracle," *High Technology Special Report: Japan,* August 1985.

U.S. Embassy. "Government of Japan-Subsidized Computer, Software, and Integrated Circuit R&D by Japanese Private Companies," Tokyo, June 25, 1982.

Strategy 2: Strategic International Alliances

Shaku, Atsushi. "Towards Revitalization of the World Economy: Japan Responsible for Four Projects," *Look Japan,* May 10, 1983.

Tatsuno, Sheridan. "East Meets West: A Surge in Joint Ventures and Licensing Agreements," *Dataquest Research Newsletter,* December 18, 1984.

Strategy 3: The Technopolis Concept

Japan External Trade Organization (JETRO). "Technopolises," *Now in Japan,* No. 34, 1983.

Furutate, Hidetatsu. "Technopolis Construction Concept: To Bring High Technology to Provincial Regions," *Journal of Japanese Trade and Industry,* No. 5, 1982.

Strategy 4: Telecommunications

Kitahara, Yasusada. *Information Network System: Telecommunications in the 21st Century.* London: Heinemann Educational Books Ltd., 1983.

Strategy 5: Venture Capital and Venture Businesses

Boyer, Edward. "Start-Up Ventures Blossom in Japan," *Fortune,* September 5, 1983.

Business Week. "A Broader Over-the-Counter Market Takes Off Fast," November 21, 1984.

Business Week, "Planting U.S. Seed Money in Japanese Start-ups," April 23, 1984.

Choy, Jon. "Venture Capital in Japan," Japan Economic Institute Report, No. 39A, October 12, 1984.

Hirschmeier, Johannes S.V.D. *The Origins of Entrepreneurship in Meiji Japan.* Cambridge, Mass.: Harvard University Press, 1964.

Japan Economic Journal. "MITI Formulates Venture Business Promotion Law," February 14, 1984.

Japan Economic Journal. "High-Tech Start-up Firms to Be Subsidized by MITI," February 28, 1984.

Japan Times. "High Tech Funds Show Sharp Rise," Feb. 27, 1984.

Kerns, Hikaru. "Time to Take A Risk," *Far Eastern Economic Review,* May 19, 1983.

Kishimoto, Yoriko. "Venture Capital in Japan: A Industry in its Infancy," *Venture Capital Journal,* February 1984.

Strategy 6: Selective Import Promotion

Consulate General of Japan. "Prime Minister Nakasone's Open Market Initiatives," San Francisco, January 13, 1983.

Choy, Jon. "Japan Considers Software Legislation," Japan Economic Institute Report, January 6, 1984; "Japan's Debate over Software Safeguards Intensifies," February 3, 1984; "U.S.–Japan Talks Focus on Software Rights," March 16, 1984.

Chapter 4. From Ancient Capitals

deBary, William Theodore. *Sources of Japanese Tradition,* Vol. I. New York: Columbia University Press. 1967.

Hall, John Whitney, "The Castle Town and Japan's Modern Urbanization," in *Studies in the Institutional History of Modern Japan,* edited by John W. Hall and Marius B. Jensen. Princeton, New Jersey: Princeton University Press, 1968.

Nitobe, Inazo. *Bushido: The Warrior's Code.* Burbank, California: Ohara Publications, Inc., 1975.

Plutschow, Herbert E. *Historical Nara.* Tokyo: Japan Times Ltd., 1983.

Plutschow, Herbert E. *Historical Kyoto.* Tokyo: Japan Times Ltd., 1983.

Sansom, George. *A History of Japan to 1334.* Stanford, California: Stanford University Press, 1958.

Sansom, George. *A History of Japan (1334-1615).* Stanford, California: Stanford University Press, 1968.

Takeuchi, Norizo. *Japanese History* (Revised Edition). Ministry of Education. Tokyo: Jiyu Shobo Publishing Co., 1967

Tsurumi, E. Patricia. "Historians and Japan's Ancient Female Emperors," *Bulletin of Concerned Asian Scholars,* Vol. 14, No. 4, 1982.

Yazaki, Takeo. *The Japanese City.* Tokyo: Tokyo News Service, Ltd., 1971.

Yazaki, Takeo. *Social Change and the City in Japan.* New York: Japan Publications, Inc., 1968.

Chapter 5. Tsukuba: The City of Brains

Aoki, Masaaki. "Scientific Research Vigorously Underway," *Journal of Japanese Trade and Industry,* No. 3, 1982.

Asahi Shimbun. "1984 Tsukuba Report," May 29-June 10, 1984.

Focus Japan. "Building a Technology Link," Vol. 10, No. 3, March 1983.

Japan Economic Journal. "Government-Industry Joint Development of High Technologies: MITI," August 7, 1984.

Japan Housing Corporation. *International Brain City Looks toward a Bright Future* (Meinichi o mitsumeru Kokusai Zuno Toshi). Tokyo: 1982.

Japan Industrial Technology Promotion Association (Nihon Sangyo Gijutsu Shinko Kyokai). *Research Plan for AIST's Testing Laboratories* (Shiken Kenkyujo Kenkyu Keikaku). Tokyo: 1983.

Journal of Japanese Trade and Industry. "Scientific Research Vigorously Underway at Tsukuba," No. 3, 1982.

Kawamoto, Tetsuzo. *Tsukuba Research Center* (Kenkyu Sentaa to shite no Tsukuba). Tsukuba University: Tsukuba Environment Group, 1983.

Kusayanagi, Fumie. "The City of Brains Supports International Technology Cooperation" (Kokusai Gijutsu Kyoryoku o sasaeru Zuno Toshi), *Tsusan (MITI) Journal,* November 1982.

Matsuda, Yasushi. "The Moonlight Project: Massive Conservation Effort," *Look Japan,* December 10, 1981 (Part 1) and January 10, 1982 (Part 2).

Ministry of Construction, Building Research Institute. *Outline of Research Activities.* Tokyo: 1983.

MITI, Agency for Industrial Science and Technology (AIST). *Tsukuba Science City Handbook* (Tsukuba Kenkyu Gakuen Toshi Yoran). Tokyo: 1982.

MITI, Agency for Industrial Science and Technology (AIST). *Tsukuba Science City* (Tsukuba Kenkyu Gakuen Toshi). Tokyo: 1975.

MITI, Agency for Industrial Science and Technology (AIST). *Research Institute 1983 Annual Report.*

Namiki, Toru. "Tsukuba Science City Preparing for 1985 International Expo," *Look Japan,* May 10, 1982.

Science City Problem Research Association (Gakuen Toshi Mondai Kenkyu-kai). *Tsukuba Science City* (Tsukuba Gakuen Toshi). Ohtsuki Publishing Company, 1985.

Science and Technology Agency (STA). "Private Sector Research Organizations in Tsukuba Science City," *Science and Technology in Japan,* Vol. 2, No. 5, 1983.

Science and Technology Agency (STA). *Overview of the Tsukuba Science City* (Tsukuba Kenkyu Gakuen Toshi Yoran). Tokyo: 1982.

Simmons, Lewis. "A High-Tech Expo Opens in Japan's City for Science," *Smithsonian,* April 1985.

Suzuki, David. "The Nature of Things: The Superachievers," PBS TV broadcast, July 6, 1984.

Tanaka, Hisayasu. "Pioneering Large-Scale Research Projects to Meet Societal Needs," *Look Japan,* April 10, 1984.

Tanakadate, Hidehiro. "Japan's City of Brains", *U.S. News & World Report,* January 10, 1983.

Tsukuba Science City Liaison Council for Promotion of Research Exchange. *Tsukuba Science City: Research Institutes and Universities.* March 1984.

Chapter 6. The Technopolis Concept.

Asahi News. "My Opinion on Technopolis," March 2, 1984.

Asahi Shimbun and Japan Industrial Location Center. "21st Century Super-Vision: Advanced Technology and Regional Development," MITI Symposium, Tokyo, February 5-6, 1985.

Asahi Shimbun. "The Road to Technopolis: Regional Revitalization through High Technology" (Sentan Gijutsu de Chiiki Kasseika: Tekunopurisu no Michi), Symposium Speeches, February 13, 1985.

Chunichi Shimbun. "Little Central Government Support," March 24, 1984.

Dempa Shimbun. "Which Technopolis Will Be Chosen?" November 21, 1983.

Dempa Shimbun. "Techno-Ninja Seek Technopolis" (Tekuno Kakeru Tekuno-Ninja), November 22, 1983.

Dempa Shimbun. "Concern over Charade" (Hayaku mo Kanban-Daore Shimpai), February 10, 1984.

Dempa Shimbun. "Zero Ceiling Budget May Extend Technopolis Construction to Year 2000," July 14, 1984.

Dempa Shimbun. "135 Candidate Regions for MITI's New Media Concept," June 8, 1984.

Dempa Shimbun. "MITI Announces Techno-Mart Concept," Oct. 10, 1984.

Dempa Shimbun. "Ten Teletopia Model Cities to be Selected by the End of 1984," October 2, 1984.

Fortune. "The Japanese Spies in Silicon Valley," February 27, 1978.

Furutate, Hidetatsu. "Technopolis Construction Concept," *Journal of Japanese Trade and Industry,* No. 5, 1982.

Gresser, Julian, with Koichiro Fujikura and Akio Morishima. *Environmental Law in Japan.* Tokyo: Tokyo University Press,1982.

Hiramatsu, Morihiko. *The Challenge of Technopolis* (Tekunopusu no Chosen). Tokyo: Japan Economic Journal Press, 1983.

Hiramatsu, Morihiko. "Regional Industrial Activation and Technopolis" (Chii-kei Sangyo no Kasseika to Tekunoporisu), *Sangyo Ritchi,* Vol. 23, No. 9, 1984.

Hokuriku Chunichi Shimbun (Hokuriku Regional News). "Favoritism to Politicians" (Seijika no Rigai Yusen), February 11, 1984.

Honbu, Kazuhiko. "Present Status and Problems in Silicon Valley" (Shirikon Baree no Genjo to Mondai), *Sangyo Ritchi,* Vol. 24, No. 5, 1985.

Iijima, Dr. Sadakazu (moderator), "Future Regional Development and Central Industrial Areas" (Kongo no Chiiki Kaihatsu to Chukaku Kogyo Danchi), *Sangyo Ritchi,* Vol. 23, No. 8, 1984.

Imai, Kenichi. "Japan's Industrial Policy for High Technology Industries," paper prepared for the Conference of the High Technology Research Project, Northeast Asia-U.S. Forum on International Policy, Stanford University, March 21-23, 1984.

Ishii, Ibo. "Activation of University Research and Industry Exchange" (Daigaku Kyushu Kikan no Kasseika to Sangyo to no Koryu), *Sangyo Ritchi,* Vol. 24, No. 4, 1985.

Japan Economic Journal. "Technopolis Program Gets Underway in 14 Areas throughout Nation," March 6, 1984.

Japan External Trade Organization (JETRO). "Technopolises," *Now in Japan,* No. 34, 1983.

Japan Industrial Location Center (Ritchi Center). *Technopolis Basic Concept Survey: Comprehensive Report* (Tekunopurisu Kihon Koso Chosa Sogo Hokoku-sho); *Regional Committee Report* (Chiiki Bunkakai Hokoku-sho); *Industrial Complex Model* (Sangyo Konpurekusu Bunkakai Hokoku-sho). March 1982.

Japan Industrial Location Center (Ritchi Center). *Japanese Industrial Location Systems and Incentives.* March 1983.

Japan Industrial Location Center (Ritchi Center). *Summary of the Technopolis Development Concept Survey of 19 Regions* (Tekunopurisu Kaihatsu Koso Chosa no Gaiyo). April 1983.

Japan Industrial Location Center (Ritchi Center). "Approval of Technopolis Development Plans" (Tekunopurisu Kaihatsu Keikaku no Shonin ni Tsuite), *Sangyo Ritchi,* Vol. 23, No. 3, 1984.

Journal of Japanese Trade and Industry. "Irrashai! Japan Opens its Doors to Foreign Firms," No.1, 1983.

Journal of the American Chamber of Commerce in Japan. "An Update on Japan's Technopolis Plan," June 1984.

Kiyonari, Tadao. "The Three Conditions for Technopolis Success" (Tekunopurisu: Seiko no San-Joken), *Voice,* June 1984.

Konaga, Keiichi. "Prospects and Policies for the 21st Century Economy and Society" (21 Seiki e no Keizai Shakai no Tenbo to Seisaku), *Sangyo Ritchi,* Vol. 24, No. 3, 1985.

Kumamoto Prefecture. *Kumamoto Technopolis Development Concept.* June 1983.

Ministry of International Trade and Industry (MITI). *Technopolis '90 Committee Mid-Term Report* (Chukan Hokuku). June 18, 1982.

Nagai, Yasuhiro. "Infrastructure Assistance Activities in the Technopolis Regions" (Tekunopurisu Chiiki ni Okeru Shisetsu Seibi Josei Jigyo ni Tsuite), *Sangyo Ritchi,* Vol. 23, No. 11, 1984.

Nihon Kogyo Shimbun (Japan Industrial Newspaper). "MITI Chooses Eight New Community Model Regions," October 16, 1984.

Nishikawa, Taizo. "New Media Community Concept" (Nyuu Medea Komyunitei Koso), *Sangyo Ritchi,* Vol. 23, No. 7, 1984.

Noyce, Robert N. "What Makes Silicon Valley Grow?" Statement before the Joint Economic Committee of the U.S. Congress, Sunnyvale, California, August 27, 1984.

Sangyo Ritchi. "Technopolis Development Plan—Five Designated Regions" (Tekunopurisu Kaihatsu Keikaku Shonin Chiiki), Special Issue, Vol. 23, No. 12, 1984.

Tajima, Kazuo. "Building the Foundation for the 21st Century" (21 Seiki ni Mukete no Kiban-Zukuri), *Sangyo Ritchi,* Vol. 24, No. 3, 1985.

Takazawa, Nobuyuki. "MITI's Technopolis Concept: Cities of the High-Tech Era." *Look Japan,* October 10, 1984.

Tanaka, Kakuei. *Building a New Japan: A Plan for Remodeling the Japanese Archipelago.* Tokyo: Simul Press, 1972.

Tsukamoto, Shunichi. "Promoting the Techno-Mart Concept" (Tekuno-Maato Koso no Suishin ni Tsuite), *Sangyo Ritchi,* Vol. 23, No. 12, 1984.

Tsukamoto, Yoshiaki. "Japan's Prospects for the 21st Century" (Nihon: 21 Seiki e no Tenbo), *Sangyo Ritchi,* Vol. 24, No. 3, 1985.

Tsuhashi, Shuichi. "Trends in Regional Airport Network Infrastructure" (Chiiki Koku Nettowaku Seibi no Hoko), *Sangyo Ritchi,* Vol. 23, No. 10, 1984.

Yamamoto, Keisuke, "Regional Development and the Teletopia Concept" (Chiiki Kaihatsu to Teletopia Koso), *Sangyo Ritchi,* Vol. 23, No. 7, 1984.

Chapter 7. The New Castle Towns

Hamamatsu

Advanced Production Machinery Technology Promotion Association. *Survey on the Introduction and Nurturing of Leading Industries* (Sentan Sangyo no Donyu—Ikusei Joken ni Kansuru Chosa Kenkyu). March 1983, pp. 115-146.

Dempa Shimbun, "Hamamatsu Technopolis," April 11, 1984, June 28, 1984, September 11, 1984, October 23, 1984, April 26, 1985, and May 24, 1985.

Hamamatsu Local Technology Development Association (Rokaru Gijutsu Kaihatsu Kyokai). *America's Leading Technology Industrial Regions*

(Beikoku Sentan Gijutsu Sangyo Chiiki: Kansatsu Hokoku-sho). March 11, 1982.

Japan Industrial Location Center. *Technopolis Development Plans: Special Issue* (Technopolis Kaihatsu Keikaku Shonin Chiiki Tokushu-go). *Sangyo Ritchi*, Vol. 23, No. 5, 1984.

Nikkei Sangyo Shimbun (Japan Industrial Journal). "Hamamatsu Technopolis," December 11, 1984 and April 9, 1985.

Nihon Kogyo Shimbun (Japan Industrial Manufacturing Journal). "Hamamatsu Advanced Technology Show," November 21, 1984.

Shizuoka Prefecture. *Hamamatsu Regional High-Tech Industrial Development Plan* (Kodo Gijutsu ni Rikyaku shita Kogyo Kaihatsu ni Kansuru Keikaku). November 1983, pp. 19-20.

Shizuoka Prefecture. *Hamamatsu Regional Technopolis Development Concept* (Hamamatsu Chiiki Technopolis Kaihatsu Koso). March 1983, p. 67.

Nagaoka

Dempa Shimbun. "Nagaoka Technopolis," April 3, 1983, December 30, 1983, June 25, 1984, and March 27, 1985.

Fukuoka, Masayuki. "Tanaka Kakuei's Grassroots," *Japan Echo*, Vol. X, No. 1, 1983, translated from *Chuo Koron*, January 1983.

Japan Regional Development Corporation. *Nagaoka New Town*. March 1981.

Kondo, Takehisa. "Nagaoka a Frontrunner in MITI Technopolis Race," *The Japan Times Weekly*, May 15, 1982.

Look Japan. "Niigata: A City of Technology and Culture Open to the World," January 10, 1985.

Nakahara, Eiichi, "Buying the River Bottom" (Kawa no soko o kau), *Chuo Koron*, Kakuei Tanaka special issue, November 20, 1983.

Nihon Keizai Shimbun (Japan Economic Journal). "Pioneering Technopolis: Nagaoka's Experiment," December 30, 1983.

Nihon Kogyo (Japan Industrial Manufacturing Journal). "Nagaoka Technopolis Becomes Concrete," September 29, 1984.

Niigata Prefecture. *Nagaoka Regional Development Plan* (Nagaoka Chiiki Kaihatsu Keikaku). November 1983.

Toyama

Japan Industrial Location Center. *Technopolis Development Plans of Designated Regions: Special Issue* (Tekunopurosu Kaihatsu Shonin Chiiki Tokushu Go). *Sangyo Ritchi*, Vol. 23, No. 5, May 1984.

Look Japan. "Toyama: Building World Leadership in Technology," February 10, 1985.

Nikkei Keizai (Japan Economic Journal). "Toyama Technopolis' Three Pillars of Leading Technology," January 29, 1982.

Toyama Prefecture. *Toyama Prefecture Commerce, Trade, and Labor* (Toyama Ken no Shokyogyo to Rodo). March 1983.

Toyama Prefecture. *Toyama Prefecture Major Plant Listing* (Toyama Ken Juyo Kojo Meibo). July 1983.

Toyama Technopolis Promotion Association. *Toyama Technopolis Development Concept.* May 1983.

Toyama Prefectural Office. *Investing in Toyama.* 1983.

Okayama

Dempa Shimbun, "Okayama Technopolis," August 5, 1984.

Hayashibara Group. *A Hundred Year Retrospect.* May 1984.

Nikkei Sangyo (Japan Industrial Journal). "Okayama Technopolis," August 11, 1984 and October 23, 1984.

Okayama Prefecture. *Kibi Highlands Regional Technopolis Development Plan* (Kibi Kogen Chiiki Tekunopurosu Kaihatsu Keikaku). November 1983.

Saito, Hidemasa, "Hayashibara: Hamsters and Hotels," *Journal of Japanese Trade and Industry*, No. 3, 1984.

Hiroshima

Chukoku Shimbun. "Hiroshima Central Technopolis," February 5, 1984.

Chugoku Shimbun, "Hiroshima Small and Medium Size Businesses," April 12, 1984 and April 29, 1984.

Dempa Shimbun. "Hiroshima Central Technopolis," November 29, 1984 and December 20, 1984.

Hiroshima Prefecture. *Hiroshima Central Technopolis Development Concept* (Hiroshima Chuo Tekunopurosu Kaihatsu Koso). March 1983.

Hiroshima Prefecture Software Industry Association. *Software Venture Businesses*. February 1984.

Nihon Keizai (Japan Economic Journal). "Hiroshima Central Technopolis," May 4/10/15/17/24, 1984.

Nihon Kogyo (Japan Industrial Manufacturing Journal). May 24, 1984.

Nikkan Kogyo (Japan Daily Industrial Journal). March 28, 1984 and May 24, 1984.

Nikkei Sangyo (Japan Industrial Journal). May 24, 1984 and September 29, 1984.

Yamaguchi

Asahi Shimbun, "Ube Technopolis," October 12, 1984.

Chukoku Shimbun. "Ube Technopolis," February 29, 1984.

Dempa Shimbun. "Ube Technopolis," April 9, 1984.

Japan Industrial Location Center. *Special Issue on the Technopolis Plans of Designated Regions* (Tekunopurisu Kaihatsu Keikaku Shonin Chiiki Tokushu Go), *Sangyo Ritchi*, Vol. 23, No. 5, 1984.

Look Japan. "Bringing Yamaguchi Back into the Mainstream," December 10, 1984.

Nikkei Sangyo (Japan Industrial Journal). "Ube Technopolis," February 27, 1984 and July 9, 1985.

Ube Technopolis Construction Promotion Association. *Ube Phoenix Technopolis Development Concept* (Ube Fenikusu Tekunopurisu Kaihatsu Koso). May 1983.

Chapter 8. Silicon Island

Kyushu Overview

Asahi Shimbun, "The Industry Invitation Battle Intensifies" (Kigyo Yuuchi Sensen wa Gikika), March 11, 1984.

Dempa Shimbun, "Technopolis Makers in Kyushu Silicon Island" (Special Issue), August 30, 1984.

Japan Quarterly, "Silicon Island—Tomorrow's World Leader?," Vol. XXIX, No. 4, October-December 1982.

Japan Times, "Kyushu in Process of Switching Economy to IC Track," December 15, 1982.

Japan Times, "Kyushu Shifts Emphasis from Tourism to High-Tech," Kyushu Supplement, November 18, 1983.

Journal of the American Chamber of Commerce in Japan. "Kyushu—Special Investment Supplement," December 1983.

Kyushu International Investment Exchange Promotion Conference. *Kyushu: Invest in Success.* 1983.

Ministry of International Trade and Industry, Kyushu Area Industrial Bureau. "Kyushu Regional Industrial Vision for the 1980s" (80 Nendai no Kyushu Chiiki Sangyo Vision), August 1981.

Ministry of International Trade and Industry, Fukuoka Bureau. *Aiming for Techno-Island Kyushu* (Techno-Island Kyushu o Mezashite: Kyushu Chiiki Gijutsu Shinko Keikaku). September 1983.

PHP Institute International. "Silicon Island: Gateway to the Japanese Market," Vol. 14, No. 10, October 1983.

Kumamoto

Dempa Shimbun, "Citizens United to Build a Prosperous City," August 30, 1983.

Dempa Shimbun, "Prospects and Problems for the Kumamoto Technopolis," (five-part series), May 8-13, 1984.

Dempa Shimbun, "Advanced Technology Activities," May 12, 1984.

Dempa Shimbun, "A Mountain of Problems," May 14, 1984.

Journal of the American Chamber of Commerce in Japan. "Kyushu—Special Investment Supplement. Kumamoto: The Center of Kyushu," 1983.

Kumamoto Prefecture. *Setting Up Business in Kumamoto.* 1982.

Kumamoto Prefecture. *Kumamoto Technopolis Development Concept.* June 1983.

Oita

Dempa Shimbun. "Japan Development Bank Loans Extended to Foreign Firms," June 22, 1983.

Dempa Shimbun, "High Technology and Industrial Exhibits in Oita," October 8, 1984.

Hiramatsu, Morihiko. *The Challenge of Technopolis* (Tekunoporisu no Chosen). Tokyo: Japan Economic Journal Publishing Company, 1983.

Nihon Kogyo, "The Status of Industry-University Cooperation at Oita University's Engineering Department," July 23, 1984.

Oita Prefecture Trade Association. *Marinopolis Project.* March 1982.

Oita Prefecture *Oita Technopolis Development Plan.* May 30, 1983.

Tharp, Mike. "Making of the Precedent," *Far Eastern Economic Review,* February 17, 1983.

Kagoshima

Asahi Newspaper, "Kyocera to Hire 1,500 for Kawauchi Plant," April 24, 1984.

Kagoshima Prefecture. *Rinku Kokusai Sangyo Toshi: Kokubu-Hayato Technopolis Kihon Kozo* (Open Space International Industrial City: Kokubu-Hayato Technopolis Basic Concept), March 1982.

Kagoshima Prefecture. *Rinku Kokusai Sangyo Toshi: Kokubu-Hayato Technopolis Kaihatsu Kozo* (Open Space International Industrial City: Kokubu-Hayato Technopolis Development Concept). March 1983.

McKnight, Susan. "Japan Considering Ambitious Space Launch Vehicle Program," Japan Economic Institute Report, March 9, 1984.

McKnight, Susan. "Japan's Satellite Development Program," Japan Economic Institute Report, March 16, 1984.

Mainichi Newspaper. "Hitachi Opens Kagoshima Software Development Plant," February 16, 1984.

Minami Nihon Shimbun (Southern Japan Newspaper). "Kagoshima Fujitsu Opens Design Development Center," August 4, 1983.

Minami Nihon Shimbun. "12 Firms Plan to Hire 858 High School Graduates," September 30, 1983.

Nishi Nihon Shimbun (Western Japan Newspaper). "Sony Strengthens Three Plants in Kokubu Area," December 11, 1983.

Yomiuri Shimbun. "U-Turn Entrepreneur Starts Local Computer Firm," March 12, 1984.

Miyazaki

Davis, Dwight B. "High-Speed Trains: New Life for the Iron Horse?" *High Technology*, September 1984.

Japan Economic Journal. "Suntory and Miyazaki University Succeed in Developing New Hormone," July 17, 1984.

Miyazaki Prefecture. *A Guide to Investment in Miyazaki Prefecture.* January 1983.

Miyazaki Prefecture. *Miyazaki Sun Technopolis Development Plan* (Miyazaki Sun Tekunoporisu Kaihatsu Koso). March 1983.

Miyazaki Prefecture. *Miyazaki Prefecture Industrial Technology Promotion Association* (Miyazaki-Ken Sangyo Gijutsu Shinko Kiko). June 1984.

O'Neill, Gerard K. *The Technology Edge.* New York: Simon and Schuster, 1983.

Chapter 9. Will Technopolis Work?

Malone, Michael S. *The Big Score: The Billion Dollar Story of Silicon Valley.* Garden City, New York: Doubleday & Company, Inc., 1985.

Rogers, Everett M., and Judith K. Larsen. *Silicon Valley Fever.* New York: Basic Books, Inc., 1984.

Wilson, John W. *The New Venturers: Inside the High-Stakes World of Venture Capital.* Menlo Park, California: Addison-Wesley Publishing Company, 1985.

Chapter 10. Japan's Pursuit of Creativity

Adams, James L. *Conceptual Blockbusting: A Guide to Better Ideas.* New York: W.W. Norton & Company, 1974.

Hall, John Whitney. *Japan: From Prehistory to Modern Times.* New York: Delta. 1971.

Kuroyanagi, Tetsuko. *Totto-Chan: The Little Girl at the Window.* Tokyo: Kodansha International, 1982.

Rohlen, Thomas P. *Japan's High Schools.* Berkeley: University of California Press, 1983.

Rosenfeld, Robert, and Jenny C. Servo. "Business and Creativity: Making Ideas Connect," *The Futurist*, August 1984.

Suzuki, Daisetz Teitaro. *Studies in Zen.* New York: Dell. 1955.

von Oech, Roger. *A Whack on the Side of the Head.* New York: Warner Books, 1983.

Ye, Oryon. *Japan's Ethos of Miniaturization* (Chijimi Shikou no Nihonjin). Tokyo: Gakusei Company, 1982.

Chapter 11. Whither America?

Brody, Herb. "The High-Tech Sweepstakes: States Vie for a Slice of the Pie," *High Technology*, January 1985.

Business Week. "America Rushes to High-Tech for Growth," March 28, 1983.

Business Week. "The High-Tech Renaissance in Southern California," September 17, 1984.

Business Week. "Why Austin's Hills Are Looking like Silicon Valley," May 16, 1983.

Electronics. "Texas Cash Fuels Electronics Boom," June 16, 1983.

Forbes. "The Beltway Bandits," October 8, 1984.

Japan Economic Journal. "Oregon Attracts Japanese Investments," August 14, 1984; "Oregon's Silicon Forest Attracts Japanese Electronics Companies," September 11, 1984.

Naisbitt, John. *Megatrends*. New York: Warner Books, 1984.

Posner, Bruce G. "Report on the States", *Inc.*, October 1984.

San Jose Mercury. "High Tech Gets its Place in the Sun," October 10, 1983.

San Jose Mercury. "High Tech in Santa Barbara," November 31, 1984.

San Jose Mercury. "Oregon Basks in Afterglow of Repealing Unitary Tax," October 13, 1984; "Oregon Harvests New Industries," December 23, 1984.

Task Force on Technological Innovation. *State Initiatives in Technological Innovation*. National Governors' Association, 444 N. Capitol St., Washington, DC 20001, February 1983.

U.S. Congress. Office of Technology Assessment. *Technology, Innovation, and Regional Economic Development*. Washington, DC: U.S. Government Printing Office, May 1983.

The Wall Street Journal. "Development Aid from States Is a Growing Factor for Firms," October 8, 1984.

INDEX

Hayashibara Biochemical Company,
156
and bioelectronics, 161
and cancer research, 158
Heihachiryo, Horiuchi (Hamamatsu
planner), quoted, 117
Hewlett-Packard, 19, 44, 182, 239
in Silicon Valley, 244
High-tech regions, U.S., 232-242
Hirai, Toru (governor of Yamaguchi
Prefecture), quoted, 168
Hiramatsu, Morihiko (governor of
Oita Prefecture), 22-24, 115,
121, 129, 133, 173, 184-187,
202
Hiroshima, 63, 86, 130, 133, 162-167
Atomic Bomb Dome in, 163
and computer software industry,
163-164
land speculation in, 166
Technology Exchange Plaza, 165
and Technopolis concept, 165-167
budget for, 166
transportation links to, 166
Hitachi, 7, 8, 15
and biotechnology, 105
HIPAC-1 computer, 9
and IBM lawsuit, 68, 116
and Kilby patent, 13
and office automation products, 15
software plant in Kagoshima, 192
and technology agreements, 10, 14,
44
and VLSI Research Association, 16,
18
Honda, Namio (electronics), 5
Hosoda, Toshiaki (Hiroshima
Software), quoted, 163-164
Hosokawa, Morihiro (governor of
Kumamoto), 133, 180, 181,
183-184, 202

IBM, 9, 10, 19
domination of Japanese industry by,
15-16
Future System, 15
in Hiroshima, 165
and Hitachi espionage case, 68, 116
Model 370 series, 14
and patent licensing, 44
in Silicon Valley, 244
System 360, 12

Ibuka, Masaru (Sony), 3
Igarashi, Mineo (Oita planner), 186
Iijima, Sadakazu, quoted, 125
Ikeda, Hayato (former Prime
Minister), 25, 95
Ikoma, Masaaki (Kagoshima planner),
quoted, 191
Ikusei, 51
Imai, Kenichi (chairman, Technopolis
'90 R&D), 123-124, 136
Imports, selective, promotion of, 36,
64-69, 71
and semiconductor industry, 66-67
and software industry, 67-69
and U.S. protectionism, 65-66
weaknesses of, 71-72
Inamori, Kazuo (Kyocera president),
193
Information Imperialism (Fukuma),
68
Information Network System (INS),
52-53, 54-56, 57, 71, 191, 204
and Technopolis concept, 136, 197
Integrated circuits (ICs)
large-scale (LSI), 15
production of, 13-14
in Kyushu, 176, 177, 178
in Technopolis cities, 180, 192,
193, 196
in U.S., 11, 14
Texas Instruments patents on, 13
three-dimensional, 104, 230
very large scale (VLSI), 15, 40, 41
Interferon, 158-159
Ishii, Ibo (Toyama), 153
Ishii, Takemochi, 120, 121
Ishizuka, Masahiko, quoted on
creativity, 221
Iwase, Shingo (transistors), 6, 10

Jacobsen, Stephen (biomedical
engineering), 239-240
Japan Broadcasting Company (NHK),
4, 57, 191
Japan Development Bank (JDB), 22,
25, 38, 185
and low-interest import financing,
64, 65
and Technopolis concept, 47, 50,
134-135
Japan Electronics Computer
Corporation (JECC), 9-10